COLUMBIA COLLEGE CHICAGO

3 2711 00145 1453

DISCARD

DATE DUE

B 0 2 2009

Music, Meaning and Transformation

Music, Meaning and Transformation

By

Steve Dillon

CAMBRIDGE SCHOLARS PUBLISHING

Music, Meaning and Transformation, by Steve Dillon
Series: Meaningful Music Making for Life

This book first published 2007 by

Cambridge Scholars Publishing

15 Angerton Gardens, Newcastle, NE5 2JA, UK

British Library Cataloguing in Publication Data
A catalogue record for this book is available from the British Library

Copyright © 2007 by Steve Dillon

All rights for this book reserved. No part of this book may be reproduced, stored in a retrieval system, or transmitted, in any form or by any means, electronic, mechanical, photocopying, recording or otherwise, without the prior permission of the copyright owner.

ISBN 1-84718-213-5; ISBN 13: 9781847182135

TABLE OF CONTENTS

Foreword by Elizabeth Mackinlay	ix
Preface	xi
Acknowledgements	xiv

Part I: Position — 1

Chapter One: Designing and managing the cultural lives of children — 2
- Some key concepts in this book — 3
- Modelling the development of a personal philosophy of music education: A teacher's journey — 7
- What we can do — 9

Chapter Two: Locating myself in the discourse — 11
- The big picture issues — 11
- Culture, technology and popular music — 13
- Emerging cultural understanding — 14
- The benefits of an Australian position — 16
- What technology reveals — 18

Chapter Three: Putting the meat on the bones of theory — 20
- Project 1: Researching the meaning of music to students in a school context — 20
- Project 2: Researching meaningful engagement with music technology — 40
- Project 3: Indigenising the curriculum and community music research — 41

Part II: Theoretical — 45

Chapter Four: Music making and flow — 46
- About Csikszentmihalyi and "flow" — 46
- Four areas of meaning — 50
- Autotelic behaviour and personalities — 51
- Early childhood music experience — 52

Institutional music learning	63
The location of musical meaning: Where is it?	68

Chapter Five: Designing meaningful and engaging environments — 71

The intrinsic nature of music experience	71
Meaning and experience design	72
Experience design and culture	73
Problematising music technology in experience and curriculum design	80
A context analysis framework	80
Observing meaningful engagement: A matrix	84

Chapter Six: The student as maker — 88

The relationship of theory to the idea of "student as maker"	88
What we can do	92
The student as maker: A definition	93
Dewey and art as experience	95
"Student as maker": The student–teacher relationship and the environment	97
The "student as maker" and the postmodern condition	99
The "student as maker" and culture	101
The "student as maker" and technology	102

Chapter Seven: The teacher as builder – the making of meaning — 105

Teaching and embodied relationships in the instrumental studio	106
Studio teaching and meaning	109
Classroom music	113
Performance	127
Building context, embodying understanding	133
Teacher as builder and the concept of culture	137
Teacher as builder and technology	141
What we can do	143

Part III: Practical — 145

Table of Contents

Chapter Eight: Meaningful engagement with music and personal meaning — 146
    Defining personal meaning — 147
    What is a music teacher? — 156
    Personal meaning and culture — 160
    Personal meaning and technology — 162
    What we can do — 164

Chapter Nine: Social meaning and meaningful engagement with music — 165
    Relational knowledge and common ground — 165
    Building of a sense of unity — 170
    Teacher qualities, organisational principles and processes — 171
    Social meaning and culture — 172
    Social meaning and music technology — 173
    What we can do — 175

Chapter Ten: Meaningful engagement with music and cultural meaning — 176
    A projection of self — 176
    The power of music in cultural identity — 177
    Case study — 178
    What are the characteristics of the teacher? — 181
    Cultural meaning and "other" cultures — 183
    Cultural meaning and technology — 186
    What we can do — 188

Chapter Eleven: The school as village — 189
    A philosophical basis for the school as village — 191
    The physical environment — 192
    The social environment — 193
    The psychological environment — 195
    The institutional environment — 196
    The educational environment: Classroom and curriculum — 198
    The school environment — 202
    The world beyond school — 203
    A changing environment: Tasks for the new millennium — 207
    The school as village and technology — 209

Building community with technology	211
The school as village and culture	212
What we can do	215

Chapter Twelve: Meaningful music making for life — 216
- A summary of the journey — 216
- A summary of insights — 219
- Knowing where we need to go next — 229

Appendix A: Meaningful engagement matrix — 231

Appendix B: Philosophical Checklist — 233

References — 237

FOREWORD

How many of us experienced music lessons in primary school where the music teacher shook her recorder at us like a dark sword when we could not play in tune, in time and together? Do you have memories of sitting at a rickety desk, painstakingly copying notes onto a music stave until your hand hurt, and you no longer knew what you were doing or why? Perhaps, like me, however, you have other memories of music education, which bring a smile to your face rather than a frown. I cannot recall many moments of pleasure in my formal music lessons with a specialist music teacher at primary school but I do remember the joy of making music in school with generalist teachers who loved music, could play a musical instrument and were passionate about using music as a vehicle for giving, sharing, teaching, learning and ultimately, making meaning. My grade 4 teacher brought his guitar into class every day and we began our lessons with a song—my favourite was "All day all night Miss MaryAnne". He would smile at us as he sang and I would watch him intently, trying to mirror the sound of his voice in my own song. My specialist music teachers at high school brought me the same sense of pleasure, passion and engagement.

It is this sense of engagement with meaningful music making that this series of books on music education in Australia explores. What types of teaching and learning process in music education bring to students and teachers alike not only knowledge of music per se, but also an understanding of self, others and the worlds we live in? Is this what we mean by meaningful engagement in music making? What are the ways that music educators—specialist and generalist—bring to their classrooms a meaningful engagement with music? What is that "magic" ingredient that "livens up" music classrooms and restores their "groove" capacity?

In this first book of this series, Steve Dillon shares with his audience his own love of music and his passion as a music educator for making music meaningful and transforming. Through personal reflection, in depth critique of relevant literature, and dialogues with teachers and students involved in music education classes in a diverse range of ways, Steve considers what meaningful engagement with music means in educational contexts. In this
intimate sharing of insights, Steve also asks the reader to take a personal, professional and musical journey with him—a crossing over and into our memories and experiences as learners, teachers, and/or performers of music—to think deeply about what music means in our lives, and how we can enact a

pedagogical process which passes on and sustains that kind of passion for music making and education. The conversation that Steve begins here in *Music, meaning and transformation*, opens doorways to create, as bell hooks (1994) urges, a music classroom bursting with possibility. As part of this dialogic process, we encourage readers to interact with the authors of each book in the series via a research BLOG that can be accessed at http://www.savetodisc.net/. Here readers can see media examples referenced in specific book chapters, participate in discussions about their experiences with music education as students and teachers, and in this way create a critical, engaged and transformative community of practice.

Elizabeth Mackinlay
Series Editor

PREFACE

For most of my life, I have been a singer, composer and teacher of music. My musical background is eclectic, for me "music is music" and whether I am singing bass in a world music a Capella group, fronting a punk band or "scatting" in a jazz ensemble, I count them all as worthwhile music experiences. As a composer, I have published rock music, jazz and music theatre and music resources for education. The distinction between style and complexity has never been an issue—I have come to see them all as musical experience. The line between teacher and musician is also a blurred one; what I have learned about musical knowledge from teaching is complemented by what I have learned about education from being a musician. All of these experiences are, as Csikszentmihalyi (1994) describes, "flow" activities. I draw upon this construction of teacher as artist in my approach to research in music education. I hope to bring an openness that flows from the eclecticism of these experiences and seek to contribute a sense of unity of purpose that can be drawn from my experience as a teacher and musician.

This book is the result of many years of academic study beginning with the development of a conceptual framework for a pragmatist approach to music education. I was fortunate to be in a position to apply these theoretical tenets to practice and through observing theory in practice completed a doctoral study, which forms the basis for the book. During that process, I gained a real passion for qualitative research and a thirst for understanding the role of the arts in community and curriculum. Like many teachers of the arts, I began with the anecdotes from my teaching experience that questioned the ways in which arts education was taught in schools and the ways in which curriculum was interpreted. I wondered why music making was not intrinsically motivated in schools, why the interpretation of curriculum ignored much of the music that children were passionately involved with, why good musicians were often not good teachers of music. I also asked why the students did not see the role of music as relevant to the school as a community, why school administrations did not appear to value music whilst simultaneously using music as a way to promote their school image.

As a teacher and head of a performing arts faculty I also saw the arts segmented and separated from one another-a notion that ignored the conception of integrated arts curriculum advocated in curriculum documents. Through these experiences I began to see the idea that curriculum is a dynamic process, which in part embodies the teachers, themselves and their ability to build and interpret the environment.

From little things big things grow

The above title comes from a song written by Australian Indigenous songwriter Uncle Kev Carmody and singer songwriter Paul Kelly. The title further describes what has happened to the ideas that emerged from my doctoral study, which was further amplified through academic research and teaching of pre service teachers at Griffith University and at Queensland University of Technology where I was able to see first hand the formation of music teachers and general primary/elementary school teachers. This position enabled me to apply the emergent theory of meaningful engagement to new contexts and with new teachers. From this interaction it became clear that there was a need for an infra structure for a more coordinated research agenda which has led to the formation of a research network that focuses upon meaningful engagement and the qualities of good practice in music teaching. save to DISC (Documenting Innovation in Sound Communities/Curriculum) was conceived to provide a framework for a dynamic network of passionate and committed researchers, music teachers, graduate students, music industry professionals, health researchers and community members with a focus upon documenting innovation and access to shared knowledge and hybrid methodology. From humble beginnings, this network has grown both in numbers and research projects to span six European countries, China, Australia, New Zealand and has growing representation in North America and Canada.

Philosophically, the position I have taken embraces what could be described as a "pragmatist aesthetic" (Schusterman 1992). This idea has been drawn initially from John Dewey's instrumentalism/pragmatism (Dewey 1970) and an existential philosophy of relationships from Martin Buber (1969, 1975). The notion of unifying the practical and pragmatic and aesthetic, or the reunion of "praxis and poesis" holds the key to understanding how I have used the term "pragmatist aesthetic". The work of these philosophers most clearly influences my approach to curriculum and to teaching and learning in the arts. The emphasis here is upon unifying these ideas rather than perceiving them as being exclusive or opposing.

I spent a total of seven years both working at the case study site discussed in this research and as a researcher/participant observer. The first of these years was spent redesigning the curriculum and the next five involved the introduction and implementation theoretical research to the curriculum and school community. Throughout that time, I documented the process and kept records in diary and journal form, collected video and audiotapes of music within the school and documents describing the curriculum and process of music education. I collected these records to document the effect of the ideas drawn from the research and as example and evidence of the interaction of policy, theory and practice that occurred within the case study school.

In the fourth year, I began doctoral research using participant observation case study methodology. I focused this research upon examining what it is about music and music experience that children find meaningful in a school context. It is my hope that this knowledge will reveal ways to provide access to that meaning for students. I hope this research will have implications for the interpretation of curriculum, the clarification of the role of the music teacher and the structure of learning experiences. This book embodies both this long-term study that examines theory in practice and subsequent iterations of research published in scholarly journals.

I began this research with these kinds of thoughts, experiences and questions in my mind. Like most teacher/researchers, I hoped that there would be some kind of reasonable explanation for my perception that music education practice often fails to engage and be relevant to students. I also hoped research would reveal some useful ideas for teaching and learning in music.

In this preface, I simply seek to place myself in this research and display my role, preconceptions and influences in an open and informative way. I hope that the commitment, energy and enthusiasm I have for music making in education and the community at large comes through in this research. I wish to make it known that I sought to undertake this research in a balanced, trustworthy but uninhibited way and hope that the results of this study contribute to the knowledge in the field of music and arts education. It is my sincere belief that all humanity needs access to meaningful music making for life and the understanding of where music is in their lives, where it is in the lives of children and where it is in the life of a community. It is especially important in the twenty first century that how we express ourselves in sound and creative production in sound is acknowledges as a way of knowing. Creative sound pervades every aspect of our lives and communities and meaningful music making for life proposes a way of engaging with the tensions at the interfaces between cultures and times and a way of making sense of it all that effects transformation of consciousness and self. The book is titled *Music, meaning and transformation* because it simply provides a journey from the music makers perspective of how they construct meaning in their lives from musical experience and how that meaning leads to a transformation of self. The questions of how we facilitate and design experiences, which have this effect I hope flows naturally from this understanding.

ACKNOWLEDGEMENTS

This has been a different and very personal experience spanning 14 years. I have many people to thank. In the first stage of this project I wish to acknowledge the wise counsel, encouragement and support given to me by my academic supervisor Professor Lyn Yates now at the University of Technology in Sydney, Australia, whose scholarship serves as a model for supervision and whose interest and faith in my research was an inspiration. I would like to thank the school and principal of my research site for giving me the opportunity to conduct this process and the privilege of sharing in their love of music. Eternal thanks to the following academics and friends who typed, read, offered criticism, argued, listened and encouraged me in the process of this research: Dr Andrew Brown, Dr Alan Cunningham, Dr Phillip Taylor, Dr Darrell Caulley, Dr Ramon Lewis, Jennifer and Jill Thornton, Lorraine Fulton, Georgina Barton and the collegial support of La Trobe and Griffith University staff and students.

When this project moved from a doctoral study to a book, I was supported and encouraged by the staff and students of Queensland University of Technology (QUT) Faculty of Creative Industries Music and Sound. The music students who helped me test theories and philosophy in practice are now wonderful teachers of music have been an inspiration to continue. At QUT in particular Associate Professor Andrew Brown has contributed a whole universe of new intellectual support for new musicianship and understanding of music technology and I am thankful for the privilege of being involved with this research as it unfolds through the Australasian Collaborative Research Centre for Interaction design (ACID). Professor Richard Vella has exposed me to a range of new philosophical and creative practice perspectives as well as great musical insights through his work "Sounds in time, sounds in space" and his creative work in composition. His personal assistance in the long journey of writing this book is greatly appreciated. Thanks also to Professor Andy Arthurs for his support and encouragement as head of the innovative music departments that I am fortunate to be a part of. I am extremely grateful to the insights and incredible knowledge about culture contributed by my editor Elizabeth Mackinlay it is a rare honour to work with such a culturally aware music educator and she has encouraged me to confront problems that many avoid in this work.

I would particularly like to thank my Indigenous friends and colleagues whose patience and generosity of spirit has inspired me on this teacher's journey of understanding in particular: Victor Hart, Gordon Chalmers, Auntie Delmae

Barton, William Barton, Robert Barton, Christine Peacock, Martin Nakata and Craig Ackland. I hope this book begins a process of modelling engagement with Indigenous knowledge from the position of an inquiring and open whitefella.

I owe a debt of gratitude to my wife Angela, for her understanding, love and support over along period of time. To my daughter Bridie, for teaching me more about how children learn than I could ever learn from books.

Finally, I would like to thank the global music education community for their encouragement. ISME has provided an amazing forum for interchange of ideas about how music is made and what it means. In particular my European colleagues: Pamela Burnard, Gabriel Rusinek, Frits Evelein, Eva Sather and Bo Wah Lueng in Hong Kong for the opportunity to discuss the issues raised in this book on a global level. Lastly, I would like to thank all of those who believed with me that documenting is the best form of advocacy and participate in the save to DISC (Documenting Innovation in Sound Communities) Research network, in particular Professor Don Stewart, Greg Dodge, Daniel Spirovski, Rachel Templeton and John Ong for his diagram designs and all the graduate students who have gathered around this unique and energetic community.

Part I

Position

CHAPTER ONE

DESIGNING AND MANAGING THE CULTURAL LIVES OF CHILDREN

> I believe that the individual who is to be educated is a social individual, and that society is an organic union of individuals. If we eliminate the social factor from the child we are left only with an abstraction; if we eliminate the individual factor from the society we are left with an inert and lifeless mass. Education must therefore begin with a psychological insight into the child's capacities, interests and habits. It must be controlled at every point by reference to these same considerations. These powers, interests and habits must be continually interpreted—we must know what they mean. They must be translated into terms of their social equivalents—into terms of what they are capable of in the way of social service (Dewey in Eisner 1994, v).

Introduction

The purpose of this book is to examine what interests and motivates children about music and what they find meaningful. This quest is bounded and focussed by the terms of their "social equivalence". It is contained by the notion that education in music is personal and individual, and simultaneously cultural and social. Meaningful music education contributes towards the education of character (Buber 1969). This book explicitly examines how curriculum and experience might be designed so that it provides access to meaningful music making as a lifetime pursuit. It is not simply a sociological or qualitative piece of research about what is happening in a single participant observation site. Rather, I focus upon what is happening in conjunction with an ongoing body of theorising about music education and explores the ideas and insights gleaned from this long term study and applies them to new contexts where music and meaning are the focus. I seek to explore how those theories should be understood, applied, and dynamically respond to the needs of practice. Furthermore, this book searches for, explores and identifies the dimensions of good practice, and in doing so, my intention is both to elaborate the meaning of music to young people in a school or community context and its relationship to music teaching.

Some key concepts in this book

The education of character

Philosopher Martin Buber, in his discussion about the inclusive relationship between teachers and students proposed that education worthy of bearing the name is the education of character (Buber 1969, 104). It is this notion of education as being transformative, which is the focus of this discussion about music making and meaning. This philosophical position, which describes learning relationships, forms part of a holistic approach to philosophy in music education. Rather than ascribe to a "one size fits all" philosophy I have blended the notions of an aesthetic education (Reimer 1989), an education of perception (Gardner 1993b), music education as initiation into a discourse (Swanwick 1994) and a praxial music education (Elliott 1995). These views of arts, and specifically music education, capture the essence of what is being educated. I find merit in each argument and even in each philosopher's criticism of the other. My pragmatist leanings clarify this ideological position.

Art, according to Dewey, is "what the product does in and with experience" (Dewey 1989, 3). Whether what is being educated is the aesthetic, the perception, an initiation into a discourse or through a process of praxial education, there is no doubt that ultimately what is being educated is "the live creature" (Dewey 1989). The live creature is simultaneously a social being, an individual in relation, and a person whose consciousness may be changed through experience. Certainly, critical philosophical discussion about the precise nature of the psychological aspects of learning is a necessary and important pursuit, but it is not necessary here to choose a preferred position, or construct a set of binary oppositions. Rather, I believe that each philosophical position provides a particular "lens" upon the understanding of how we think and how art affects our feelings and intellect. Each argument is also profoundly limited, filtered and shaped by the context in which it was conceived and most importantly seems to focus upon music as a cultural object or an act of participating in culturally bounded experience.

Despite the now hackneyed and misunderstood concept of child centred approaches, music education—and indeed those that discuss philosophy of music education—always begin with a cultural framing (Bernstein 2000) of music as an object or "musicing" as an experience which frames the perceived value of sound in that community. In this discussion I will explore an approach that whilst acknowledging the influence of the cultural framing of musical experience focuses more clearly on the student's experience as he or she moves between cultural experiences and how this influences their development. The education of character always involves some kind of change in the way we think, act or know. Sometimes these changes are incremental and within the domain and other times, they have transferable qualities and are able to be conceptualised and reapplied in new domains, cultures and contexts.

From transfer to transformation

David Perkins (1988) discusses the concept of teaching for transfer—that is, the ability for a concept in education to be transferred to another context or domain. Reflecting on my observations of children growing up, and through a tacit awareness of my own life, I have become aware that the way I think "musically" has affected the way that I do things and solve problems, beyond the process of making music, in fact my music making experiences have had generic consequences. The processes and interactions involved in music making have educated my character; I have been able to transfer the skills and knowledge gained in making music to other domains. Indeed, I believe this research to be heavily influenced by such thinking. Through the process of making and thinking about music, I have also been "made" by it. For example, the idea of student as maker described in Chapter 6 is primarily about the role that music education can play in the education of character: identifying and defining the processes that refine, reify and make music experience meaningful. This refers to music making as a transformative experience. At every point in this book I have tried to refer to the child's capacities, interests and habits (Dewey 1989) and bound these within a context that refers to the social, and that contributes a benefit to society.

Music making has a powerful influence on emotions and can contribute to our identity and its formation. Musical experiences can help us know ourselves, communicate with others in wordless ways and contribute to our understanding of our place in our own distinctive culture. These experiences in these locations have the capacity to be meaningful and lead to transformation of self.

The phenomenon of meaning in music

As I described in the preface to this research, I have had a deep association with the phenomenon of the meaning of music as a music teacher in a school. I wanted to utilise this association to advantage to gain an understanding of the phenomenon of meaning and the processes that facilitated or gave access to that meaning from the inside. In this process, I became the instrument of measurement, reflection and analysis, conflict and argument, and eventually understanding. In doing so, I was able to take fundamental values, philosophical principles and practices, and test them rigorously within a unique school environment. The opportunity to observe theoretical concepts in action and gain an insight into the logistical and educational affects of this "theory in action" presented to me an opportunity for fascinating ethnographic research. Further to the case study, which forms the major part of this book, I have been able to apply and test many of the findings from that earlier study in new contexts. I have since observed the relationships between meaning and contexts, and the characteristics of student experience and teachers practice in detail, as part of ongoing and comparative research with colleagues in Europe, the USA and Asia. The process of putting the meat on the bones of theory and developing an appropriate methodology for research that allows students to speak through me as a researcher is discussed in Chapter 3.

While this book is principally intended as a philosophical study I do not directly pursue the philosophical debates that are the concern of music education globally. These debates have informed the study and my practice but because of the contextual limitations of the discussion, I would argue they tend not to have solutions for three major issues confronting music education internationally. The issues of technology, culture and the value of popular music still seem to be peripheral to the culturally framed philosophical positions. They are still "problems" for music educators whose principle position is a colonial "Western art music" one. While it may appear cowardly for me not to evidence this grand critical statement immediately, I will say that this book proposes to demonstrate how it is possible to confront these issues by shifting the focus of music education from a cultural framing to the child's experience of meaningful music making. In Chapter 2, I will outline my position and experience with research particularly focusing upon music technology and cultural understanding. The role of popular music in music education is interwoven throughout the case study and research contexts here and is in no need of separate treatment. In each chapter, I will discuss the issues of technology and cultural understanding against the theoretical focus of the chapter. As a further measure to expose music education theory to practice and critical review, I will also draw upon current research findings that examine and problematise these issues to extend the debate.

Music, meaning and transformation

The purpose of this book is to examine how meaningful music making can lead to transformative experience and a sustained interaction with music making for life. In this respect, the ideals or areas of social formation are important because they seek to address the aspects of the post-modern condition that have an effect upon self-formation and social life. I define these experiences as "aesthetic grounding", which suggests that the activities and associated reflective practice are those which ground students in present relationships with others and develop and increase the store of social capital within a community (Cox 1997). They are able to contribute both to self-development and self and community. Throughout exploration of the case study data and subsequent iterations of research into music and meaning I was able to support and evidence the idea that the ability to be critical, reflective, and perceptive is an essential skill that counteracts the advance of homogenised meaning. The ability to be creative and to use lateral thinking skills becomes a mandatory vocational and life skill for survival in our society (Burnaford, Aprill and Weiss 2004, Robinson, 2001). It is a realisation of humanity's needs to be expressive, and communicate through all media—verbal, written visual and aural. I would suggest that it is essential in aesthetic education for us to learn in these kinds of ways and with these kinds of foci and hope to provide evidence from practice that amplifies these ideas as ways of being and acting for music teachers and coaches working in contemporary communities and schools.

Decolonisation and music education

Recognising that music making has the potential to facilitate social and personal transformation is an important insight, as is acknowledgement of the embodied nature of music learning, the pervasiveness of music across cultures and the potential to harness music experience to affect changes in values and attitudes across cultures as well as inside them. In a global context—or indeed in the multi-cultural contexts where we live and learn—mono-cultural perspectives and cultural framings that colonise expression in sound are at risk of diluting their own importance as cultural knowledge and miss an opportunity to gather on common ground at the intersections between cultures. In this kind of approach there is a risk of mono-cultural framings taking on neo-colonial positions—one of the issues with a colonial approach is that it refuses to see the damage it is doing and it's power as a political dominating force—this kind of position is dangerous, even more so, for Indigenous cultures or the "others". Perhaps the most cogent position in this kind of realisation of an approach to music education practice is to be continuously conscious of the power differential my white, European position affords me. Indigenous scholars notions of acting at the borderlands or engaging with the tensions at the interfaces between cultures (Nakata 2002), suggests that this is not a tension that leads to resolution but of continuous engagement. It is fundamentally a politically activity and is enacted through the struggle and a relationship that is open and seeking criticism. Music making however can afford us a relationship between cultures that has potential to foster understanding.

Music making has the power to connect people in non-verbal ways. It has a potential to convey something of "others" through embodied understandings and unify people in shared time and space. More importantly than this clichéd insight, music making has the potential to engage people across cultures in ways that can be themselves transformative because they challenge our colonial position and introduce the concept of the other in musical ways. So while I am at the early stages of this understanding I have chosen to examine the idea of music making as a decolonisation process as a part of transformation of self through the deeply political notion of decolonisation.

Modelling the development of a personal philosophy of music education: A teacher's journey

The tone of this book I hope is one that describes my own personal journey as a music teacher. What I hope to do is to amplify the voices of children, teachers and parents I met along the way. The aim is that through observing how I have undertaken this process and by trying to apply some of the analytical tools and philosophical principles described here that the reader could undertake the development of their own continuous and dynamic development of philosophy in practice. I have been fortunate enough to guide many pre-service music teachers through this process and some of the tools and processes have been developed specifically to assist pre service music teachers to develop their own music education philosophy. The feedback from them is that it works and so in each Chapter I summarise what we can do in each context to provoke discussion and understanding of the ideas in the Chapter and seek to encourage their application to your context and culture.

The book is laid out in three parts. Part 1 positions and locates me as a teacher and as a researcher. It provides detail about the important issues that have emerged from data and my interaction with practice. In this Part I discuss their pertinence, their origin and outline my experience with them both empirically and from the perception of a music teacher in a school and a university. Following on from this, I then outline my approach to methodology and research design examining in detail the principle case study site and the subsequent research about music and meaning in the context of music technology and cultural understanding.

Part 2 provides a theoretical perspective but not one that simply speaks of philosophy. Rather it demonstrates how philosophy can engage dynamically with practice and can provide new understandings about how theory might be refocused to draw upon the students' experience of meaning in context. I begin with a discussion of the concept of "flow" and its connection to the intrinsic nature of music making. I then examine the practical concerns of teachers in designing meaningful and engaging environments. I discuss the central idea of the student as maker not only of music but as a self-formative activity. The conclusion to this section examines the idea of the teacher as builder of context where students encounter meaning through music making which is transformative.

Part 3 examines "practice" through the voices of those who are making music in practice. Here I focus upon the personal, social and cultural locations of meaning and then examine a unique reinterpretation of Rousseau's theory in an examination of a real school as a village where music making provided access to meaning and engagement with expressiveness, social inclusion and feelings of belonging and most of all the education of character.

Appendix B refers to a set of fundamental philosophical ideas, which seem to have a large basis of support amongst philosophers, curriculum designers and practitioners. It is useful to consider these against the ideas raised in each chapter and undertake a personal reflection on what issues are raised in relation to the assumptions that surround these ideas. These constitute ideas that I took into the field to examine in practice and in subsequent iterations of research about music and meaning. They describe the relationship of the chapters to the ongoing body of thought and provide criticism of them also that suggest a need for new principles or expansion of existing values and assumptions.

Conclusion

In this book, I have applied the concept of the "student as maker" as a tool for analysis in music education research that allows us to refocus upon the students' experience of meaningful engagement with music making. Philosophically I am able to draw some fundamental pointers that suggest that the adoption of a particular approach to curriculum and practice would lead to educational or social transformation. I suggest that students who experience this approach might gain a particular kind of social formation as an outcome that is more responsive to contemporary conditions and needs. Put simply, this book seeks to reinterpret the Deweyan approach to experiential learning in a way that enables students to respond to arts education in the twenty-first century in a way that would enhance their understanding and provide experience and tools for critical analysis that are relevant to twenty-first century constructions of how music is perceived and interpreted.

The model discussed in this book was used in the design of curriculum, philosophy and practice at a case study school and in subsequent research contexts both live and virtual. The ways in which these ideas were "worked out" in these contexts form the basis of the empirical study detailed here. This research is intended as an expansion, empirical investigation and further conceptual elaboration of the ideas of the student as maker and the implications of this for the interpretation of curriculum, the design of experience and the approach taken by teachers and coaches to provide access to meaningful music making for life. The idea here is to provide an opportunity for music teachers and coaches to manage the cultural lives of children (Dillon 2005a) and design experiences that take a full account of the affordances of the environment and the need for students to express themselves in sound within that context in a way that is both relevant and reverent to the communities values.

 *What we can do*

Much of how we teach music comes from our embodied understanding of music making. Before you can understand the meaning of music and its effects on students, it is therefore important for you to understand what music means to you. For you to begin, continue or restart your reflective journey as a music educators, at the end of each chapter in this book I have included a set of reflective questions and exercises—those included here are preliminary and will be asked again many times throughout this book in the light of new information. My wish is that as you respond to each question, your answers to them will evolve and your understandings grow.

Where is music in your life?
Where it is in the life of a child?
Where it is in your context /community and what do you perceive it to mean?

Using the answers to these questions begin to construct your music life story and focus on moments when you felt that you underwent a significant shift in your understanding.

CHAPTER TWO

LOCATING MYSELF IN THE DISCOURSE

Introduction

Since 1989, I have taught pre-service music teachers and general primary music education. Each year I am away from the school music classroom I am self-conscious that my credibility as a practitioner might wane with these students—I ask myself, am I still a "real music teacher"? What is my relationship to practice? How would I respond to the new contexts I encounter in this state? Do I really understand what it is like to be a music teacher in this place and with these people? How does my theory and values fair here and now? As I ask these questions, I realise that the fact I am asking questions is part of the continuous evolution of my position as a music educator and as a reflective practitioner and critical researcher. I now have the privileged position to observe theory in practice made by other teachers and pre-service teachers—to hear their stories, their successes and failures, to see them develop as music teachers and develop their own personal and dynamic philosophies of music education and value systems. Here, I want to step back to better understand my own positioning within the many different discourses that underpin, drive and sustain music education. I feel that it is important to share this more evolutionary approach of a music teacher's critical practice as well as positioning myself as both a teacher and researcher.

The big picture issues

From these interactions and from ongoing research projects about music and meaning, issues arise constantly for me, gather voracity, and elevate in importance. The issue of the value of popular music has been one of those and as I am from a professional popular music performance and song writing background, my embodied understanding of how popular musicians learn has been useful in the structure of a curriculum that is inclusive of musical forms as a source of musical knowledge (Green 2001). The other issues that arise consistently are those of music technology and cross-cultural music studies.

All three of these issues can be confronting for those whose backgrounds as musicians are grounded in live, Western art music performance. It is rare indeed to find students who have genuine embodied understanding of "other" culture's music, knowledge of popular genres and styles, and a genuine working understanding of how music technology might be used to enhance and engage learning in music education. Fear of non-Western music, fear of technology and fear of popular music was and still is common amongst pre-service teachers of music. I came to realise that this was because of how they constituted themselves as musicians, how they constructed their identity as musicians and their whole sense of self. So when I proposed assignments that involved resource production, peer performance in multiple genres and cultures that were to be developed, presented and produced using technology for many I threatened their very identity as musicians. Nevertheless, this process has been a provocative one that has led to success. Students were able to share their understandings and resources for use in their first year of teaching and the process of interacting with a range of musical styles did have an affect on their understanding of musical style and cultural framing of music.

The idea that I could create a classroom environment that would challenge student's sense of self and identity and provoke self-critical awareness about "otherness" in music education was appealing and seemed to be successful. What I did not realise at the time was my "elemental" approach to music education was still framed by Western art music theory and pedagogy—asking students to notate embodied cultural materials using a notation program on a computer, for example, hardly challenged their Western art music values. Others students when completing this task appropriated cultural materials or presented them in ways that made me cringe. I wondered at the ethical considerations underlying these experiences and why students were not engaging with them. I wondered too how working with a common practice notation program on a computer enhanced their contemporary musicianship in a world where digital recording is the dominant representation system and CPN filters the essence of groove from popular and cross-cultural music. At international forums and in music education journals these issues still arise consistently yet popular music and its appropriateness for the classroom has been debated regularly for the entire 30 years I have taught. Music technology seems to have earned itself an entire subject or course status in many Universities, while cross-cultural understandings have been offered through ethno-musicological studies for many years.

When interviewing music teachers for a study about the qualities of good practice in music teaching I discovered a profound insight. Every one of the teachers I had interviewed who was considered a "good/successful teacher" had "embodied" experiences with cross-cultural musicianship and popular music, and used music technology effectively integrated in their practice. Similarly, of the pre-service teachers who achieved high standards in the "resource-making" assignments all had embodied experience in cross-cultural musicianship, popular music and used music technology as a normal part of their music performance and production processes. What this says to me is two things. First, that these qualities of good practice are "teachable"—they are not simply a personality trait or as result of an individual teacher's charisma. Second, these issues signify something quite important about the kind of musicianship required for the twenty first century.

Culture, technology and popular music

In international forums, I have repeatedly observed that it is the issues of culture, technology and popular music, which problematise contemporary discussions of music education. In an attempt to engage with these issues I have included in each Chapter a brief discussion of the relationship that culture and technology have to each chapter foci, the effects of culture and technology on the case study school discussed, and draw upon subsequent research contexts to explore these issues in more detail. It is intriguing to me that the issues of the value and appropriateness of popular music in music curriculum are still being argued some 50 years after the beginnings of what can be referred to as "youth music" (see for example, Agardy 1985, Gans 1975, Green 1988, 2001, Swanwick 1984a, 1984b, Vulliamy 1981, Vulliamy and Lee 1976, 1982, Vulliamy and Shepherd 1984, 1985). What this suggests is that this issue is not one which is simply about musical knowledge or relevance, but that the perspective which is culturally framed forbids its inclusion in the curriculum without discussion. In recent times Lucy Green's work in particular has established the values and musicianship associated with popular music as important aspects of music education in contemporary life (Green, 1988, 2001). In this book I will not directly deal with this idea but you will find that integrated throughout in what participants in the research call the "music is music" approach you will I hope see how Green's and Swanwick's theories function in practice.

Technology however has also become a problem for music educators whose eyes glaze over at its mention and try to dismiss it at "just a tool" or dedicate whole sections of curriculum time in reifying it to a level of essential technical competency. The position adopted in this book is to examine technology as it refers to the students' experience of creative production. Hence, every chapter will have a section dedicated to discussing technology in relation to the focus of the chapter. Primarily these sections ask Heidegger's question about what technology reveals and what it conceals (Heidegger 1977), and further whether what technology conceals functions as a pedagogical device for focusing learning. In this sense in each chapter, I will examine recent research in music technology practice and thought, which works through contemporary practice and examines the new forms of musicianship that are associated with twenty-first century music making.

Culture, cross-cultural music and its teaching in ethical ways is a concern also in music education. It is becoming even more apparent that our frameworks for music education and our philosophy are West centric and European in origin and this context serves as a colonial framework for how musical otherness is perceived. Globalisation and appropriation of music from across cultures and times is expanding at a great rate and I have examined the idea of music education and culture from the perspective of research I have undertaken into Indigenous standpoint theory and knowledge which problematises the notions of existing cultural framings. Each chapter will examine the themes in relation to Indigenous knowledge from the point of view of a teachers experience with engaging with tensions between cultures as a conscious political act rather than a colonial perspective. While this is perhaps under developed at this stage, as research it does however present the issues and some potential solutions, which have been applied in my own context and found to be effective.

Emerging cultural understanding

I will interrogate the ideas of culture, appropriation, representation and ethics in each chapter of the book in relation to the students experience of meaningful engagement with music. Now I would like to provide a positioning that explains why these issues are of importance to me as a music teacher and what I need to do to engage effectively with the problems that have arisen from this practice. I am convinced of the worth of engaging with the inherent politics of culture and of the potential for such activity to be transformative. What concerns me is how this can be done ethically and how we can construct embodied understandings rather than filtered and watered down experiences.

At this point, I feel I need to define what it is I mean by culture, popular music and music technology and how this affects my practice. The concept of "culture" as described by the Encarta World dictionary is an interesting and revealing description:

cul·ture n
1. art, music, literature, and related intellectual activities
2. enlightenment and sophistication acquired through education and exposure to the arts
3. the beliefs, customs, practices, and social behavior of a particular nation or people
4. a group of people whose shared beliefs and practices identify the particular place, class, or time to which they belong
5. a particular set of attitudes that characterizes a group of people
9. the development of a skill or expertise through training or education
(*Encarta® World English Dictionary* 1999).

This definition highlights the Western importance of art and initiation into an arts discourse as central to how cultures are represented and defined. It recognises that culture is about the social aspects of shared values and rituals, and most clearly that to belong in a culture we need to be educated about what the culture is and means. This concept of "culture" signifies both our identity as a member of "a distinct culture" and the "otherness" of those that belong to different cultures and not to our own—according to this definition then, culture both unifies and divides.

Music as a signifier of culture also does this—it is as evident within youth culture styles as it is with national anthems at the Olympics. Music says in an instant who we are and where we belong. Culture therefore provides what (Bernstein 2000) would call "strong framing" and "strong classification". In music classrooms, the "strong framing" and "strong classification" is distinctly Western art music in origin. This becomes problematic when those that are receiving the education may not be natives of the culture so music becomes a means of colonisation. The proliferation of multi-cultural schools, influxes of non-Western immigrants and refugees, and the pervasiveness of popular culture challenge both the framing and classification of what is being transmitted. The complexities of this strong framing of culture are perhaps most transparent when we are exposed to "otherness". Music is no stranger to a trading or exchange or appropriation of sounds and structures across cultures and alternatively there is potential for music to become a site of cultural interchange and understanding through interaction with embodied experiences and critical reflection of both musical and political agendas. But how is this done in relation to context—how can such a process become something more than a benevolent, liberal and colonial position?

The benefits of an Australian position

I began this book wondering what an Australian perspective might be able to offer the music education world. My own position as an Australian from British immigrant origins suggest that my experiences of music making and philosophy are framed by colonial ideology and theory and yet this is somehow distorted by the distance from the centres of Northern hemisphere thought and practice and more importantly the very different physical and intellectual context. This may seem like a disadvantage when commenting upon global issues in music education. Nevertheless, the Australian influence on music education is quite profound not the least from its expatriate representatives. Through my own recent journeys to international forums, I have come to enjoy the unique perspective that our "mixed bag" of philosophy, method and practice has come to provide. However, in Australia I have also observed otherwise internationally "successful" methods turned into dogma as they are inappropriately applied in a colonial way. I have come to question the study of European musical history in a context where it has only been a part for two centuries and struggled for relevance—philosophy and practice become distorted by the differences of Australian values and its unique environment.

In Australia, I have access to wonderful experiences with cross-cultural music in thriving and diverse cities. I am invited to participate in communities where music takes on different roles as has been my experiences with the many and varied Islamic communities. Most significantly I have been privileged to be invited to gain an understanding of Indigenous standpoint theory and Australian Indigenous knowledge (Nakata 2002). These experiences began for me when I was charged with the responsibility to "Indigenise curriculum" in music and sound at the University. This process involved examining the potential and impediments to cultural inclusivity and in particular identifying methods and resources to undertake this task across the faculty. What began as a process of "consultation" with Indigenous Australians, became a relationship with individuals, communities and knowledge frameworks that have had a profound effect upon my thinking about music as knowledge and about how cultures interact with music. I have found this emergent understanding to be profoundly different from what I suggest is the naïve position of many who encounter music as an object and study other cultures as interesting artefacts without experiencing and understanding or engaging with the ethical concerns that are inherent with this kind of experience. To know that in Australian Indigenous culture that "without a song you are nothing" (Dillon and Chapman 2005, Mackinlay 2004), that the human voice in song so affects the emotions that it is sacred in Islam and should only be reserved for talking to God—these are the kind of diverse experiences that perhaps our isolation from European culture have afforded me. They are a blessing carried by generous people who share a meaningful relationship with music and recognise openness and respect as a passport to entering into a relationship of understanding.

With this invitation to participate or to enter into a relationship of understanding, I have also taken on the responsibility to question my own colonial position and the power relations that this implies. Aspiring to be a transformative teacher rather than a mimetic one has been a philosophical goal since my early teacher training but this approach does not prepare us to engage with the politics and the tensions between cultures. To ask questions about our colonial positioning and the cultural framing that influences what we do and how we do it. I resonate with Mackinlay who states, "I hold strongly to the belief that we have a moral responsibility to engage in such questioning to work towards an ethical, moral and socially just research and educational praxis" (Mackinlay 2005, 114).

My own journey thus far has only brought me to a point where I understand the need for this moral, ethical and socially just approach and have begun a deeply personal and at once professional process of questioning. What I hope to do in this book is ask these questions and perhaps explore my emergent ideas about music as a metaphorical common ground where cultures can meet, learn embodied knowledge from each other and perhaps forge new syncretisms, and how we might do this in an ethical framework. What appears to be common across cultures and is represented strongly in Australian Indigenous culture is that music represents knowledge and is a container and vehicle for knowledge transfer which can potentially lead to understanding of the knowledge of "others". I hope that this "need to understand" is not perceived as another colonising desire but one that seeks to have embodied experience of the "others" music and reflect on it in context with deep and critical self-reflection. I would suggest it is more clearly focused upon experiencing music as a way of knowing others and of knowing self and therefore provides an opportunity for meaningful and transformative interaction—as Nakata (2002) suggests, we need to engage with the tensions at the interfaces between cultures.

There are many tensions—ownership, identity relationships, knowledge and context are all ready to be misunderstood just as signs in a foreign language are. I have come to the conclusion alongside Mackinlay that "participation in music–culture as a path to learning then has the potential to encourage students not only to theories about their experiences, but also to actively engage with the political and the ethical"(Mackinlay 2005, 115). This is indeed a bold step for teachers and one that I recognise as important to my practice. Further, talking to me about the process of teaching a world music course to pre-service music teachers, my colleague Jim Chapman found that:

A unit on World Music was most meaningful if it made an opportunity for Australian students to experience some part of the reconciliation process between black and white Australians. Before real understanding of the music could occur, understanding of the people and culture and the historical and present relationships between the dominant white culture and the peripheral indigenous culture must occur (Dillon and Chapman 2005, 192).

In our discussion, Jim and I recognized two things in the context of teaching this course. First, the process was a political one that challenged and asked questions about self, self and others, and as Mackinlay suggests, "holds promise as a process for deconstructing the borders and boundaries of colonialism in all guises" (Mackinlay 2005, 116). Such an approach is an act of "decolonisation" and is deeply political. This is confronting for many music teachers—it challenges our identity and values and asks us to in turn challenge the values and identity of our students. In music education the strength of the cultural framing and classifications are evident within the struggle for cultures to be represented rather than acquired and appropriated. It is most evident within cultural identity but even more visible when we understand how music technology and popular music seem to question or generate new forms of skill and musicianship. These ideas have become extremely important to me and over the course of this book; I hope to struggle further with what an ethical approach to music education might involve and what decolonisation means to our practice.

What technology reveals

Having spent much of my professional career as a rock musician, my relationship with technology has been an integral part of practice and the development of philosophy. As with music and culture I frequently observe a lack of fundamental understanding as to the role of technology in music education, philosophers generally fail to deal with it, practitioners are frightened by it (Dillon 2006a). I have been fortunate to be involved with new software developments and research into interaction design at the Queensland University of Technology and as a touring musician was part of the first wave of electronic music live performers in the 80s. I have worked with generative music making for children for many years now as a philosopher and curriculum designer (Dillon 2003, 2004a, 2004b, 2005, 2006b). This kind of cross-disciplinary research has profoundly influenced how I consider the role of technology as an expressive force in the future of music education.

It is from the philosophy of (Heidegger 1977) that we can begin to understand the nature of technology and of the relationship that humanity has as tool users. Through observations of how musicians interact with technology in the creative production of music, Brown (2006) suggests three metaphorical perspectives that describe usage of the computer as either a tool, medium or instrument. This framing allows us to perceive the specific function of the technology as music makers in practice use it. What Brown's approach to the idea of technology as an amplifier of musicality suggests is that we need to examine what the technology reveals, what it conceals and identify whether what is concealed, functions as a focusing mechanism for pedagogy or a limiting and filtering mechanism for expression or understanding. Throughout this book I will examine these ideas against research concerned with meaningful engagement, seeking to reintegrate tool use within creative production of music as an amplifier of musicality (Brown 2006).

Conclusion

This chapter has sought to simply position myself in respect to emergent issues of what I perceive to be important in music education. At the heart of these issues is the thought that music education for life is intimately linked to issues of cultural understanding, popular music and technological mediation of experiences. Throughout the book, I hope to display and model how I have encountered these issues and the effect that reflection on these experiences has engendered. Certainly, we need to be reflective practitioners but we also need to examine the definitive concepts that frame what we do. In the next chapter, I would like to discuss my position as a researcher and introduce the story of the research projects, which form the empirical basis of the study of music and meaning and its potential for transformative experience.

CHAPTER THREE

PUTTING THE MEAT ON THE BONES OF THEORY

Introduction

In the previous chapter, I located myself within discourses of music education. I would like to now position myself as a researcher and tell the story of the research which underpins the ideas presented in this book. My work here takes a pragmatist philosophical approach and is essentially about a dynamic interaction between the "live creatures" interpretation of philosophy and practice where we are able to observe and measure the voracity of the claims made by theorists about meaning and human behaviour. The voices and music of students, teachers and community are heard loudly in this chapter as a way of putting the meat on the bones of theory. Methodologically the data that informs this study has been unique. It involves a long-term participant observation case study at a single schools site as a basis for the discussion. The school as village that provides the large and deep body of data is described and two other ongoing areas of research that have I have been involved with over the past seven years in relation to meaningful engagement with music making—music technology and the process of Indigenising curriculum in a tertiary context—are also discussed. Both of these later studies also widen the context of the research beyond schools to community music contexts. This chapter then serves two purposes. First, to contextualise and introduce the participants represented in the study, and second, to provide a description of the methodologies used and propose some newer approaches to methodology that allow music to be heard rather than silenced by the filter of text.

Project 1: Researching the meaning of music to students in a school context

Selecting an appropriate methodology

The selection of appropriate methodology that will most effectively and rigorously reveal information about research questions is the first problem encountered by every researcher. The problem of paradigm issues is involved in this process. As a researcher, there is a fundamental choice between positivistic methods that measure phenomena through the elimination of variables and from the viewpoint of the dispassionate objective observer, or alternatively a naturalistic post-positivist approach that emphasises the wholeness of the context and the researcher as instrument. Of most importance to me as researcher are the kinds of information, the depth of data and the ability of the instrument to reveal insight into the phenomena under study.

The central question that binds and focuses this study is; what is the meaning of music to young people in a school? Meaning in this study is defined as what students find involves and engages them with music making and listening. Related questions are: What are the processes that give access to and facilitate those meanings? What are the implications of this knowledge for teaching, learning and community? For this reason, I considered an interpretive case study method to be a good way to get at these questions. This study then is clearly grounded within the interpretive paradigm of qualitative research that recognises participant observers as interpretive, sensing and reflective, and acknowledges that they are in themselves the instruments of research.

The appropriateness of the interpretive paradigm

Sloboda and Howe's (1992) quantitative study examined the system of music learning in early childhood. Their study had many similarities to the school case study described here, in particular the descriptions of teachers and processes, but little about meaning. Their study revealed, for example, that the music students' "first teacher" was significant in influencing continued interest in learning music but because of the structure of the research was unable to reveal what qualities that teacher might have had. Sloboda and Howe also interviewed teachers, students and parents to gain a broad perspective of the students' "music life" beyond the classroom, in the school community and in their families.

Sloboda and Howe's study, which focused upon student's early music learning experiences, used a relatively small sample, which perhaps reduces the significance of the outcomes. Sloboda and Howe's research has similarities of sample and context with those of the current study and a comparison would provide an understanding of what each methodology is able to reveal about music learning. The data presented by Sloboda and Howe revealed some generalisable results but was unable to provide a basis for an understanding of the phenomena as part of a system. As these kinds of research methods are "adapted from the physical and biological sciences they are not always adequate for the study of human behaviour" (Borg and Gall 1983). It is the idea of observing how people interpret the world in action and in context, and what they find meaningful that was the most pressing concern in the selection of methodology for this research.

Csikszentmihalyi (1996), in his study of creativity, suggests that only by examining all of the factors that comprise the system within which a phenomenon takes place can a true understanding of it be formed. Music is made and experienced in a school in a number of contexts. The process of learning music involves many different activities and encounters. Students in schools may experience music in the classroom, the instrumental studio and a range of ensembles, or as part of family and youth subculture. To gain an understanding of the factors influencing, and giving access to meaning in music it was imperative that the study was inclusive of the relevant contexts. As Csikszentmihalyi (1996) demonstrates in his study of creativity, the observation of a total system can be usefully researched using qualitative methods. These kinds of methods related to anthropology and ethnography could provide a "thick description" of the phenomena of music meaning in context, which is the focus of the current case.

As this participant observation case study research is directly concerned with "human meaning and interaction" (Jorgensen 1989), a kind of methodology was required which would lend itself most favourably to examining both meaning and process within a naturalistic setting. As a member of staff at the case study site, access as an unobtrusive observer was guaranteed. I saw myself as a "deep insider" researcher and sought to identify and acknowledge the influence provided by the position of power that I might have brought into the context, I undertook to also employ crosschecking mechanisms to compensate for and to reflect on this effect continuously. My position enabled me to take on several research roles as teacher, researcher, reflective, practitioner and non-participant observer. My established presence at the site ensured a kind of transparency or more natural response than that afforded an observer whose presence may have predisposed participants to perform or change the way in which they might act normally. Indeed, Jorgenson suggests that participant observation is most appropriate when certain minimal conditions are present as follows:

- the research problem is concerned with human meanings and interactions viewed from an insiders perspective;
- the phenomenon of investigation is observable within an everyday setting;
- the researcher is able to gain access to an appropriate setting;
- the phenomenon is sufficiently limited in size and location to be studied as a case;
- the study questions are appropriate for case study; and,

- the research problem can be addressed by qualitative data gathered by direct observation and other means pertinent to the field setting (Jorgensen 1989).

The size of the school and my own prior knowledge of the site provided an intimate and compact knowledge of the case. The "deep insider's" view provided me with privileged access, a clear perspective of who to ask and where to look and an established understanding of the history and development of the site and the people in it (Edwards 1999). An illustration of this occurred when I was able to make connections between historical incidents that I shared with students and teachers. I was able to use prompts that referred to those shared experiences for example: "what about when we had the synthesizer concert– how did you feel parents responded to that?" In this case, the shared memory helped me to prompt a situation that we both had knowledge about. However, I was also placed in a position where I needed to be critical of the effect that I might have upon the data collection and analysis.

General advantages and disadvantages of the approach

The methodology of participant observation seeks to uncover, make accessible and reveal the meanings (realities) people use to make sense out of their daily lives. In placing the meaning of everyday life first, the methodology of participant observation differs from approaches that begin with concepts defined by way of existing theories and hypothesis (Jorgensen 1989). The experience of the insider is different from that of aliens; it constitutes a reality for those inside it and even erroneous beliefs have real consequences (Jorgensen 1989). The advantage of this kind of access is its familiarity and the notion that the participants within the site are most likely to continue their daily lives relatively unaffected by the known insider observer. The methodology "provides access to the insider's world of meaning" (Jorgensen 1989, 15).

As meaning is a central question of this book, this perspective potentially offers an interesting and distinctive lens on the phenomenon. This access is to be celebrated and valued as a privileged view. Nevertheless, despite this privileged access, there is a need to incorporate measures to ensure the trustworthiness of the research, so that the effect of my own values is considered in the interpretations. In this research, I had intimate knowledge about the students. I had taught them all for five years. I knew their parents and had influenced their music learning and personal lives. What guarantee did I have that these students, when interviewed, would not simply tell me what they thought I wanted to hear? What measures did I have to ensure that staff for whom I had been "boss" would not also tell me what I wanted to hear or act how they perceived I would like them to act in observation? How could I see what was not already familiar to me? How could I check that my data reconstruction and analysis were not driven by my preconceptions about what I hoped to find?

To address the problems of influence and the value-laden qualities of data interpretations, a number of procedures were undertaken. First, I decided to implement a pilot study, to examine student and teacher responses and observer influence. The pilot study further served to refine the interview instrument and sample. In the research design, I also incorporated the following procedures for crosschecking and self-checking measures to increase the trustworthiness, authenticity and fairness (Lincoln and Guba 1985, 295) of the data collection and analysis; member checking of interview and observation transcripts and triangulation or what Janeseck terms "crystallization" (in Denzin and Lincoln 2000, 393). The term, "triangulation", it is argued, tends to fix meanings rather than reveal shifting changing nature of truth (Taylor 2000, pers comm., 20 June). In this research, I use it to describe the use of different methods of data collection such as interview, observations and cross sampling to provide a multiple lens upon the phenomenon. In this process, I also collected data in a number of media: text, video, audio and digital form. I discuss the detail of these procedures later in this chapter. Furthermore, I also made a conscious and deliberate search for things that surprised me as part of data analysis as well as following negative cases such as examining student's off-hand treatment of classroom music. These kinds of measures, I hope, enabled me to overcome the problem of being unable to see what was not already familiar.

Ethics

Proceeding ethically in any research is about engaging with the research site and the people in it in such a way that it does not harm the participants or environment but more importantly so that it is done with rigour and accountability so that the voices of the participants can be amplified and focused by the research. Ethical approval for this research was obtained from the La Trobe University Human Ethics Committee in 1996. Permission to use the school as a case study site was obtained from the school principal and signed participant consent was obtained from teachers and the parents of students. Ex-post-facto data that included teachers' journal, video and audio recording and documents analysis was also collected which involved data from 1991 onwards. The last phase of the study was done in a situation where I had withdrawn from teaching the students, and in which I would not be using things they said in evaluating their work or in evaluating teachers. The study was not primarily directed to evaluating or critiquing particular individuals (students or teachers). It was intended, and understood, as a study about an approach to a music program. For the school, the study offered some potential benefit, as part of a program to build and reflect on innovative and extensive commitment to good music education. Although the case study uses the conventions of anonymity, it cannot totally disguise all participants, who are identified by their role in the school. Care was taken in the writing of the study and in publications from it to avoid any form of reference that might identify them to negative effect. In my research journal, I noted that in the member checking process, students and teachers expressed a pride in their involvement and a sense of the importance of their contribution. This attitude was reflected particularly in the thorough nature of their checking and offers of additional material.

The pilot study

In qualitative research if we need to further understand and refine the question we are asking of the case and its participants and we need to examine the effectiveness of our research data collection strategies, a pilot study or focused preliminary field study offers the opportunity to do these things. The pilot study used in this research comprised interviews with a music teacher, a Uniting Church minister, who also serves as a counsellor and family social worker at the school, and four student members of an electronic music ensemble. The students represented were highly involved music students who participated in a variety of ensembles, had experienced music as elective classes and in the studio, and had actively performed music in school ceremonial events. The rationale behind the selection of these students was that if useful data could not be collected from these students, then either it did not exist or the interview was not an appropriate research instrument to gain this kind of data.

The pilot study revealed some useful findings. First, it was difficult for students to comment on their own personal growth. Second, I noted that it was difficult for students to isolate music experiences as a source of personal growth from other experiences that might just be a part of "growing up". This meant that information about the affects of music making experience upon personal and social development of the student was difficult to gain from interview alone or it may be inextricable from all the other influences and context. Alternatively, others more easily observed student development such as other students, teachers and counsellors. Third, the interview process needed more prompts to gather information about classroom music, as the focus of answers to open questioning was upon instrumental/studio learning and solo or ensemble performance. Fourth, students seemed very honest, open and critical of their music experiences, both in school and out. Indeed the feeling I got from interviews with students was that, because critical reflective discussion had been part of their classroom music activity, we had built up a relationship that was open to such discussion.

Students' intimate and confidential comments about each other, teachers, and even about me, provided credibility to the view that they were making open and honest comment because of my presence, rather than in spite of it. The enthusiasm with which each student and teacher spoke about their music making and their music biographies also suggested the importance of these constructed memories to the participant. For example, in this brief extract, Peter, a primary-music teacher, comments about the role of music and his family:

> Music was very important to us as a family. Music was always part of our worship and celebrations. I was exposed to a lot of singing and playing; it was just a part of our life (Peter 1998, pers comm. with teacher, 10 January).

Linda, a 16-year-old music student passionately describes her first recollection of music in her life:

> I don't remember anything else about being four except just this vision of a violin player getting a standing ovation from so many people, and sounding so good. And I just went [loudly]: "Mum I want a violin, now" (Linda 1997, pers comm. with student, 5 March).

These recollections were often moving and open descriptions of their involvement with music making and suggested that music was indeed intrinsically engaging and meaningful to these people. Their stories also revealed something about the context and ways in which they gained access to this meaning. This suggested that, by asking these students to discuss their music biographies, I might also gain a description of the process and context of that meaning.

The results of the pilot study suggest that musical biography, and focussed questions about aspects of the school, could generate useful data that was important to understanding the phenomenon of meaning, and provide a valuable lens on the context. I felt that interview questions that dealt with personal development needed to remain part of the interview prompts but that these needed to be crosschecked against observations and comment from teachers and counsellors as external observers. Extra prompts needed to be added to the interview guide to gain more information about classroom music. Examples include:

- Let us focus upon the environment at school, what effect has it had on your development as a musician?
- Firstly, classroom music, (emphasise this question for a story of the effect it had upon access and exposure, reflection and music thinking).
- What was beneficial?
- What was not?

There were also prompts about ensembles, place and access to equipment to contextualise their experiences; and the effects of teachers on their musical development, e.g., "what effect have the teachers/musicians had upon your development?"

The combination of music students, teacher conductor and the school minister constituted a mini-community of interactive parts. Crosschecking and coding of data across interview sources generated multiple perspectives of the phenomenon of the meaning of music to the students and the community. Recording the teacher's music biography added a complexity to the understanding of the meaning of music that extended beyond the present time or place. What I gained from his description was narrative of his own early memories of music experience and what it meant to him. All interview transcripts were member checked, with individuals providing extra comment and validation of the accuracy of transcription. Data analysis was also discussed with participants, which further added to the honesty of the interpretation. For member checking, the pilot study results allayed many of the feelings of self-doubt about the data collection and method.

The research framework

The research was a participant-observation case study. The instruments for data collection were: interview, participant observation, historical document, audiotape, videotape, and observer's journal. The interviews took place over three ten-week school terms. Observation of rehearsals in preparation for major performance events occurred throughout a full school year and included after school and weekends. The participant observations took place at the end of term three and included a further ten weeks of observation in term four.

Description of the site

The school is an independent school of the Uniting Church. The school population at the time of the research was 590 students, from pre-preparatory (three year old) to Year 12 (18 year old). Music was a compulsory classroom subject from pre prep to year eight. In Years 9 and 10, music was offered as an elective subject. At Year 11 and 12, the final years of secondary education in Australia, VCE (Victorian Certificate of Education), and music performance was offered for advanced students. There were classroom instrumental lessons from Years 3 to 8 and within their time at the school, the students are able to experience playing instruments from a variety of instrument families. There were up to 20 ensembles at the school. These ranged in size and style from a large wind ensemble and big band to rock bands and creative art ensembles. Up to one third of the school's population participated in parent-funded private instrumental lessons.

Data collection

The process of data collection involved: semi-structured interviews; observation of ensemble rehearsals and performances; participant-observations of students in classroom music; summaries of curriculum and policy documents; videotapes and audiotapes of students' music making in ensembles and classrooms; and, the maintenance of a researcher's journal. It was most important in this study to gain a systemic view of the phenomenon. To this end, sampling of teachers and students interviewed was purposive. Twenty-one students were chosen because of their experiences with different musical styles and instruments and their involvement with ensembles and classroom music. It should be noted that all students at the school had been involved in music activity as part of the core curriculum in primary school and Years 7 and 8. The students selected for interview were chosen on the basis of their involvement with particular aspects of music making within the school such as classroom music electives, instrumental and vocal ensembles, musical styles and instruments. The focus was deliberately upon those with a high involvement as they were considered to have a distinctive association with the phenomenon being studied. The research follows the experiences of these students in the classroom, ensembles, performances and ceremonies, and in the wider community through their music biographies.

A brief description of students interviewed

Twenty-one students were interviewed—12 male students and nine female. All interviews were recorded on audiotape and transcribed onto a word processor. Grouped according to ensemble, the students were:

- Four student members of a synthesizer ensemble
  Bronwyn: Plays synthesizer, piano and is a self-taught rock guitarist
  Teresa: Plays woodwinds, wind controller, piano and sings
  Dennis: Synthesizer, electronic music composer
  Brian: Synthesizer, voice

- Two students from the school jazz big band
  Colin: Trumpet, piano, bass guitar
  Jason: Trumpet, rock guitar

- Two students from an all-female rock band
  Wendy: Voice in choirs and rock band, songwriter
  Fiona: Voice in choirs and rock band, songwriter

- Two students from a male rock band
  Edward: Clarinet, rock/jazz guitar
  Luke: Rock guitar

- Two students from classroom elective programs
  Daniel: Saxophones
  Phillip: Voice and piano

- Two percussionists
  Janet: Mallet and un-tuned percussion and drum kit
  Jack: Drums and percussion, guitar, bass guitar

Other students:
- *Linda*: A student from the large wind ensemble (note several other students in this sample also play in this compulsory large ensemble), plays woodwinds and violin
- *Holly*: A singer
- *Margaret*: A composer, plays piano and synthesizer

Four ex-students:
- *John*: A rock guitarist
- *Sandra*: A choral singer
- *Michael*: A Piano player and composer
- *Bradley*: A drummer/percussionist

A brief description of teachers interviewed

Ten teachers were interviewed. They were permanent members of the music teaching staff who directed ensembles and taught in the studio and or the classroom. Home room/pastoral care teachers were selected to gain a perspective of the effects of music on the student's general life. The school minister and counsellor were interviewed to gain a perspective of the phenomenon as it relates to community and personal development, social inclusion and self-esteem.

The teachers interviewed comprised:

- *James*: Keyboard teacher/junior-classroom/synthesizer-ensemble director
- *Simone*: String teacher
- *Matthew*: Brass teacher/conductor/senior classroom
- *Janet*: Woodwind/classroom/conductor
- *Peter*: Junior classroom-music teacher
- *Robert*: Guitar teacher/rock band director
- *David*: Pastoral-care teacher/pianist
- *Jessica*: Pastoral-care teacher/drama/English
- *Barbara*: School psychologist counsellor
- *Mark*: School minister/counsellor

Observation data

Observation of school music camp/ concert preparations

The school had a major concert event in the middle of the year, and in preparation the music department held a two-day, weekend, and in-house music camp. Students and teachers were observed in preparation for this concert. The concert was also observed and recorded on videotape. Observation was also made of performance of Year 8 preparation for a "Blues Brothers' Rhythm and Blues" performance evening where four groups of seventeen students formed rhythm and blues bands and performed both original compositions and cover versions of rhythm and blues classics. "Highlights" of this event were also videotaped.

Observation in the classroom

During the fourth term of the school year, I observed and taught music at the school in Year 7, 8, 9, 10, 11 and 12. In addition, I conducted a junior classroom string program and took a class of four-year olds in the pre preparatory school. All observations were recorded on a laptop computer immediately after the class or at the end of each day. Video and audiotape recordings were made of classroom performances and reflective writing was collected.

Researcher's logbook

Throughout the research, I maintained a journal of my reflections and observations about the research and the site. Often at the end of each day I recorded reflections verbally onto a tape recorder and later transcribed them on to a word processor so that I could let my thoughts flow through conversation rather than purely in a textual way. I also used a laptop in the field, for typing up textual comment and observations. In this book I kept records of times and places of interactions and events. I recorded my own impressions of each interaction and thoughts about emergent theory and personal reflections. I listed questions and prompts to follow up on data that I felt needed further explanation.

Audiovisual data

Over the period that I worked and researched at the school, I collected videotapes and audiotape recordings of concerts, student performances and compositions. During the specified one-year observation period and the intense twelve-week observation time, I also recorded visual and audio information in support of field notes. These data were collected primarily to illustrate and give some concrete context to descriptions of music performances and student compositions. They also provided a reference point for field notes and interview data and served to provide audio-visual evidence for some of the claims of text data. Subsequently these data have become more important under re-analysis because of the meanings contained in them that were silenced by the textual research methodologies. It is this aspect of the research, which has problematised the notions of music making and its ephemerality as data.

I have subsequently found that it is the audiovisual material collected in this research, which more readily captures a clear and present description of the student's experiences of meaning in music making. This has led me subsequently to question the absence of the presence of music itself in research that discusses music. It is to this end that research that is more recent has focused more clearly on creating an audiovisual documentary of music experience rather than filtering these meanings through text. Music is only ephemeral because of its time dependence and if we record an artefact of music making, while this is not the experience itself but a representation of it, the artefact is more able to capture sonic events and visual impressions of engagement that a text description. This is not to belittle the excellent work that qualitative narrative has brought to research in our domain but to add to it by allowing technology to reveal and make present something that was once ephemeral and unable to be preserved in anyway but memory.

Analysis

All data were transcribed as text files and the computer program QSR NUDIST (Richards and Richards 1999) was used to organise coding, data retrieval and theorising. I used NUDIST, primarily as a way of accessing and managing the large body of data that I had collected. Theory in this research is emergent from data and the analysis looked for themes that seemed to recur within a body of data and across data forms. For instance, at one stage I examined how teachers and students talked about "openness" in interviews and followed this theme using NUDIST to group and contextualise each response. "Openness" was a strong factor used in a number of ways by teachers interviewed and I wrote data summaries about each of the categories mentioned and crosschecked them against field observations. What resulted from this quite large exploration was that the concept of openness was reduced to a "valuing of the child's interest". What students valued in teachers was their ability to value their interest in music rather than pretending to "like" a musical style or instrument with which they were unfamiliar. The concept moved from openness to recognition of the unique values of each individual. In the process of analysis, I also made deliberate searches for negative data and pursued them to extinction. Furthermore, I grouped data by examining what surprised me about the case and what I found that did not surprise me was used to vary the lens I held on the phenomenon.

Cross checking of data analysis

The following measures were adopted to crosscheck value-laden data reconstruction, coding and analysis and aid trustworthiness, authenticity and fairness:

Member check interview transcripts

All interviews were recorded on audiotape and transcribed on to a word processor. The complete transcripts were then returned to the participants to check for accuracy of transcription. Participants were encouraged to comment, add further reflections and make additions and changes to the transcript. This process resulted in the following changes to transcripts:

- changes to punctuation to improve the clarity;
- removal of references to "known musicians", who were discussed in a negative light (Note: this was not relevant to the data but seen as not desirable to make public);
- addition of extra thoughts and reflections. This was a common occurrence; suggesting that the participants enjoyed the process and acknowledged its importance and accuracy;
- clarifications of names, times and dates, typing - errors, unclear - recording of transcriptions.

The member checking process also enabled further informal discussion with participants and follow up of further questions about emergent theory. Theory that related to particular incidents recorded in interviews was also followed up informally and recorded in my research journal. This enabled further clarification and gave depth to data reconstruction and analysis.

Establishing trustworthiness and authenticity

A broad range of data was collected so that a fuller picture of the system of music making and the context in which it was made could be constructed. The interviews were internally diverse, representing a broad range of teachers and students. Observations of curricular, co-curricular and extra-curricular activity were used to examine the whole community and its interaction with music making. The data were gathered over a prolonged period of engagement. They included interviews and observation collected over a year of field research plus a further five years of "ex post facto" data drawn from audio-visual, teacher journal entries and students work samples and recordings. It is hoped that the breadth of data sources and the methods included to crosscheck data will help to provide a view that acknowledges the observer influence and seeks to provide multiple perspectives.

Negative case analysis

Across both data collection and analysis, I consciously pursued negative cases. I actively sought students who were prepared to discuss negative experiences with music at the school and found that these students only expressed a lower level of engagement rather than negative experiences. One of these students whom I interviewed informally spoke of how his ability to discriminate instrument timbres had much impressed his peers despite having a semester where his own instrumental experience involved avoiding playing as much as possible. He reported "feeling great" when he participated in an end-of-term concert in front of parents and peers. This analysis of negative data produced a similarity of perspective in relation to the location of meaning for both musically experienced and non-musically experienced students that were useful in understanding data. Driven by the comment that classroom music was lightweight or "a little light on" (Interview Student: Jack), I examined classroom music in more detail. This resulted in gaining a perspective on the role of the classroom teacher and greater understanding of the structure and depth of content. These kinds of active investigations of negative cases in the field and within data analysis provided means to make data descriptions thicker and to allow me to challenge and make sense of my own value-laden views.

Seeking a number of lenses on the phenomenon

Crosschecking and triangulation of data served to thicken the description of the phenomenon under examination and provide a multiple lens on the phenomenon. By this, I mean that some aspects of people are better observed by a third party, music is better recorded on tape than written about, and some things are better observed in action rather than reflected upon after the fact. Throughout this research, I was particularly conscious of the need to use the most appropriate tool for capturing the data and the need to examine it as a system, in action and in context. I also sought a variety of views of the same subject to provide a broad description of the phenomenon.

Auditing of transcripts and data reconstructions

All transcripts were line-numbered in NUDIST (Richards and Richards 1999), enabling easy data retrieval and viewing. A disinterested, competent third party who systematically undertook a random audit trail audited data reconstructions. The auditor is a psychologist who holds postgraduate qualifications in research methodology and design. The auditor checked three interview transcripts, examined member check records, randomly examined "other media data" against descriptions; and randomly checked three data reconstruction following themes. The auditor also acted as a "devil's advocate"—deliberately searching and questioning emergent theory/themes and where possible providing plausible alternatives. Over the research period, Professor Lyn Yates from the Institute of Education, La Trobe University in Melbourne an experienced and highly developed qualitative researcher, acted as a "peer de-briefer" in regular fortnightly discussions about data reconstruction and analysis. Professor Yates actively challenged and questioned reports on data and the ways in which I used data in the written analysis. Other peer comment was gained through the publication of journal articles in subject association journals and through presentation at conferences in music education and education (Dillon 1995a, 1995b, 1999, 2000).

Criticism of participant observation

There is no doubt that in this research, I am indeed a deep insider. As stated earlier, this position is one of advantage and unlimited access and knowledge of the site and the people in it. It is also a position that is fraught with critical issues of value-laden reporting that could affect methodology, data reconstruction, and analysis and interpretation. The approach can be perceived as lacking objectivity. Despite the dangers of criticism and potential value-laden qualities of this approach, I believe that the case study site and my position as a teacher researcher offered an opportunity to observe theory in practice. This position also enabled access and a perspective not available to an external researcher. This perspective is privileged and particular to the process and approach of deep insider researcher. As Edwards outlines in his portrayal of deep insider research, "unknown objects can be identified through single, seemingly insignificant signs, rather than through the application of laws derived from repeatable and quantifiable observations" (Edwards 1999, 72). Deep insider research, "carries with it the potential for deeper understanding and greater insight" (Edwards 1999, 73). What is important for this research is the perspective that this methodology reveals about the system and the parts of an organisation as an organic whole. It provides access to insights about the organisation, the people in it, and the dynamic interactions that take place between them.

In undertaking this participant-observation case study, I became aware that all research is value-laden and that no question is without preconceptions and prior theoretical assumptions. Certainly any question worth answering and spending such a large portion of one's life engaged with carries with it guesses, assumptions and creative hypotheses. These are the very reasons that the questions were raised in the first place. It gives them meaning and sustains the interest required to engage in a study of this dimension. My approach to value-laden research has been to acknowledge it, be "upfront" about it, and to put into place ways of teasing out and exploring it fruitfully so that it adds to the process of making theory.

Within positivistic methods, we hypothesise, eliminate variables and test these assumptions rigorously. Qualitative research as an interpretive paradigm is nonetheless rigorous but more appropriately conscious of the researcher as an instrument of data collection and analysis. In this model of researcher as instrument of research, there is an acknowledgement that as a sentient being we are able to critically observe, participate, reflect and synthesise an understanding of phenomena. In this process, we take into account the context and our role in it as a system of human behaviour and develop our sensitivity and awareness of the case. As a musician, this kind of integration of intuitive awareness and analytical understanding is highly valued and developed. In this study, the awareness of my influence upon these processes has been attended to with self-checking, crosschecking, critical discussion and auditing serves as a constant reminder and "independent conscience" of the value and honesty of my interpretations. In terms of the research questions, these acknowledgements are part of the consciousness that I am the instrument of research. I believe that a deep insider researcher can fruitfully observe the phenomena of meaning and process in a way that can contribute to our understanding of music education. In this respect, I believe the approach has distinct advantages.

Knowing where to look, and who to ask

As stated earlier, as a teacher at the school site for six years, and as head of performing arts, I had taught all students interviewed. All the teachers interviewed were well known to me. Samples of their work were available on video and audiotape as well as an intimate knowledge of their history and even body language. In interviews, I purposively chose participants who had experience with the phenomenon. Each participant had a story to tell about his or her experiences with making music. Their involvement with music making was over at least a five-year association with the school and they were actively involved in music activity. Csikszentmihalyi (1996) in his study of creative individuals used a similar biographical approach to interviews but focussed upon those who had a "creative life" from which to observe the phenomenon. Sloboda and Howe's (1992) study of early musical careers also utilised an elite music school to examine children's musical biographies.

At this point, I could be criticised for seemingly not including young people who did not have a satisfactory or lengthy association with music making and such criticism is indeed valid. This study sought to identify what it is that student's find involves and engages them with music making and listening, which I define as meaning and the processes that facilitate that meaning. To identify this—as with Csikszentmihalyi, and Sloboda and Howe—I needed to examine the phenomenon where and when it occurred, not look where it was not. Participant observation in the field study takes into account the demographic of non-music participants and examines the phenomenon in context. Consequently, students who participated in compulsory music activities were observed and interviewed within the day-to-day classroom music lessons and school environment. Negative cases were actively pursued within the participant-observation field and data drawn from these observations. Interactions were recorded in field notes and the researcher's journal. While access to the site was assured by familiarity, during the participant observation I taught new students whom I did not know prior to the research and who were not aware of me. In that sense, I also had the additional perspective of students who had entered the school system without a prior expectation of me as a teacher or of music classes at the school.

Ready access to site and natural response

My access to the site was relatively unobtrusive and the notion that the response to me was "natural" was particularly apparent in the field observation. Students and teachers seemingly went about their daily interactions without a consciousness that they were being observed. With interviews, my long associations with the participants gave me access to historical and detailed knowledge of family, instruments and in many cases shared memories and experiences. My initial concerns of a power differential between the students and music teachers were allayed by the results of the pilot study. The study suggested that students were comfortable in interview and that I had developed a habit of reflective discussion as their classroom music teacher. I also believe the responses of staff were honest. It was the openness, criticism and frankness of the discussions recorded that suggested that my position was not influencing these responses. On the contrary, participants appeared to value the process and were passionate about accuracy and the perceived importance of telling their music stories.

Access to people

The access to people was informed by intimate knowledge of the culture and those within it. Students and teachers alike mentioned in their interviews a "special kind of knowing" that is associated with the kind of relationship one has with persons that you play music with. This kind of association, I have come to realise, was also part of my relationship with students and staff in this study. There is a sense of shared understanding that is not necessarily more intimate but certainly based upon more intuitive and wordless understandings than "normal" teacher-student or collegial relationships. This is indeed a privileged access, as Edwards so perceptively described— it facilitates access to part of the body language and "seemingly insignificant signs" (Edwards 1999, 74) that would not be recognised by the outsider researcher.

The methodology at "face value": A summary

In summary, I put a number of measures in place to establishing trustworthiness and authenticity in this research. Beyond these measures, I suggest that I have developed a policy for treating analysis of interview data at "face value" rather than imposing deeper values upon data. Where possible, I will allow the data to speak with its own voice. Csikszentmihalyi in his discussion of creativity when commenting on the interview process and the positive nature of his transcripts proclaimed, "Instead of suspecting these stories of being self-serving fabrications, I accept them at face value—provided they are not contradicted by other facts about the person or by internal evidence" (Csikszentmihalyi 1996, 16).

Within the structure of the methodology, crosschecking and variety of data sources serve to establish truthfulness of statements made in interviews. The notion of taking interviews at face value is one that acknowledges that the interviews do not constitute truth but that the participants chose retrospective recollections of those moments that made up their story. It is what the participants choose to relate that is important, and this reveals what the participant perceives as valuable and meaningful. Indeed the act of memory itself says something about its significance and the values placed upon the recollection.

As meaning and values are the focus of this research, I feel that this speaks positively about the ability of this instrument to provide useful data about that phenomenon. This is not to say that transcripts are not actively interpreted, but that I have not attempted to "read into" sub-text of transcripts or seek psychological implications of text. I have not gone beneath interpretation. Where questions arose from interviews that needed clarification or generated a need for more depth or explanation, these questions were taken back to the participant and discussed.

I believe that the use of a participant observation case study methodology serves to reveal deep understandings and descriptions of the phenomenon. It is able to do so without dissecting and disturbing the wholeness of the system. It is able to observe philosophy in practice and generate thick description capable of putting meat on the bones of theory. The diversity of the instruments used provides a variable three-dimensional view. The design is flexible and responsive to emergent themes and theory. Most importantly, the design recognises the particular and distinctive opportunity for the researcher to gather a unique view of the phenomenon in its native environment. The method recognises and values this association while also putting into place rigorous self-checking and crosschecking devices to question and strengthen emergent theory.

Finally, I would add that this methodology is most appropriate to me as a creative musician. I believe that making music affects and changes the person who makes it and that the effect of this interaction is meaningful. The same is true of all creative acts. Interestingly, I found this research to be a something like a "random stochastic algorithmic" composition. This form of electronic music making involves decisions about the parameters of each element of music in a creative and thoughtful musical structure. Each time the music is played, the performance will be randomised within the parameters set by the composer. Although the composer has a strong idea what the affect and outcome of each performance may be, he or she is always surprised by the subtlety of the changes that occur at random in performance. This research and teaching has been full of surprises and exciting discovery beyond anything that I could have anticipated. I know the next note will be C above middle C, but what timbre will it be? How long will it last? Moreover, what dynamic will it be?

Research, like composing, is a creative and dynamic process full of surprises and challenges, excitement and interest and even pain and boredom—making art has these qualities too. Both hold the joy of unexpected discovery and are potentially "flow" activities (Csikszentmihalyi 1994). Both take skill, time and dedication to achieve. The maker too is changed, made more complex by the act of making—I feel that this research has done that to me, perhaps even educated my character (Buber 1969) and led me to more complex consciousness (Csikszentmihalyi 1996). As with composing, the task that follows is to communicate and present expressively and in such a way that it affects the audience—this methodology provided me with the structure and form for this communication.

Project 2: Researching meaningful engagement with music technology

The case study described above generated some primary principles of meaning, which will be further described in the next chapters in more detail. At the time of completion of the case study, I had the opportunity for ongoing examinations of these ideas in the context of observing students interaction with music technology through a process of software development as research (Brown 2006). This provided a unique moment to combine the research from the original case study and combine it with research about how students engage with creative production (Brown 2000, 2003, 2006). This process which is presently ongoing has taken place over a further six year period beginning in 2001 through continuous annual iterations of the research in case study sites in Australia, the USA and Europe (e.g., Brown and Dillon 2007, Dillon 2001, 2004b, 2004c, 2005, 2006b, 2006c). This research has focused upon applying the philosophical aspects derived for both research projects firstly to the design of a unique piece of networked performance software and secondly the creation of a framework for observing how students engage meaningfully with music making using music technology (see Appendix B). Each case has involved action research cases involving children from 4-14 years of age. To date over a thousand students have interacted with the software and been observed and recorded using digital video recording playing with the software in a variety of settings.

While this is not the forum to discuss the detail of the research into Networked Improvisational Musical Environments, what this research reveals that is of importance to this study is firstly, a way of problematising the relationship we have with music technology in the production of music in a simultaneously virtual. Secondly, the development of research strategies that allow philosophy to be modelled in software development which provides for music education research an approach to modelling theory that an astronomer might use to model the universe. jam2jam (Brown, Sorensen and Dillon 2002) is a shareware program developed in java that uses music algorithms based upon specific pitch, timbre and rhythmic qualities that can be manipulated in real time with a simple interface that a child can control. The process of interaction with these software instruments is called "networked improvisation", which can be broadly described as collaborative music making over a computer network (Brown and Dillon 2007).

Research for iterations of this study have occurred in schools and communities and involved a network of 8 to 12 computers. Generative algorithms based upon student musical preferences were constructed and applied to the software and then students were observed interacting with the software and each other in jam/networked improvisation sessions. Each iteration of the research was video taped and observed to combat the criticism of early research to filter meaning through textual analysis alone. Analysis of observations, which affected the design of the interface or the implementation of theory, was incorporated into the next version of the software. Situational analysis and observation was reviewed and fed back into the experience deign for the teachers and the development of curriculum materials. Data from these case studies and the large body of published research about meaningful engagement with music technology provides evidence and a basis for the discussion about how students interact with music performance using music technology and how music technology raises new questions about the nature of musicianship in the twenty first century.

Project 3: Indigenising the curriculum and community music research

This project draws upon data from two sources. Firstly a participant observation case study approach to Indigenising curriculum in a tertiary music department and secondly a series of community music research projects conducted with graduate research students in community music settings where the participants in the programs were from diverse multi cultural backgrounds and urban Indigenous Australian origin. Insights from the analysis of data from these projects represent both a personal involvement with curriculum development that considers cultural difference and observational data in school and community settings.

The participant observer research I undertook myself began as part of a University led and faculty initiative supported by a grant to 'indigenise curriculum in music and sound courses delivery and the identification of resources to support and enable this process. This resulted in the publication of a number of academic papers, and policy and teaching and learning initiatives within the music and sound curriculum offering. As a participant observer in this process it further opened up a dynamic relationship with the Aboriginal and Torres Strait Islander Oodgeroo Unit at the University and began a personal journey of understanding about Indigenous knowledge frameworks and ethical engagement with music in this context.

In 2002, Queensland University of Technology (QUT) Music and Sound Department undertook a shift in the fundamental ontology for aural musicianship based upon a model provided by Richard Vella (2000) through his work that examined Musical Environments. This model, while still framed by Western art music composition, utilises a time and space model of aural perception rather than a musical elements approach. This approach provided a potential framework for a more culturally inclusive approach to aural perception and analysis and led the way for the incorporation of Indigenous perspectives with the tertiary music and music education course of study at QUT. What this framework alerted us to was that to realise the need to examine the underlying structures of how music is perceived and valued within a culture (Dillon and Chapman 2005, 197). The effects on how cross-cultural musicianship was learnt and taught were quite profound. This research, which examines the embedding of Indigenous perspectives with the music curriculum has taken place over a four-year period and has also provided a foundation for asking new questions about the ethical inclusion of Indigenous music in music education and syncretic appropriation of music (Dillon 2006d, Dillon and Chapman 2005, Dillon, Stewart, Brown, Arthurs, Dodge and Peacock 2004).

While this research is in relatively early stages of development of two case study iterations, the idea of being a teacher researcher and reflective practitioner has become a part of my approach to learning and teaching at the University level. These case studies when combined with research that also involve multi-cultural communities provides the basis for a discussion about music making, meaning and culture that is represented in this book (e.g., (Dillon 2004a, 2004d, 2004e, 2006a, 2006e, Dillon and Stewart 2006, Dillon, Stewart, Brown, Arthurs, Dodge and Peacock 2004, Spirovski 2004). These cases provide data that can be compared to the literature from Indigenous Australian education and critiqued by Indigenous scholars. It is this approach to reflective practice as a teacher in a university music program, and as a researcher working in community music contexts, that constitute new field research that contributes to my present understanding of the relationship between music and culture. While I am aware that this is a contentious position and in no way meant to be authoritative, I do however, suggest that it is one that holds promise for understanding the relationships and effect of music in cross-cultural and inter-cultural learning contexts for music.

The community music projects involved three iterations of a town council funded project-involving youth based at a multi cultural school with high representations of Aboriginal and Torres Strait Islander. These projects involved a music teacher who had been an undergraduate student in the Music and Sound

Education degree, community music coaches from the local community, and CreActives, an organization that facilitates contemporary community music experiences for youth. This research focused upon the qualities of good practice and curriculum development of teachers and coaches and upon documenting the effects of music making on youth. The participant observers in this project have been graduate students from the save to DISC (Documenting Innovation in Sound Communities) research project. The observations reported on in this book have been drawn from pilot and preliminary studies and graduate publications. These provide a link between the approaches to Indigenising curriculum and cultural management as a strategy for undergraduate teachers and the application of these music education processes in complex multi cultural communities. They also provide an opportunity to observe meaningful music making in quite different context to the school case study.

Conclusion

My journey that examines music and meaning across contexts is an ongoing one. What I have sought to provide here is a sense of the wide variety of sources of data that inform this study and the evolution of methodological strategies. Primarily it is a teachers' journey of understanding through engagement with the context but this process of engagement, documentation and analysis is nonetheless a rigorous and accountable one that has involved continuous engagement over a long period and replication of theory testing within a variety of contexts. The central case study provides a solid foundation for this research and subsequent research contexts involving music technology and Indigenous and cross-cultural perspectives have provided ways of problematising theory. The main purpose of this approach to methodology has been to put the meat on the bones of theory through observing how the theory affects music makers and documenting and evaluating their interaction with theory and the effect of context.

Part II

Theoretical

CHAPTER FOUR

MUSIC MAKING AND FLOW

Introduction

My earliest memory of an engaging experience with music making was singing. I was entranced by the pure tone of my own boy soprano voice. I was engaged with how my voice blended with others in a choir and I was intrigued by the sense of belonging I felt when the sounds I made and those of the ensemble I was part of was valued by an audience of my community. Early in my research about music and meaning, I identified these kinds of early experiences with music making as a micro-aesthetic or small experience which led to an interest in music making. After a career as a singer and composer, I still find that when I sing with *The Esplanados* a capella group, I still get that feeling of losing track of time and being immersed in the intertwining textures of the voices in the choir. I realised long ago that what I had experienced as a child and had driven my enduring interest and passion for music making was "flow".

The concept of "flow" is a significant aspect of happiness and of understanding how happiness is achieved was an aspect of theory that was consistently evident in the field data across the whole spectrum of research projects that inform this study. The idea of flow is inextricably linked to intrinsicality and engagement and provides a long term and replicable body of research to evidence its existence and connection to happiness. The work of Mihalyi Csikszentmihalyi is extremely influential in this research. Indeed life story interviews, which were used by Csikszentmihalyi in his study of creativity provides a key data gathering strategy in this study.

About Csikszentmihalyi and "flow"

Csikszentmihalyi spent over 30 years researching the qualities of happiness. He identified that people who are challenged and have the capacity to meet that challenge feel "flow". He recognized arts and sporting activities most likely provide these kinds of challenges and "flow". He suggested that people who experience "flow" find it significant, valuable and meaningful. In music making, we can get flow from two distinct kinds of activities and also when these two areas of knowledge act in consort. The graph below (see Figure 4.1) represents what Csikszentmihalyi (1994) calls "flow".

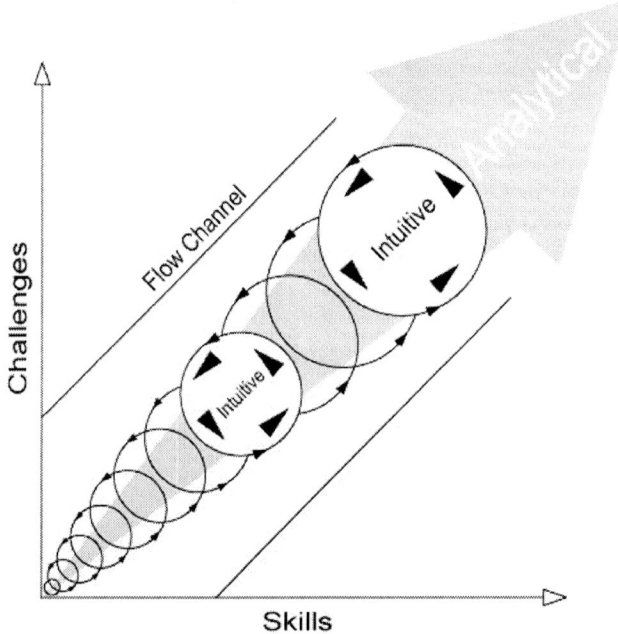

Figure 4.1 Flow and musical experience

If a task is too challenging then the result is anxiety while if it is not challenging enough then the result is boredom. The flow channel represents the point where the challenge and the ability to meet the challenge (skills) intersect. The result of "flow" is a state of consciousness where there is actually less brain activity because of the high degree of focus upon the task. The result is a feeling of the task flowing from our bodies and mind effortlessly—hence the term flow to describe the feeling. In arts activity many artist report this sensation as they do in sports and many other human activities. Arts making has the potential to deliver flow to participants if the task enables access to achievement without boredom or anxiety. Arts' making and sports are considered intrinsically motivated and this is flow—where we loose ourselves in the intrinsic pleasure of the task.

Musical knowledge as described by Swanwick (1994) can be divided into two distinct areas: analysis and intuition. The analytical knowledge is linear and we gain it by being constantly challenged by such things as technique, accuracy and clarity. These aspects of musical knowledge are measurable. The expressive and intuitive qualities of musical knowledge however are more cyclic in nature. We get deeper in the groove when we play jazz or blues we feel the elegance of phrases in a melody. In terms of flow, music provides opportunities that are both linear challenges and cyclic depth. Musical activity and the acquisition of musical knowledge provide multiple opportunities for meaningful engagement that leads to flow.

Flow in therapy, curriculum and experience design

In therapeutic terms for health professionals, this is valuable information because if we can identify activity that can provide meaningful engagement then we have a powerful weapon against depression. In therapy, this means that a therapist may be able to help clients to identify activity that provides "flow" or to recognise the characteristics that are without meaning or engagement. Often in depression, clients disengage with personally meaningful activity, social engagement and cultural or universal values. This is a problem also amongst youth in our communities and so often it is arts led and creative activities, which provide a means of expression and a pathway to engagement for troubled youths. In schools and communities achieving engagement and meaning in educational and social settings is an important aspect of motivation to participate in activity and in the outcome being educative, socially inclusive and transformative. In learning and teaching, the understanding of what motivates the student is of key importance in the construction of curriculum and the design of experience.

Flow and intrinsic experience

Csikszentmihalyi (1994) in *The psychology of happiness* provides a clear and appropriate description of the encounter that leads to "flow". These encounters are significant, meaningful and lead to intrinsic motivation and willingness to be involved with an increasingly more complex encounter with music experience. This results in a change in self that is gained from the "meaningfulness" of the encounter and "transforms self by making it more complex" (Csikszentmihalyi 1994, 74). Buber's (1969) philosophical notion of the education of character and Gardner's theory of the education of perception

(Reimer & Smith 1992) both suggest that experience effects a change in the consciousness of the individual.

Czikszentmihalyi observed that artists and musicians appeared to achieve "flow" more frequently. He concluded that aesthetic activity provided an endless supply of ever-increasing challenge to the participant and was a constant source of opportunity for "flow". He describes "flow" experiences as providing "a sense of discovery, a creative feeling of transporting the person into a new reality" (Csikszentmihalyi 1994). Put simply, "flow" occurs when a challenge and the ability to meet challenge intersect. Both the analytical and the intuitive tasks in music provide an endless supply of such challenges. This adds to the explanation of music making activities as intrinsically motivating. The question this raises for educators is how we facilitate and structure experience so that student can gain access to "flow".

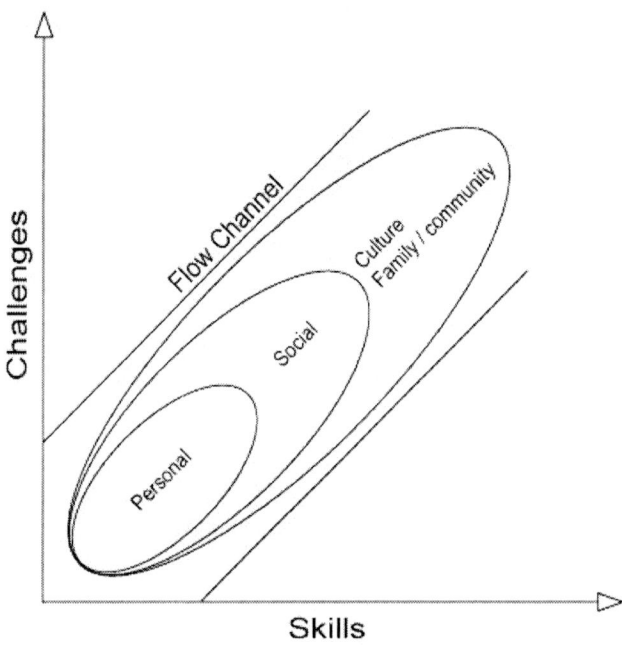

Figure 4.2 Meaning and flow

Four areas of meaning

Csikszentmihalyi's describes four areas of meaning in relation to "flow". The first relates to the "needs of the organism". The other three are termed "self-interest", "community/family" and what he calls "reflective individualism" (Csikszentmihalyi 1994, 222), which is where the individual forges a unity with cultural values. The areas of meaning described above are similar to the three areas evidenced in this research. The meanings are described as being made through interactions that are personal or located in self, social or located in relation to others and as a projection of a reflective individual. These constructs provide an analytical tool for understanding the system in which meaning is made. Figure 4.2 above illustrates how the location of meaning radiates from the personal through social interaction towards a cultural or community interaction.

Czikszentmihalyi's (1994) research and theory refer more specifically to adults than children but the sorts of themes that emerged from interviews with students for this study resonated strongly with the narratives Csikszentmihalyi associated with adult flow experience. Like Swanwick, he describes what he terms as a dialectic tension between differentiation and integration of consciousness (Csikszentmihalyi 1996). Swanwick divides the experience in the discourse between the intuitive and analytical aspects of music making (Swanwick 1994). These ideas were also supported by the themes that emerged from the central case study data for this research. The problem this raises for educators lies in motivating the analytic experiences and creating and structuring an appropriate pedagogy for teaching the intuitive and integrated activities.

In a therapeutic relationship, the client can discover these qualities through cognitive behavioural therapy sessions and eventually learn to recognise and encourage these kinds of relationships and activities within their own lives. In the classroom or community setting, a teacher can recognise what it is that triggers engagement and leads to meaning and transformation for the students. Appendix B provides a way of locating, observing and describing this kind of meaningful engagement. By identifying and understanding, the things that we find meaningful and engaging we can find alternative as well as well-worn pathways to happiness. The purpose of "flow therapy" or indeed "flow in learning" is to provide an opportunity to discover or rediscover what gives us flow, and plan an approach to successful engagement with the task.

Autotelic behaviour and personalities

Csikszentmihalyi (1994) suggests that personality type has an effect upon the individual's predisposition to flow. The "autotelic" personality is describes as a person who seeks and can construct his or her own challenges, which lead to flow. He suggests that such personalities may occur naturally or they might be encouraged through encounters with "flow" producing experiences. This is an important concept especially in the light of an epidemic of depression across human society. If we can identify the qualities and conditions that nurture and encourage autotelic self-actuated challenging behaviour and we can identify the kinds of activities, which lead to flow, then we have a powerful weapon against depression. Certainly, the power of music activity has been identified as a strong effect on social inclusion (Dillon 2004d, 2006a) but what are the psychological implications of the behaviour, which encourage positive thinking and resilience? While it is not within the scope of this research to answer this question we can begin to identify the activities that lead to meaningful engagement and this may lead to a clearer understanding of the relationship between music making social inclusion and resilience (Dillon and Stewart 2006).

During the process of analysis of data for the central case study for this research, I was consistently reminded of the "flow"-like experience that students and teachers described in relation to their musical encounters. The narratives examined lend qualitative support to many aspects of Czikszentmihalyi's theory of flow and support for the intrinsic motivation of arts activity. The question that arises from this insight is whether those interviewed were autotelic personalities, who were attracted to music making, or whether they became autotelic because of the encounter. This is an impossible question to answer from this data and most "nature/nurture" questions present similar cyclic arguments. What I would conclude is that both occur when an environment that encourages and is open to making experiences of all kinds is provided. What is important here is access to experiences that facilitate the making of meaning while engaged with music making.

I know I am autotelic—my continuous involvement with creative activities have given me the opportunity to develop this personality trait through imaginative play throughout my life, but where did I get this? In addition, if it was not naturally occurring, what activities led me to perpetuate this behaviour? When I think about what autotelicism is, I am reminded of one of my daughter's favourite episodes from the quirky Nicktoons cartoon character "Spongebob Squarepants". In this episode, he and his friend Patrick Star order a wide screen television and when it arrives they throw the television away and play in the cardboard box, preferring to play with their "imagination". Each time they say the word they gesture in front of them and a rainbow appears. This is autotelic behaviour. Perhaps it is stronger in some of us than others, but it is most evident in all of us as children, at least until seven years of age.

Robinson (2001) suggests that school de-skills our children in these creative behaviours. I too wonder at the lack of recognition of the intrinsic qualities of many activities in school and the need for "discipline" to ensure learning rather than teachers awareness of this fundamental understanding of learning. Reminiscent of my own early experiences with music making, Custodero clearly links the ideas of "flow" to music learning in early childhood suggesting that, "music challenges us to be responsive to personal and cultural meanings" (2002, 1). Further, Custodero asserts, "children actively seek musical challenges and in doing so guide teachers in designing appropriate strategies to assist in the acquisition of musical skill" (2002, 8). I would also add Perkin's (1988) idea that these skills and the process of creating challenges in music learning are transferable to both near and far activities both within music making and to other creative applications.

The significance of autotelic behaviour and its effect on motivation to engage and participate in activity is important for my discussion here and I will explore the idea of the intrinsic nature of music experience in the next chapter. What is important to consider is that the data analysed from interviews I conducted with musicians of all ages, teachers, students and community members, strongly supported the idea of autotelic behaviour and engagement with music making at a very early age which gave access to flow and was the basis of a sustainable involvement with music making activity for life. These aspects of music life stories as told by participants in the school case study site provide an interesting and important understanding about flow, autotelicism and meaningful engagement. They also tell us something significant about the characteristics of teacher, student, significant adults, environment, and approaches to learning, which affect a students potential to engage and sustain involvement in music making as a lifetime pursuit.

Early childhood music experience

To examine these ideas further I would like to explore data gathered from interviews in the case study concerned with the early childhood music experiences of students and teachers. The idea of asking participants about a first remembered musical moment evolved from the notion of a micro-aesthetic experience I had discussed in my master of education thesis. I explained the first musical memory as an experience, which is very attractive. Rather than constituting a complete aesthetic product, it is in fact the smallest unit of creative experience. It is the "seed of creativity" and is associated with what

Csikszentmihalyi calls "flow" (Csikszentmihalyi 1994). It is a strong initial attraction to music making (Dillon 1995). This significant relationship with music was noted amongst students interviewed and seemed to me to be related very strongly to the question of meaning and music, hence its inclusion as an interview question.

The vivid descriptions of early music experiences detailed here are important to our understanding of the meaning of music to these students as it gives a sense of the value they place upon it. It is significant that most of them have a vivid early memory. Even if this is not simply "what happened" (there may have been other things that did happen), it is how they construct themselves in their own autobiography that is important. They see and remember the experiences in this way and as an important part of their life and of who they are. It is also significant that they recognise the experiences, processes and people who have provided access to flow and potentially expressiveness and happiness through music making.

I interviewed 10 teachers and 21 students and asked both the same questions. The data presented here was taken from interview material, presented as narratives, and are primarily retrospective reflections on early childhood music experiences. The intention is to explore the meaning now given to those experiences by the individuals interviewed and their views on the processes they experienced. I began by asking the individuals to recall a first remembered music experience ("What was your first remembered moment of a musical experience?") and followed this with a more open question, which asked the participants to outline their own personal music story ("Can you tell me your music story?"). The "first remembered moment" of music experience and the circumstances and context that surround it can be important events that are carried into adulthood along with the associated learning patterns, behaviour and skills that are attained at this time. It is here that we are able to see the first recognitions of experience, which engages, and are able to identify what that is and how it differs between participants. The selected stories present a range of types of recollection and provide what I believe to be a multiple lens upon the phenomenon. Essentially, this enables me to display the notion of meaning from a variety of perspectives.

Peter's story

Peter taught primary classroom music at the case study school for five years. His story of early childhood musical experiences raises several aspects about the meaning of music for this analysis. Here is an excerpt of our conversation:

Steve: Peter can you remember the first and any small moment in your life when you first became interested in music and music making?

Peter: It's very hard to pinpoint one particular moment. My father is a musician, he plays the piano, and being from a church family background, music was very important to us as a family. Music was always part of our worship and celebrations. I was exposed to a lot of singing and playing; it was just a part of our life.

I remember when I was living in Israel as a six year old, one of my American friends, was learning the recorder and they were playing quite well. I was interested in what I saw, and heard and really wanted to join in. The teacher was an old German lady who lived in the same big house that a number of us expatriates shared. Her husband was the main director of the hospital that my dad was working in as a surgeon. During my first recorder lesson I remember her pinching my fingers to tell me exactly where my fingers should go in the holes. I really enjoyed the whole idea of learning an instrument and making musical sound.

We returned to Australia when I was starting Year 3 and I was very fortunate to be at a State Primary School that offered guitar lessons. Mum bought me a cheap three-quarter-size nylon string guitar, which I soon got the hang of. For some reason I had the ability and motivation to make sounds easier than the other kids and I was being acknowledged for my efforts. It was something I could do that my dad couldn't do. I was able to pick up chords fairly simply; I knew most of the basic chords by the end of Year 3.

It was also in Year 3 that some Year 7 students came back to primary school to demonstrate their electric guitars to us. This kick-started my fascination with Rock and Roll.

Later in the interview, I asked Peter to build on this early micro aesthetic experience and tell me his music story:

Steve: Now you've moved around a bit in your life. Can you tell me your music story, how you started to play, people who may have influenced you, circumstances or environments?

Peter: I've already touched on some. I think my father was a big influence on me musically. Even though he was classically trained, his love of performing and his love of music is something that I emulate. My German recorder teacher is still alive, and I saw her only a few years ago and told her she was a big influence.

There have been lots of teachers that I've had. One that stands out was my woodwind teacher Mr. D at the new school that I attended from Year 5 to Year 12. He was a Scottish jazz saxophonist who used to be a professional musician during the War years. His love of music just spilled on to me as I learned the clarinet and then the saxophone through his guidance. He inspired to learn, enjoy and appreciate jazz music.

At that stage there weren't a lot of opportunities at the school for me to be involved in jazz and other contemporary groups so I tried to create the opportunities for myself. I formed a band outside of school, more a rock band than a jazz band, and got involved with what jazz there was at the school.

Steve: Can you tell me about the relationship with this teacher being "inspiring"? Can you tell me why that might be?

Peter: I remember listening to him play but also listening to him tell his story about life in Scotland back in the 40s and 50s. I was inspired by the way he dedicated his whole life to music and the way he instilled his love of music into his students. I aspired to be like him (Peter 1998, pers comm.. with teacher, 10 January).

The meaning of music for Peter

Peter outlines quite clearly what music meant to him. Music is meaningful in a social sense as it extends through his family, church, primary and secondary school music experiences. He shows an attraction to it through friends and family and even seeks it through starting his own groups both in school and out. This is indeed autotelic behaviour where the music makers create their own challenging circumstances and activities. In a relationship context, the social extends to his desire to "emulate" his father's love of music and he sees a competitive side to learning an instrument that his father does not play. He "aspires to be like" his saxophone teacher and I might venture to suggest that he wants to share in the personal meaning shown by his teachers and family. In a sense, he is attracted to their love of the instrument and playing and seeks to share in that meaning.

He suggests that the image of playing and the achievement of playing have been great motivators for him. The encouragement he received from his immediate cultural setting was significant for him. He "really enjoyed the whole idea of learning an instrument and making musical sound" and his ability to "pick up chords really simply". There is evidence here of the internal and personal satisfaction, the social relations and the reciprocal response of his family and community.

This story is about personal achievement but also something that is projected publicly. Peter was interested in "what he saw and heard". He was attracted by the image and sound of playing music. The recorder players, his father, the saxophone teacher and the young rock guitarist's—all influenced his perception of music. He was drawn into different aspects of the discourse through these aural and visual experiences. In terms of process, Peter is acknowledging the strong influence that teachers and parents making music had upon his attraction to music making.

Edward's story

I would like to pursue these ideas about meaning further here in an analysis of a narrative that shows a recollection of personal meaning. At the time of our interview together, Edward was a 17 year old who played both clarinet and guitar, and began experiencing music with his father as a toddler:

Steve: Now Edward, can you tell me about your first memories of involvement with music?

Edward: Well, I can't remember the age, but it would have to have been before the age of five.

Steve: So preschool?

Edward: Yes, my father was a rather good clarinet player and his father was a great, jazz clarinet player and used to play around quite a bit and Dad loved music and loved playing his clarinet. Quite often on weekends he would pull out his old music box from the cupboard and play a few songs through and I used to love sitting there listening to him. And one day he bought me a recorder and he used to play his songs and I used to pretty much ruin them by playing the recorder all through them, but it was good fun—I used to love doing that. Then my Dad passed away so I sort of wanted to continue the love of music type of thing partly because of that and because I really enjoyed playing music as well, so that's probably my earliest recollection.

Steve: So does it make you feel close to him when you play?

Edward: Especially when I'm playing the clarinet.

Steve: So you are now playing clarinet and guitar. Tell me your life story as a musician, .the teachers that have influenced you—your relationships with them, good and bad

Edward: Well my next step would have been that I would have been in early primary school years and the Australian Boy's Choir came and I did a few auditions for that choir and I got in. So I was a second soprano, I think, and I sung with them for about five years and apart from anything else they gave me a good background in theory and that. I had a pretty good idea of theory side of music, more than most of my friends. Also my aunty was a big piano player, she still is and she one day for one of my birthdays when I was in Grade 5 she gave me a glockenspiel and I used to love that thing and I listened to all my favourite songs and figured them out on my glockenspiel. Doing things like that I didn't find that very difficult and everyone was incredibly impressed and in Grade 6 we had a little glockenspiel ensemble and we played (Edward 1997, pers comm., 9 July).

The meaning of music for Edward

For Edward there is also an explicit family connection here and a clear expression of his, own love of music. The personal aspects of music related to closeness to his deceased father through clarinet playing provided a touching moment in the interview. Similarly to Peter, his musical achievement impressed his family and friends, giving him an encounter with the cultural aspects of music meaning that affirmed the value of his involvement. The encouragement and sense of belonging to the family and community provides a strong motivation for continued involvement. His experiences with music as a social experience in the Australian Boy's Choir are also mentioned. He attributes the development of his analytic understanding of music to these experiences. People playing and people who are prepared to share their playing, and involve him in playing music are also prominent in this interview. He mentions his father, grandfather and an aunt as important influences. As with Peter's story, these people demonstrate their own love of music and involve him in music seemingly without judgement. They encourage involvement and provide the opportunity to share their experience. Both participants describe a similar immersion in music making, beginning within family and then radiating outwards to new experiences in institutional music making. The idea of a relationship where the student is taken into the life of the musician, be it a relative or teacher, suggest, evidence of Buber's (1969) concept of immersion in music learning as an inclusive relationship. Aronoff's (1969) notion of maintaining and developing the child's natural aesthetic response is also apparent in these transcripts. These notions alone provide interesting ideas, which might inform the process and development of music learning during this time.

Linda's story

Linda is a 17-year-old student saxophonist in Year 11 who began her music education as a violinist. This extract describes her first experience and the effect it had on her family:

> *Linda*: I was four years old, and it was just before my birthday and I still remember the picture of me sitting in front of the TV and there was a Philharmonic orchestra or something with a solo violinist and I remember exactly when I first went "ohhh" [gasps and laughs]. I don't remember anything else about being four except just this vision of a violin player getting a standing ovation from so many people, and sounding so good. And I just went [loudly] "Mum I want a violin, now". And she had never seen me so instantly interested in something and she said "Oh my God better get her a violin now". So, I got one for my birthday. And I loved just the whole thing from there, from this one vision.
>
> *Steve*: So you heard really nice playing? What attracted you about the playing, was it the whole thing?
>
> *Linda:* Just the whole concept of so many people being so interested in something that you had a talent for. And just being able to stand up in front of so many people and saying look, this is what I'm good at (Linda 1997, pers comm. student, 5 March).

The meaning of music for Linda

In the interview with Linda, she mentions that her experiences of the violin on television at age four included the idea that "it sounded so good". However, the comment about how it sounded is not as strong in her re-telling of the story as her comment about what she saw happening there: a vision of a violinist, "the standing ovation", this one "vision". As interviewer, my follow-up question "Was it the whole thing?", tried to probe further about what was important here, "". Her answer does not refer to the aesthetic experience of sound at all, but to social and personal meanings. Even more importantly, she describes how doing "something that you had a talent for" would place you in relationships with other people and the community.

This kind of inspiration is common amongst young children and I am moved to ask why this instance is different. Why does Linda move beyond an image of herself playing to a reality? The answer may lie in her parent's response and the quality of interaction she had with her first teacher. What is outlined here might be seen as an exemplification of what Aronoff has pointed to as a music experience needing to build upon the natural aesthetic responses. Linda described her teacher in the following way:

> *Linda:* I had a very good violin teacher. She was incredibly patient but she was always pushing me to be better but without pushing me too hard. And I had lessons with her for six years. And she saw me all the way through...like she was so incredibly positive about everything that I did that it gave me the basis for, do you know what I mean?
>
> *Steve:* The foundation for your talent for music?
>
> *Linda:* Yeah.
>
> *Steve:* Was she a particular kind of teacher? Was she a Suzuki teacher or were you at Steiner school at the time?
> *Linda:* Yeah she was a Suzuki teacher and I was at Steiner but she taught me privately, outside of the school thing. But she encouraged me to be in things at school like the school orchestra.
>
> *Steve*: So, what was so special about her? How did she teach you? Did she make it fun? Was she firm and fun? So, what was the character that this teacher had that made you really enjoy it for that six years?
>
> *Linda:* Well because it was so long ago that when someone says "Lana", I just get this picture of her. She was always smiling. She was never "No that's wrong" (affected voice). She was never, she was always positive. No matter how badly I played; she could always pick out the positive things. And she was never in a bad mood, never had a bad day.
>
> *Steve*: Did she play for you?
>
> *Linda*: Yes and she accompanied me. Because that's what I wanted to be, I wanted to be the solo person. And so from five years old I was playing with an accompanist and being the one in charge, and going, look, this is how it goes. And she was always (pause) like, she'd point out the things that I did wrong, but she wouldn't dwell on them (Linda 1997, pers comm. with student, 5 March).

I then asked Linda about her teacher's teaching style:

> *Linda:* I just had a connection with her. I just thought.... it was just awe, I just thought, every time she picked up a violin my mouth would just drop open. And it was having such a great respect for how good she was. And how good she thought I was.
>
> *Steve*: She made you feel confident?

Linda: Yeah, that I could be as good as her or as good as the guy I saw on TV. And she'd always make a connection between what I was doing at the time and what someone else did in front of ten thousand people (Linda 1997, pers comm. with student, 5 March).

Linda's story displays what appears to be an effective building upon her natural responses. In her recollection, the teacher appears to have understood her attraction to the violin and built upon it. She took the child into her own life as a musician and provided the child with experiences and "tastes" of realising her ambitions. She made Linda feel that she "could be as good as her or as good as the guy [she] saw on TV". Presented here is a strong emphasis upon Linda sharing in the teacher's love of music, experiencing through her as well as having an experience of her own. This kind of music interaction is intimate and intense.

Apparent in all the interviews presented is an attraction to music as an image. There was a very strong association with the sound made by the teacher or parent playing. The students's felt that they could make sounds like that themselves, and they were attracted by their own achievement toward those ends. There is a sense of personal satisfaction in music making, an attraction to making music collaboratively in a social sense and a conscious awareness of how their music making is received and responded to by family, friends and community.

These transcripts represent the "lucky ones"—those fortunate enough to have musical or appreciative families and with the financial resources to facilitate private lessons. These students also expressed an interest in music themselves. Amongst those interviewed there were those who came to music through parent-guided experience and who did not find music immediately attractive. There were also those who may not have been in a position to access private music lessons. The next section of this analysis examines these through two interviews.

James' story

James is a 24-year-old piano/synthesizer teacher. He talks here about why his parents introduced him to music and how he felt about it.

James: I can't remember, I think my parents thought it might be a good idea for me to learn piano or to learn an instrument, and piano was what they ended up deciding. I can't remember whether or not at the very early stages whether I was excited about it or...I really can't remember what my reaction was, but I know the reason that my parents wanted me to do it, was because they both enjoyed music themselves. They both thought that it would be a worthwhile thing, that I could get some benefit from it. They are both musical in a sense, neither of them call themselves musicians, they wouldn't call themselves musicians in that sense, but they both enjoy music. Like, my father comes from a musical home and my Mum plays a little piano and that sort of stuff. But I think that they were keen for not only myself but also my brother and sister to have some musical experiences and they thought it was worth something (James 1996, pers comm. with teacher, 28 October).

James' parents believed that music was "worth something". They involved him in their valuing of music and he shared in this despite, as revealed later, not feeling particularly motivated by it. He explains:

James: I started first, being the eldest, and although I can't remember what I thought of it initially. I know that a year or so into it I didn't enjoy it a lot. I was in about Grade 3 or 4 when I started. It might have even been the end of Grade 2. I know that when you're in grade three or four you don't really care about stuff like that. It's more fun mucking around with your mates, on your bike and things like that. So I much preferred doing that sort of thing and I found practising and going to lessons a real chore. And often I would try and do anything I could to get out of it. And so at that age it wasn't something that had much of an impact on me in terms of something I really enjoyed and looked out for. It was just part of the week that I just had to do.

But my parents said that they wanted me to keep learning until I reached a certain grade of exam or something—I think it was Grade 4—and once I reached Grade 4 [Australian Music Examination Board Grade] I could make a decision as to whether I wanted to continue or not. They felt that it was important that I stuck it out for a period of time where I would get a good enough experience of it to make an informed kind of decision, where I was just saying, "I hate it, I hate it, I hate it". I think the reason I hated it was it involved the type of learning where I had to sit down in a room, and there's no way that you can get around practising, you can't just do it. You've just got to spend that time at your machine, which for me was the piano, and just work on it and it was such a frustrating thing when you don't know how to play it. It's a hard thing to learn and I think that was why I didn't like it so much I was much more interested in a lot of other sort of young boy things, I guess (James 1996, pers comm. with teacher, 28 October).

James like many children responds "dutifully" to his parents' request to involve him in music learning or is doing it without questioning it. When he does suggest that he does not like the experience because he prefers to spend his time "mucking around with his mates", his parents' response is to give a structure to the learning that they value. They also place a further emphasis upon commitment. It is the inescapable "hard work" that is the turn-off for him. In this next narrative, you can see that the social holds an appeal to James. This is further developed later in the interview when he talks about beginning to learn the clarinet:

> *James:* My parents were my initial influence in that they wanted me to start and I perhaps became more interested in music in general when I changed primary schools and some of my friends and a couple who were cousins of mine were in the school band. We had a little band at the primary school and they had things like clarinets, brass instruments, and things like that. And it was run by a very nice elderly gentleman bandmaster who came in once or twice a week and I really wanted to be in the band 'cause some of my friends were. I really wanted to play drums, like everybody. This is when I was in Grade 5, or something. I really wanted to play drums and the bandmaster said "we've already got a really good drummer", and I still know that drummer, he's been over in New York and I use to bump into him occasionally. One day he came into the class and he said, "I know you wanted to join the band but there are no drum spots available but I do have a spot on clarinet". And I had no idea what a clarinet was I didn't even know if you hit it or blew into it or what! I said, "Yep I'll play that."
>
> *Steve*: You were still playing the piano?
>
> *James*: Yeah I was still playing piano, but I think what I really enjoyed was being able to play with other people and participate in an ensemble situation. And I got relatively good at clarinet for my age and for the intensity that I was having lessons. It was a fairly relaxed affair, but I guess you could say that I proceeded to be one of the more proficient clarinettists, by the time I was in Year 6 that was as high as that school went to, so I began to enjoy things. And also, I think it was because I had the friends who were playing, too. It made me a bit more motivated; just turning up to band with a couple of my mates was a bit of fun. And I don't know whether I related much of my piano playing to what I did in the band. I think it was more a social experience, but it probably wasn't until I was in Year 7 at high school that I met a whole bunch of other people and I happened to meet a whole load of people that enjoyed music and started seeing these other bands at school like the concert band, and some kids started making a rock band (James 1996, pers comm. with teacher, 28 October).

The meaning of music for James

James' story shows a journey through isolated music learning associated with piano and the change of environment to a social one where there were more of his friends and relatives who played music. The social aspects of music making became James' micro aesthetic, but for him it was not an instant experience, rather one that took several years before it was realised. The idea of gaining access to meaning "later" in the student's experience, and as a result of parent structured learning, is noteworthy and also is representative of the experiences of a number of other participants in the study. James' movement into a career as a musician pivoted upon his gaining of a social meaning. Once activated, his prior learning became valuable, and gave him access to personal expressive meaning and associated cultural meaning.

There is a synergy that connects these levels of meaning and that allows them to exist independently and in powerful consort. The difficulty lies in the productive tension between the analytical experiences of practice and repetitive learning and the intuitive "flow" experiences gained through more intrinsic means (Swanwick 1994). Students of music need to maintain the engagement in both the realms of intuitive and the analytical. The mastery of good teaching is about being perceptive about the student's development and balancing these factors. It appears that participants describe a "good teacher" as one who is aware of what motivates the child and can also take the child into their own love of music.

What of those who do not have access to music learning through a private teacher or a musical family? What can we say about those who had access and did not find the experience motivating? James was not intrinsically motivated by his music experience until he gained a social meaning through a school band. Does this suggest that commitment and motivation came from extrinsic means or a sense of "duty", or was it as it may have been for other interviewees—that the meaning was unspoken or shared? It is for these reasons that we need to examine institutionalised music. These forms of interaction may provide access to other meanings.

Institutional music learning

Among the 31 teachers and students interviewed, 12 began learning music for the first time in their primary years. Many learnt through some form of community music making institution such as a choir, while others gained access through individual or ensemble lessons at school. What is most apparent from examination of the interview data is the lack of opportunity for music learning in primary education, with the exception of those who were at an independent school. The main opportunities arose from formal choirs such as the Australian Children's Choir and the Australian Boy's Choir, some Orff percussion in classroom music, recorder or a junior musical production and one brass band. Overall, the participants' primary music experiences support research that suggests that access to music in primary schools in the state of Victoria in Australia is limited and inconsistent (Leirse 1999). In a few cases, those who attended independent schools had access to "user pays" private music lessons at school and in several cases students participated in instrumental music lessons in small groups.

For the participants who attended state primary schools, access to music appeared to be limited to choirs, recorder and musical productions. The kinds of music experience represented by choirs and productions in particular, whether in the primary school or within the community, suggest a powerful influence on early experience and musical training as a social form of music learning. This kind of music learning is accessible due to its mobility and low expense. In a negative sense, this form of music learning is often audition based and in this respect is elitist and restricted to the talented few rather than providing access for all.

The importance of the early childhood music experiences, which occurred in institutional experiences of school and community, is that they represented social and collaborative learning rather than the kind of learning found in private studio lessons. I would like to examine this phenomenon further as a process and discuss what it might bring to the meaning of music to the student. We have already seen the effect such learning had upon James and Edward, who both had access to private music lessons but also, had institutional/ensemble experiences. While asking participants to relate their music stories, I probed interviewees to discuss music at their primary school and church, and their membership of choirs and bands.

Wendy's story

Wendy is a 17-year-old singer who sings in an all-girl rock band and a female vocal ensemble. Her initial involvement with institutionalised music experience came from a children's choir:

Wendy: I did the Australian children's choir when I was about eleven.

Steve: And what was that experience like?

Wendy: I really enjoyed it, I really enjoyed performing, and I really liked the songs we played in the choir and stuff.

Steve: So, what were the learning procedures in the Australian Children's Choir? Did you learn exercises and warm ups and things like that?

Wendy: Yeah we didn't go straight into the songs. We did a lot of exercises I think. Yeah, and I had a really good teacher I was really impressed by her. I thought she was wonderful.

Steve: So describe your relationship with this singing teacher. Did she teach you in a group?

Wendy: Yeah

Steve: How large was the group?

Wendy: It was quite large it was twenty or more.

Steve: And yet she was still able to have an effect on you? A bit of magic, why do you think that was?

Wendy: She was really friendly and fun and stuff. She reminded me of my older sister I think.

Steve: Did she have a nice voice herself?

Wendy: Yeah, she had a beautiful voice.
(Wendy 1997, pers comm. with student, 31 July).

Wendy displays the positive experience of learning music in an ensemble and part of her attraction to the teacher is a positive comparison to her older sisters. The group learning is immediately social but the reference to her family provides another kind of connection to the transfer of Aronoff's natural aesthetic response.

Janet's story

Not all experiences with group learning are positive. Janet a 16-year-old orchestral percussionist and rock drummer outlines her difficulties with learning instruments in groups:

Janet: I learnt the keyboard for a little bit, but that was a whole big class. There was about fifteen of us learning from one teacher so it was very difficult especially when I didn't have a keyboard at home. And when it does take me longer to pick things up, I need to practice them more than other people. I find that in everything I do, I really need to practice to get it down, so yeah, I struggled with that (Janet 1997, pers comm., 21 December).

Numbers and access to an instrument to practice frustrated her progress.

John's story

John, a 20-year-old ex-student who played guitar in a rock band, speaks about his early frustrations with group learning in primary school:

John: The guitar teacher at the primary school, I don't think she was great; she didn't really have an approach that really made me understand the music. For the first two years, I think, I was playing sort of chordal pieces, strumming. And then in the third year, when I played at primary school, we did picking individual note, kind of stuff, and I couldn't see any connection whatsoever between these two (John 1997, pers comm., 21 December).

Later in the interview, I asked him about the relationship with his teacher and he responded in the following way:

John: I can't remember that very well, it was probably like the relationship with most teachers in primary there wasn't much there.

Steve: So she was just going through a set list of things?

John: She was just there to keep us occupied for the half-hour or whatever and that was it. We did one or two small performances for parents (John 1997, pers comm., 21 December).

John's frustration was with the quality of the teaching and his lack of understanding. The relationship with his teacher has none of the fondness of Linda's experience or even Wendy's choir leader—sadly, the teacher was perceived as there merely to keep them occupied. In students' constructed memory, recollections of music teachers, they often described what they considered to be good music teachers. They seemed to combine the personal (nice personality of teacher, as an attractive person), the talent of the teacher as a good musician, and appropriate encouraging pedagogy. John's encounter with a music teacher (above) outlines what happens when several of these elements are missing or below expectation. Social reflections of their achievement were also a part of their story: it was not simply that they enjoyed the sounds they were producing, though this was part of it, but that others—friends, teachers—gave them messages that they were achieving highly.

Holly's story

School productions/musicals are also a great social attraction, often involving several of the performing arts (dance, drama and music). Holly, a 15-year-old singer, describes her first involvement with singing at school:

> *Holly*: I used to always be vocal and just sing and that sort of thing...Then in Grade 5 when I was asked to be a lead in a play at primary school and that, really I thought "wow, I must have an okay voice" then that was the first thing that really made me interested in singing. I've always liked singing but when I was asked to be a lead in this play. There were two casts and the other girl in the other cast she was a fantastic singer and I thought I mustn't be too bad then. That was the main thing. I hadn't thought of me being a singer at all. From there I came to Farnsworth and had lessons here and I just love it, it was just something that I do as a hobby, it's just great (Holly 1997, pers comm. with student, 16 April).

Many students begin their association with music learning through collaborative activity within musical productions. There was a social affirmation or recognition of Holly's ability as a singer, which added to her self-esteem. Certainly, the social and cultural meanings seem present in these stories of institutional learning, but what they share with those who had access to private lessons is the quality of the teaching relationship. The negative cases presented highlight this factor quite disturbingly. Where students had poor relationships with teachers or the teacher focused upon drill and practice to the exclusion of the child's interest and attraction to music, participants reported being "turned off" the teacher and often music learning itself.

I would suggest that the meaning of music for a child at this age is more likely to be found in the affective, intuitive, and embodied aspects of experience rather than those that might result from reflection. This certainly supports the arguments in the literature about the intrinsic nature of music being the natural focus of music learning. The evidence presented in this case suggests a wordless meaning that is experienced as feelings rather than understandings and as intuitive embodied understanding rather than declarative knowledge.

The "meaning" of music for young people in this part of the analysis is to be found in narratives which refer to these intuitive and shared meanings. There appear to be two distinct approaches to learning music, which constitute music experience in early childhood, individual or private music lessons and group or institutional learning. Both offer a perspective on the child's perception of the meaning of music. Early childhood music experiences are defined in this analysis as those that occur before commencement of secondary school. Within the data collected, the majority of music experiences were of the studio or individual lesson variety while a few students had experiences through institutional learning such as community choirs, bands or primary school.

The location of musical meaning: Where is it?

From the discussion of early childhood musical experiences presented here, the meaning of music to young people seems to be located in three primary areas of the child's life. The first is that of the personal—where the activity and experience of making music are intrinsically motivated. This is "flow" from engaging with the act of music making itself and how the music making activity communicates with us personally. This constitutes what I would like to term "intra-personal meaning". As discussed earlier, this meaning may involve a kind of "living through" the teacher's experience at this age, a sharing in the teacher's joy of experience. Something of this personal pleasure is evident when children play along with the teacher or experience satisfaction of their achievements in playing music.

Second, music has meaning in the social sense—that is, making music collaboratively with others in ensembles, choirs, bands and orchestras. Communication and meaning is then "inter-personal" or about the relationship of self and others. The third area of meaning is located in a combination of those mentioned earlier and I have termed this "cultural" meaning. This constitutes what the individual experiences as someone who "is musical" or has musical experiences that are expressive, which results from their inter-personal and intra-personal experiences with music making. Fundamentally, this is a sense of well-being and self-esteem gained through music making and it is predicated upon a reciprocal interaction of the music product and the music maker with the community. This is a reciprocal and communicative area of meaning dependent upon affirmation of the music maker by the community and acceptance of the community's values as worthwhile by the maker.

I became aware of this idea, after interviews with school counsellors and pastoral care teachers who frequently made the comment "I didn't know he or she could do that" as a significant part of student self-esteem development. The idea of a "cultural meaning" refers to the student's performance or creative making as an interaction of self and the cultural aspects of community, which presents another side or complexity to how we are perceived by others. Csikszentmihalyi (1996) describes an area of meaning where the individual forges a unity with universal values and I believe that this was what I was able to observe in the case study. The notion of universal values is used here I believe to represent those universal within a distinct culture rather than implying a universal that takes in all of humanity. For this reason, I have chosen to use the term cultural meaning rather than universal in this study. Rather than appearing as a continuum or a progressive sequence of meanings, these meanings appear to constitute different kinds of ways in which students enter or are attracted to music making and sustain an involvement with it.

I am wary of making too broad an analysis of the information gleaned from this data. I would not suggest that the availability of quality music learning experiences in primary schools is limited to those who have access to music through independent schools or the "talent" to join public children's choral groups and school productions. In a sense the social music learning becomes a "pseudo family" experience. What appear to be successful and influential experiences are those that involve social and collaborative learning such as a choir or school production. The social and collaborative aspects of institutional learning appear to have attracted James to playing the clarinet in a more positive way than his experiences with piano. In Linda's case, learning the violin, the initial image was of the violin performer getting a standing ovation. This was an interest which when combined with the teacher, made up an important part of her initial involvement and impetus to continue.

This aspect of institutional contexts provides meaning to individuals because of its social dimensions. This aspect of meaning is one that is in need of deeper analysis within the context of school music at secondary level where the data are greater in quantity and thicker in description. The meaning of music to young people within institutional experiences of school and community is bound up with the social. This acts as part of the intrinsic motivation for involvement and continued participation. Learning in this sense and at this age is largely experiential, as is the meaning. It makes sense too that access to flow producing experience and the modelling of autotelic behaviour is integral to music learning in any context.

Conclusion

What I have suggested in this chapter is that each of the "meanings of music"—the personal, social and the cultural are potentially motivational aspects of learning music. They may occur in combination or individually. They might also not be apparent until a considerable amount of "work has been done" which enables access to them, as with James. Until this occurs, I would suggest that it might be enough for a child to be immersed in someone else's love of music—their family, a teacher, or even a group's collective fervour. This involves experiencing the meaning of music through others and sharing the family or communities valuing of music.

The most significant points raised about the processes of music learning gained from this analysis refer distinctly to the relationship between teacher and student. This suggests that teachers need to be able to involve the student in their own lives as music makers and recognise the development of the child's own aesthetic responses. Buber's (1969) suggestion that the educator stand at both poles of the bipolar relationship is "made flesh" in students' responses outlined here. The intimacy of the private music lesson represents the opportunity for musical development of individuals, which gives access to personal expression as well as to a social discourse of music making. The skills learned are conscious, deliberate and only contextual in performance. The institutional experience is built around the context of music making as a group, the aim of which is performance and the meaning of which are socially expressive and shared by the community or culture.

The meaning of music to the child is mutually dependent upon process. The "successful" processes as suggested by the stories outlined here imply a need to balance the intuitive and emotive aspects of music and the analytic and skill base required to perform it expressively. It is suggested that one may be reached through the other but it is only in making music in context that the two come together and are capable of giving meaning that communicates with others or self. Swanwick summarises this synergy and the importance of music as valued knowledge:

> This is where the ultimate value of music lies. It is uncommon sense, a celebration of the imagination and the intellect interacting together in acts of sustained playfulness, a space where feeling is given form, where romantic and classical attitudes, intuition and analysis meet; valued knowledge indeed (1994, 41).

The point this raises about theory is an understanding of what constitutes an intrinsically motivating experience. Music activity is not always intrinsically motivating. The image of playing sometimes does not match the reality. Many hours of practice precede performance. The process of repetition, analysis and skill development is not always related to the outcome. Performance and social music making sometimes constitute a frightening, self-esteem destroying experience. So what turns these potential "turn-offs" into effective music education that leads to a satisfying and meaningful pursuit? The suggestion here is that it is "living through" the experience of others and a sharing the meaning. The teacher and the student's relationship with them seem central to the success of music learning in both the private and institutional settings.

CHAPTER FIVE

DESIGNING MEANINGFUL AND ENGAGING ENVIRONMENTS

Introduction

In this chapter, I will draw on the understandings gained through the definition and examination of meaning to students and explore the some fundamental philosophical ideas. Applying an evolved pragmatist philosophical framework (Dewey 1989, Schusterman 1992) I would further like to suggest an approach for designing meaningful and engaging environments beginning with the intrinsic nature of music experience as the first premise for design and utilising some analytical tools I have found useful in schools and communities. I will then move to an approach for determining the factors which influence design decisions using two observation tools—a context analysis framework and a "meaningful engagement matrix". Following this I will re-state what I believe to be fundamental philosophical principles observed in the study and through reviews of literature and examine the implications of each principle for the design of meaningful and engaging environments.

The intrinsic nature of music experience

The intrinsic nature of arts activity has been consistently discussed amongst music and arts education theorists (Dewey 1989, Eisner 1985, 1991, Reimer 1989, Reimer and Wright 1992, Swanwick 1981, 1988, 1994). The notion of "intrisicality" is central to this examination of meaning and has arisen frequently in the data analysis. In this research I have used the word "intrinsic" to describe a natural attraction or engagement with music making—a playfulness with sound materials which may in itself be universal amongst humankind but then becomes culturally constructed when a culture imposes or shares its values for particular ways of being playful or constructive with sound. Intrinsic motivation has its prerequisites and should not be assumed as present in music encounters. As Swanwick describes, the productive tension that exists between the analytic and the intuitive in music education provides both challenge and pleasure to participants who are initiated into what he calls a "music discourse" (Swanwick

1994, 21). Both kinds of experiences can initiate flow but also the reverse is possible—a music activity can induce boredom or anxiety. It is therefore useful to understand which aspects of music making have the potential to be intrinsic and flow producing and how this might be sustained throughout engagement with music making. It is useful also to understand what and why some activities produce negative effects and how to create the productive tension that Swanwick describes between the natural intuitive flow activities and the analytical aspects which are necessary steps in achieving more articulate and expressive music making (1994, 20).

Meaning and experience design

Personal, social and cultural meaning can be present in a person independent of one another or in combination. Most poignant and useful for the purposes of education is the idea that they might all be facilitated or constructed. The participants interviewed and their observations suggest that the whole process of learning music and the meaning gained from it cannot be attributed to single aspects of education such as the studio lesson, classroom or ensemble. Students and teachers alike perceived that their growth in skill, knowledge and understanding was due to participation in a wide range of activities. This attitude was presented despite the seeming, discontinuity of the experiences.

Certainly, those who participated in all of the aspects of music experience demonstrated a diverse and mature understanding and seemed to find each area meaningful. Alternatively, those that had negative experiences in instrumental/studio, classroom and ensemble context were still able to attribute meaning to their performance experiences if they were encouraging the participation rather than judging their skill. What I am implying here is that the cultural meaning may be the only meaning gained by some students but that it may eclipse the others because of its powerful effect upon self-esteem. The opposite may be said of negative cultural experiences.

Meaning to the "non-musically experienced", or those who did not show an interest in continuing involvement with music making, was seen to display the same three areas of meaning. The depth and breadth of understanding and access to increased complexity was limited to their specific subculture and personal understanding. Interestingly the memories of these students of their musical encounters were positive, based entirely upon an affirming cultural experience rather than lack of success with personal and social encounters. This presents the problem that poor music education can be enhanced by a single successful performance. Unfortunately, this is a very common event in music education. It does not excuse or correct the problems of poor teaching or curriculum. It does explain how such approaches survive through their public perception rather than their curricula reality. Aside from this caution of false impressions created by successful performance, the most important issue is that each of the meanings described in this analysis could be facilitated through curriculum and teacher action.

This is the essence of facilitating the access to meaning and teaching the intuitive. As Jane remarked, "It's that feeling, and you can't create that, you can only create the situation that makes it possible" (Jane 1997, pers comm. with teacher, 13 February). Her comment suggests that it is possible to ensure that the environment can facilitate experience where meaning can be "caught" and "taught" (Swanwick 1994). The implication is that we need to be conscious of the curricular environment of classroom and the extra-curricular experiences of studio, ensemble and community interaction and participation when considering music learning in total. It is important to treat music learning as a total environment and a continuum of learning experience rather than a series of unrelated musical experiences. This notion provides the opportunity for students to have access to personal, social and cultural meaning. How this kind of environment might be formed is the focus of the next chapter, which examines the idea of "teacher as builder" of environments where music meaning may be caught and taught.

Experience design and culture

I would like now to draw upon research that utilises Indigenous Standpoint Theory and my own experience of curriculum design that engages with these ideas. I will begin by outlining the principle ideas of common ground and engaging with tensions at the interface between cultures and then present a vignette which highlights these tensions followed by some rules of thumb which potentially enable a way forward for experience and curriculum design.

In 2005, Jim Chapman and I discussed an approach to engage with the process of personalising our experiences of Indigenous knowledge through experience and embodied understanding. Nakata's discussion of "interfaces" between cultures provides a way forward for how to design environments which are culturally inclusive and reverent to community. He writes, "What is certain is that the intersections of different knowledge, systems concerns and priorities will converge to inform and develop new practices in this area" (Nakata 2002, 15). It is the understanding of the sites and tensions inherent within this emerging understanding of "interfaces" between knowledge systems, systems concerns and priorities which is important for our understanding of how to design culturally appropriate experience.

Too often, we tokenise cultural knowledge and filter all meaning from it through a Western art music framework or alternatively we acknowledge the importance of musical knowledge in a community as sacred and fail to engage with it at all for risk of offending the community. I would like to present here a brief set of principles that enable engagement with the tensions at the interfaces between cultures. These experiences come from my own experience with Indigenous Australian and Islamic cultures and while I acknowledge that these are diverse, complex, and not generalisable, I do believe that these rules of thumb allow access to a "common ground" (Dreise 2006) as a way of making music ethically and with reverence and respect of culture.

Tension at the interface: A brief vignette

Nakata (2002) refers to the interface of cultural knowledge being a site where activity occurs and suggested that that activity was necessarily a point of tension. The suggestion is from my interpretation is that unless there is tension then there is potentially a situation of unequal power relations. Essentially, if there is no tension then one party is in a position of dominance and quietens the activity. In musical knowledge, we understand this idea and we can distinguish between productive (Swanwick 1994) and non-productive tension. Indeed Swanwick's theory in relation to musical knowledge refers to a productive tension between analytical and intuitive knowledge in music making.

I witnessed some intra cultural tension like this at an Indigenous youth hip-hop festival. An Aboriginalist lens on urban Aboriginal musical values would suggest that both hip-hop and country music are perceived to be a less genuine expression of Indigenous worldviews than an "authentic" connection with traditional songs, which connect the participant with a genuine understanding, and connection to country. However, in Australia, Indigenous people have engaged with both of these forms of music in a creative and functional way for many years. There is also an intra-cultural tension between hip-hop and country music. Elders in communities seldom want young people to present to the world the kinds of negative and sometimes offensive ideas common to hip-hop which is strongly political and often contains sexual and drug references and can present negative lifestyle themes (see for example Indigenous Intrudaz: http://www.abc.net.au/triplej/unearthed/bands/6860.htm).

On the other hand Country music is more mainstream but because it is "about country" and relationships with country and perhaps historically because of the association of Australian country music with folk traditions which express a connection with the land and relationships in song. This scenario represents a tension between worldviews and perceptions, which occurs at the interface of music and culture. This tension can occur both in songs and about them. In Australian rural and bush areas country music has strong history, appeal and indigenous people have also made this connection with the expressive qualities of country music through Aboriginal country singers like Jimmy Little and Troy Cassar-Daly (Dunbar-Hall and Gibson 2004, Walker 2000).

Elders in the community where a hip-hop festival was held saw country music as representing a connection to country, which expressed relational knowledge. These urban elders however could also see that hip-hop, despite its potentially negative connotations, had an effect on giving youth a voice through song to express their condition. From this recognition of music as a common ground, a festival has grown from this understanding, which has genuinely, re-connected youth to their communities and provided a means of expression that brings personal social and cultural meaning.

What we can learn from this is that popular music despite the perception of its lack of "genuine" and authentic connections to a traditional culture can genuinely and authentically connect with people as a means of cultural, social and personal expression. Through an engagement with the tension, it can also provide a productive outcome. Had the elders bended to political correctness this community benefit may never have occurred. The following rules of thumb provide some ways of engaging with these ideas:

Rules of thumb (Derived from Dillon and Chapman 2005)

1. Ways of knowing: Examining underlying structures and assumptions of knowledge

In many cultures, music exists only as a functional container and communicator of knowledge. The first assumption made by Western music teachers is that a melody of a song for instance exists purely as a musical entity without reference to its context, function and relationship to culture and context. De-contextualised an Indigenous song melody is meaningless when it is separated from country and relationships with people and knowledge. A further problem is presented when we view music through a purely Western art music aural perception framework. These often act as cultural filters. In our own work with curriculum and culture we have found that rather than using an elemental approach to aural perception it is useful to adopt a "time and space" (Vella 2000) model. This allows the music to be perceived as sound in relation to context rather than imposing meanings on the perception.

2. Knowledge from country: Distributed and situational knowledge

When the role of music in a community is a means for knowledge transfer and containment it takes on a different perspective and its value is increased significantly. It becomes as reified as a library in status. In Australian Aboriginal and Torres Strait Islander cultures song performs complex and multiple functions as knowledge, container and transmitter of cultural knowledge. Song can be directly structured and linked to country or place. The law is in the songs, ceremonies and stories (Chalmers 2005, pers comm.). Places and objects are said to be sung into existence. These are complex notions of the role of song in a community and radically different from European concepts of songs as commodities or entertainment. In some respects these notions of a relationship between music and place are reminiscent of the concept of distributed intelligence where knowledge is resident in our surroundings.

The idea that knowledge is situated and directly linked to context is also an extremely different way of viewing music making. My understanding of the connection between place and music is that when a song is resident within a place and this place triggers the memory of the song, the song itself tells the keeper of that knowledge where water or food or shelter might be found the meaning of music and song becomes about knowledge transfer rather than aesthetics. I am aware that my reading here is singular and does not take into account the changes brought by colonisation to Indigenous Australian forms of cultural and performance practice—in many ways this description represents a romanticised view of how Indigenous Australian peoples connect to country, understand their place, and enact the knowledges associated with ownership and belonging to country. As I understand it, the degree to which Indigenous Australian peoples are able to sustain this connection to country through song is varied from community to community according to histories, experiences and the on-going effects of colonisation. However, what I am concerned about is that the differences in the function of song and how song is perceived between Western and Indigenous Australian cultures are highlighted.

3. Ways of representing knowledge: drawing on multiple modes/systems of representation to store, communicate and amplify thought.

Text or specifically the technology of print is a relatively new device for storing and communicating important cultural knowledge. In engaging with non-Western cultures we must consider ways of transferring knowledge, which utilize multiple modes or systems of communication. Aural/oral transfer of knowledge is common and utilising embodied knowledge approaches to learning and teaching allows curriculum to be more dynamic. We must be aware that print as a technology conceals (Brown 2006, Heidegger 1977) and filters much that is important in musical experience. So to use common practice notation in the teaching of embodied aural/oral knowledge will by its nature conceal the essence of its meaning.

4. Relational knowledge: Understanding who you are when you are on common ground.

Country music provides a metaphorical "common ground" where it is possible for people of diverse backgrounds to meet. Hip hop is a form of contemporary music that can provide a means of expression which allows political and social issues to be explored and this has potential to lead to an understanding of these conditions by those who are not part of the culture through direct experience with music making. Music educators need to consider identifying common ground in a variety of contexts asking who you are in relation to the community and place. Relational knowing involves assessing your relationship to "others"—your relationship with "others" will establish what knowledge will be revealed to you and what will be concealed.

The concept here involves drawing upon Dreise's explanation of common ground and Nakata's concept of interfaces as a way of presenting music making as a metaphorical location where cultures can interface. In musicology and in theology this is called "syncreticism". Syncretic music is described as different from traditional music in that for traditional music to change the culture itself would have to change (Vella 2000). Syncretic music involves a blending together' of musical ideas that maintains the integrity of the original cultures and brings about something even more expressive or expressive of the relationship between cultural frameworks. Syncretism is complex ethically.

While in contemporary commodity culture popular music undergoes syncretic change all the time, there are continuously aspects of appropriation of "new sounds" and structures that occur without permission or understanding of the significance of the music to its cultural origin. Nevertheless, music can provide an interface between culture and this kind of common ground where Indigenous knowledge can be imparted as part of pedagogical experience for those who seek the meaning of expression in sound. There is potential here for a non-verbal, non-textual interface and for embodied understanding to take place. Engaging politically and ethically with this kind of tension takes persistence and courage but it is extremely important that we constantly seek common ground and interrogate its potential to be a productive source of meaning, understanding and knowledge about culture and our relationships to each other.

Experience design and technology: jam2jam vignette

Advances in computer technology have made it possible to design music algorithms based upon specific pitch, timbre and rhythmic qualities that can be manipulated in real time with a simple interface that a child can control. Jam2jam is a software program that uses these ideas and enables what is called "networked improvisation (Brown and Dillon 2007). Users manipulate sliders and dials and influence changes in music in real time. This enables the opportunity for participants to interact with the sound possibilities of the chosen musical style as a focused musical environment. Essentially by moving a slider or dial the user can change the intensity of the musical activity across musical elements such as rhythm, harmony, timbre and volume and the changes they make will respond within the framework of the musical style parameters, updating and recomposing within a quaver. This enables the users to play within the style and to hear and influence the shape and structure of the music. What is different about this software is that through utilising a network you can create virtual ensembles, which are simultaneously collaborative and interactive just like acoustic ensembles.

New music technologies have for centuries provided new expressive possibilities and an environment where humans can play. With jam2jam users can play with complex or simple musical ideas, interact with the musical elements and hear the changes immediately, doing so collaboratively in a virtual ensemble and both live and virtual performances. What is significant about this case is that it enables music to be present in a conversation about music. Users can focus on the particular configuration of the parameters of musical style that make styles/genres unique. It allows the groups of users and teachers the opportunity to both play as an ensemble and discuss the ensemble performance simultaneously. The music is generative and the performance is continuous and so conversations about the sound can occur with the music present. It also allows for "what if?" scenarios—what if there was more bass? What if the tempo was slower? What if we changed the timbre of the keyboard?

The conversation becomes necessarily focused around using musical terms and musical concepts, which pedagogically scaffolds the user's reflection in and on the activity of music making. For education, creating a networked musical environment allows teachers to focus attention on the expressive qualities of composition and this leads to a musical conversation about the music with the music present. Consequently the answer to each of the "what if" questions can be heard and discussed.

While we can focus listeners on musical ideas when playing a recording with this approach, in this case we create a new kind of experience where the users can interact with the style/genre in a collaborative and safe environment where feedback is immediate. The software establishes a relationship between the user's ears, gesture and the musical ideas encapsulated by the algorithm. Thousands of children between the ages of 4 and 16 have used this software within moments of its introduction. What this research has alerted us to is that this kind of music technology allows us to be simultaneously immersed and apart from the experience of music making. It allows teachers to focus students' attention in an immersive environment and engage them with collaborative music making. It provides an opportunity to play in a playground filled with musical experiences which can be engaged with meaningfully. This suggests a shift in perspective for us philosophically in relation to performance, composition and listening and how and when these occur with the added possibility of being able to engage with these simultaneously.

Previously we described networked improvisation as defining a new form of musicianship. Musicianship in a networked environment acknowledges the computer as an instrument, a networked group as a form of ensemble and cyberspace as the venue for their music making. Since the instruments utilize digital technologies to store, represent and communicate musical knowledge and experience, it is necessary for the musician to have a reasonable understanding of how these technologies operate. For this reason, contemporary musicianship includes skills in using computer hardware and software to record, review, generate, produce and publish music. It acknowledges the unique techniques and knowledge demonstrated by DJs, sound designers, electronic composers and music producers. Furthermore, in place of common practice notation, the contemporary musician uses digital representations of music—such as waveforms, graphs, event lists, and computer code—to analyse, compose and perform (Brown and Dillon 2007).

This idea of a relationship with music technology suggests a new form of musicianship is required. It also suggest that we need to engage philosophically with what is suggested here because the implication is that this kind of experience design which utilises technology in these ways affects what we learn, how we learn and at what age or skill level we can encounter this musical knowledge. Music technology has moved beyond the dismissive "its just a tool" paraphrase it is and always has been simultaneously an expressive communications tool, a cognitive amplifier (Papert 1980, 1994, 1996) and a container of knowledge as our oral/aural knowledge systems (Will 2000) evidence for us. What is needed here is for us to continuously ask the questions about what technology reveals, conceals and highlights for us in the construction and design of experience and curriculum.

Problematising music technology in experience and curriculum design

The above mentioned networked music experience represents a shift in how technology might be used in learning. It creates a focused environment where participants can encounter musical knowledge in an intrinsically engaging and meaningful way. Indeed the software design was based on the theory discussed in this book and those of Andrew Brown (Brown 2003). The position of music technology in this scenario is one where there is a clear understanding of what the technology reveals and what it intentionally conceals to the participants (Brown 2003, Heidegger 1977). It is necessary to problematise the idea of music technology in this way because to date music educators have tended to be users or replicators of existing frameworks for the expressive use of technology in music education. We tend to run courses in music technology rather than creative production and we seldom ask what the technology enables or filters. The violin bow and the saxophone mouthpiece are perhaps the most expressive pieces of music technology in Western history yet composers and virtuoso performers did not undertake courses in these technologies. To understand them they actively explore what the expressive capabilities of these technology enable, what they revealed and concealed to us as musicians.

I have presented this jam2jam vignette simply to suggest that when we work with music technology in the classroom, studio or community we now need to ask new questions that refocus our relationship with music technology so we understand its function in relation to expressiveness in sound making. Music technology provides ways of representing sound (common practice notation is a technology), amplifying our creative thoughts, allowing these to become concrete and present rather than abstract. As Brown suggests, music technology "amplifies skills by providing leverage and extension. Just as an audio amplifier can make music louder, a computer can be a musicianship amplifier enhancing musical skills and increasing musical intelligence" (Brown 2006, 7). For the student as maker just as creative musicians in the past have explored and exploited the creative and expressive potential of the trumpet valve and the piano hammer so too do we need to embrace a relationship with technology that utilises this greater potential for expressive music making and learning.

A context analysis framework

In light of the ideas presented here, I would like now to present some tools for analysis that I have found useful when designing experience and curriculum. I will begin by presenting a simple context analysis tool, which enables the educator to perceive the factors that influence decisions about learning design. Next I present a simple matrices developed by Andrew Brown and I to examine meaningful engagement in software design and production. The tool has also been used frequently to examine human systems of learning also and provides a simple and useful lens on the relationship between the participants and the creative process. Finally, I re-present the philosophical fundamentals discussed earlier and provide a description of how these might provide a checklist for putting the meat on the bones of theory and dynamically testing practice against theory.

A basis for context analysis

Before we can adequately design experience, the context needs to be analysed thoroughly. For the music teacher there are a number of factors, which influence how they interpret curriculum. Figure 5.1 provides an overview of the" demands" made upon the teacher that influence their decisions about curriculum. Beyond the music teacher or coach's own values and experiences the school or institutional constraints influence strongly what can or may not be done within the context. The arts pedagogy, which frames the curriculum or even the focus of community music programs, strongly influences content, processes and culturally frames the music making. The traditional and colonial model for music education involves the Institution and the pedagogy, which represents mainstream musical values simply, require student to learn particular music in a distinctive way. This is colonial cultural reproduction and has been effective as a way of reinforcing mono-cultural values. In a post modern and multi cultural society, this kind of approach becomes more problematic. It is colonial, it is not inclusive of culture, gender, genre or creed but more importantly, it fails to engage all children in meaningful music making for life.

The school or institutional demands are such things as: curriculum policy, timetables, teaching spaces, resources, behaviour models, assessment outcomes or evaluation frameworks and standards and quality assurance measures. The Arts Pedagogy considerations for music education include such things as: repertoire or classic works, history and storage of knowledge, music theory, representation systems such as Common Practice Notation, notions of aesthetic development and how to measure this and initiation into a musical and cultural discourse, i.e., classical, jazz, pop or particular cultural framing or interpretation of these.

Figure 5.1 Situational analysis of context (demands on teacher)

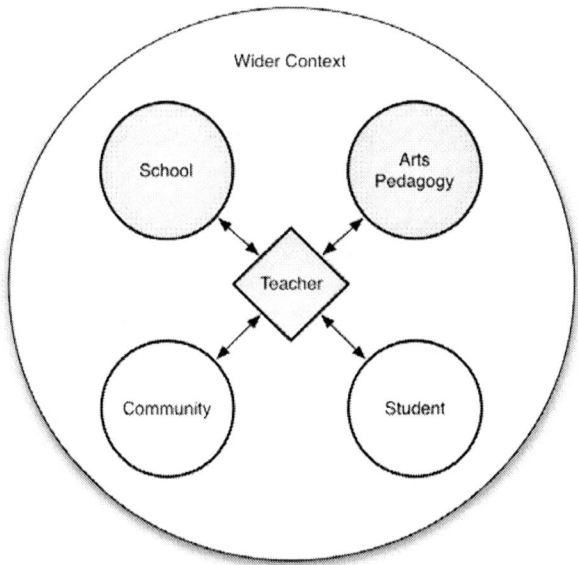

The student interviewed at the school case study site suggested that their needs were for engagement, motivation, interest and the feeling that they were making progress in their learning. The students spoke of access to a safe environment that was also challenging, meaningful and gave them a sense of belonging and affirmation of their place in the community. Each community has its own set of values and music plays integral roles in documenting, transmitting and creating a sense of the unique character of the community. In a suburban community or a school setting this will be a multi dimensional and generally a multi-cultural community. Mono-cultural communities are indeed rare today. Reconciling how multi-cultural community values music in their lives and utilising this kind of understanding is an important part of music education. It also provides a rich resource for cross cultural understanding and access to embodied knowledge through members of the community who know the role of music in the community. Furthermore, it provides the opportunity for ethical syncretic music to be made and for music to become a common ground where tensions at the interface between cultures can be engaged with in meaningful and productive ways that can lead to cultural understanding and new creative expression in music. Essentially the community requires an initiation into culture and values and for art/music that defines the community.

A bottom up approach

Designing a so-called bottom up approach is not difficult but it must be genuine. It is also not just about consultation followed by imposed action. This too is colonial. In Australia, the role of music is problematic in the traditional approach for Indigenous music where "music" per se exists with a function that is as a storage communication and cognitive amplification of knowledge. A song containing multiple layers of meaning connected to unique country, understood only by those who are the right age, gender and skin group makes the colonial approach patronising at least and culturally insulting in another. The decontextualising of knowledge in song and the appropriation of songs which are containers and communicators of important cultural knowledge brings with it ethical dilemmas that have seen the study of indigenous music relegated to the "too hard basket". Or more likely the lets do nothing because they risk offending someone.

With Islamic communities despite the strong presence of music in many Islamic cultures, interpretations of the Koran suggest that music is a recognised as a powerful force to affect emotions and communicate with God. Indeed a top down colonial approach to this context also leads to a plan to do nothing. If however "consultation" leads to a relationship with the community and an ongoing dialogue then this often leads to the teacher being invited to experience the embodied notions of music present in these cultures in an often-unexpected way. This is where the music teacher or coach can engage with the tensions at the interfaces between cultures. This is where common ground allows shared understandings and contextual and relational knowledge to be experienced first hand.

When the teacher draws from a genuine and continuous dialogue with the community and the students then music learning can be truly relevant and reverent to culture and community. The diagram above (Figure 5.1) provides a way of gathering contextual information about how the community frames, values and interprets musical signs. Applying it to a community where music is taught or plays a role in the community as a spiritual, ceremonial or practical application to community identity can provide an understanding of how the community can or needs to function and the most relevant application of music to the community that allows it to provide aesthetic and embodied knowledge to students.

Observing meaningful engagement: A matrix

Andrew Brown has been observing and examining how computer musicians engage with the act of creative production. This work has led to the development of an approach to identifying the relationship we have with creative processes and the roles of composer, process and technology in the production of creative sound (Brown 2000, 2003, 2006). In subsequent research, these ideas have been combined with the current ideas presented in this book about meaning and applied to the development of music experience software for children (Brown and Dillon 2007, Brown, Sorensen and Dillon 2002, Dillon 2003, 2004c, 2005b, 2006c, 2006d).

This approach to the identification and description of meaningful engagement has proved useful in both software development and curriculum and experience design and provided a way to balance activity and design alike. While the theory associated with this instrument is based upon two doctoral studies over five years of field study with children the instrument itself has not been formally validated. I present this matrix here at this stage to provide a simple checklist for the documenting and evaluating of the relationship we have to engagement in creative production and the potential that activity and design has for meaning. Like the usefulness of Swanwick's CLASP acronym in the creation of curriculum the Meaningful Engagement Matrix (see Figure 5.2) provides a tool for analysis that provides useful information about the construction of curricular and the approach to teaching and learning design.

Using the meaningful engagement matrix

The matrix supplies two axes. The horizontal axis provides a description of the students' processes in the act of making music and the each category is described below:

An appreciator: Listening carefully to music and analysing music representations
The active involvement of a music maker in listening to music in a way that involves an engagement with reflection embodied understanding and critical listening such that the student is able to perceive the effectors and effects of music and determine something of its expressive qualities.

Figure 5.2. Meaningful engagement matrix (MEM)

MEM	Appreciate	Direct	Explore	Participate	Select
Personal					
Social					
Cultural					

(Dillon 2006)

A director: Managing music making activities
    A director is controlling music. Traditionally this might be a bandleader conductor or musical director but in a contemporary sense, it may also be a DJ manipulating loops of music samples or a computer musician affecting real time changes to an algorithmic piece. The fundamentals of this engagement involve creative decision-making and application.

An explorer: Searching through musical possibilities and assessing their value
    Exploration, improvisation and just plain creative free play with musical materials are a useful process for musicians. It allows them to play with possibilities and construct concrete rather than abstract constructions of music ideas. This too like the appreciator involves reflective and analytical practice, which feeds back into the creative process.

A participant: Involved in intuitive music making
    A participant is essentially a musician immersed in the process of making music collaboratively or participating in an activity directed by someone else of by adherence to a symbolic representation like sheet music, an algorithm.

A selector: making decisions about the value of music or musical elements
    A selector influences change through their assessment of musical expressive value. This process could be a DJ selecting materials for performance, a composer making decisions about themes and variations or an acoustic

performer selecting the expressive interpretations of a notated work. Selecting involves the act of aesthetic judgement and expressive value.

As described tin the last three chapters meaning has been identified as having three locations. The vertical axis describes the potential for an activity to generate meaning and each location are described below.

Personal: The activity is intrinsically enjoyable
As described earlier personal meaning refers to the music makers' own relationship with music. It describes a personal experience where you and music are involved and engaged with the form such that you are engaged and connected with the music in a dialogue which is flow producing. It could be as simple as listening to music and relating its narrative or timbres. It may be the notions of relaxation described earlier or simply you and your instrument playing alone. This meaning feeds into the sense of self and constructs our identity it is a self-formative process. While it may involve critical reflection, it is primarily about simultaneously making, perceiving, and gaining "flow".

Social: The activity connects the student with others and these relationships are valued
Social meaning involves the wordless connection to another; it speaks of sharing a sonic product and embodied understandings through our connection with rhythm and synchronisation of our minds through sharing the sound in time and space. We feel its intensity its tensions and release and share non-verbal experiences framed by sound and gesture. It is self-forming because we are made by our interactions with others and this non-verbal communication provides rich understandings of others that produce flow for participants that ensure continued engagement with the activity. The participant values these activities, the members of the ensemble or group and the community to which they belong because they provide pathways to understandings and ways of connecting with cultural materials.

Cultural: The activity is regarded as valuable by the community and, by participating (or succeeding) in it; the student achieves a sense that they too are important
The application of this theory of meaning involves understanding that not only does the culture value the music made by its creative individuals and groups but utilises it to define and project its character. Music provides instant recognition of cultural identity. National anthems are testament to this idea but the creators of music who draw upon what their culture values as how sound might be organised expressively are also part of our national character or our

genre/style identity. This factor of music as a social identifier and the musician as a living (or immortal) symbol of culture and history of a community is an important consideration when observing whether music is meaningful, why it is engaging and why it is made the way that it is to reflect community values. While we also reify our sporting heroes in much the same way music and musicians are more pervasive than the image of a sporting hero. The introduction to Beethoven's ninth Symphony, the riff from Deep Purple's "Smoke on the water", the sound of Sowetto street music, a didjeridu, a sitar all identify clearly and instantly their communities and potentially evokes the values they represent. This becomes self-formative for the music maker because acknowledgement and sometimes-even rejection by a community builds a relationship with community and culture that influences the formation of self and has a powerfully transformative effect.

Conclusion

This chapter was fundamentally practical and analytical in nature. What I hope to encapsulate here has been a process, which enables the dynamic interaction between practice and theory and the active application and testing of philosophy in practice. Most significantly, I emphasise the intrinsic nature of music experience and advocate that this quality is central to the construction and design of experience for students. Furthermore, I explored the idea that music has the potential to act as a "common ground" where an opportunity for cultural awareness and embodied and intuitive knowledge of "the other" can be experienced.

This idea was problematised and I provided some rules of thumb for ethical engagement with cultural experiences. I also drew upon emergent technologies to further discuss the complexity of music making within contemporary musical contexts to enable the practical engagement of a teacher with evaluation of their context. Furthermore, I provided some analytical tools that allow us to observe meaningful engagement in music practice.

The tools presented here are useful in providing a lens of the phenomena of the unique contexts of our schools and communities. It is in no way intended to be prescriptive or even sequential although the gathering of context data normally should be a first step in a bottom up approach to the design of experience or curriculum—this is the focus of the next chapter.

CHAPTER SIX

THE STUDENT AS MAKER

Introduction

The meanings that students attach to music experience in a school and the issues raised by these portrayals of meaning are explored in this chapter. Previously I suggested that the meaning gained by students is linked to the nature of these experiences, and intrinsic motivation is derived from their success. I identified three areas of meaning—the personal, the social and the cultural. I would now like to explore these meanings further in the school context. Primarily, I will examine the meaning that students attach to music, through the students own voices captured whilst conducting music life story interviews. I will build upon themes arising from analysis of these narratives and introduce teacher's voices and my own field observations to vary the lens and thicken the description on the phenomenon of meaning. To begin, I want to review some of the theoretical understandings, which inform my framing of the student as maker. I will then discuss the sense of self that students talk about, and the part that music plays in that. The three areas of meaning outlined above will be used to structure the discussion.

The relationship of theory to the idea of "student as maker"

In this section, I represent the fundamental beliefs I have gained from the study of music education philosophy and theory and examine what these tenets mean in relation to the student as maker of music.

1. Music is an intrinsically motivated activity (Abbs 1990, Aronoff 1969, Dewey 1989, Dillon and Stewart 2006, Dillon, Stewart, Brown, Arthurs, Dodge and Peacock 2004, Dillon 1995b, 2001c).

What this means is that humans are playful beings and being playful with sound and organising it is widespread and universal amongst human cultures. So if children will naturally make sounds and be playful with sound and expressive with sound why do so many of us here have such bad memories of school music teachers and classes. Why is music not intrinsically motivated in schools except by the "gifted" elite? It must be to do with the teachers values, the curriculum and the approach or method so at the very least we should not get in the way of the intrinsic nature of music activity and aim to build on the child's natural aesthetic responses- create environments where they can both be playful with artistic materials and learn.

2. Activity and reflection should ideally complement and support each other. Action by itself is blind, and reflection impotent (Csikszentmihalyi 1996, Schon 1984, 1987).

We need a balance of these activities of experience and reflection and we need to provide structures and habits of making and reflecting. Activity and experiences in making music in real or simulated way need to be made into cognitive understanding through structured reflection. Reflection needs to be in another medium i.e. verbal, written, video audio tape—this allows another lens or perspective on the experience. Alternatively, over attention to reflective and abstract learning is impotent. Make it come alive by giving it purpose, context, and relevance and make it concrete—a making activity. The secret is a balance between analytic and intuitive learning between that which is "caught" and that which is "taught" (Swanwick 1994).

3. Music lessons should include both making and reflective activities and be taught within a context that is real or simulated so that it is relevant to life (Bruner 1960, 1966, 1972, 1986, Dewey 1916, 1970, 1989, Dillon, 2004a, 2004d, 2005a, Dillon and Stewart 2006, Durrant and Welch 1995, Hallam 2001, Papert 1996, Swanwick 1981, 1994) Saatchi and Saatchi 2000, Schon 1984, 1987).

In practical terms, this means to make music i.e. create or perform music in the classroom based upon real life activity and discuss and draw out the process and evaluation of each product through reflection both formal and informal. To make music that simulates or replicates how musicians make music in the real world is to situate music making within the functional and aesthetic worlds, which it occupies, in real life. Once a simulated experience has been designed, what makes it meaningful and pedagogically useful is to reflect on both the music making process and product. This needs to be done as Schon suggests both during and after the experience. It should also be undertaken with the music present in the discussion as an artefact/recording or live performance. Furthermore, the reflective response need not be text or words but could be visual or sonic response.

4. Music lessons should have activities that involve composing or a creative aspect, performing or a presentation aspect and listening/audition/analytic response (Swanwick 1981, 1988, 1994, 1999, Swanwick and Franca 1999, Swanwick and Tillman 1986).

Every lesson should involve the possibility of children making aesthetic judgments or creative thought. Even if it is simply deciding on the timbre and dynamic of singing the "pop" in "Pop goes the weasel", the students should be involved in making those decisions. They should always present or perform work at the end or during a lesson and they should always discuss each work in a reflective way using the vocabulary that of musical elements.

5. *In Western art music curriculum the musical aspects of curriculum refer to consistently revisiting the fundamental concepts of musical elements in increasingly deeper and more complex ways that build on understanding of music* (Bruner 1960, 1966, 1972, 1973, 1986, Pratt 1990, Swanwick 1981, 1988, 1994, 1999, Swanwick and Franca 1999, Swanwick and Tillman 1986).

It is suggested here that these elements also may need to be expanded to include more recent expressive qualities such as space. These elements of music can be used to:
- Develop compositions in expressiveness and form.
- Develop performances in expressiveness and impact
- Develop critical listening frameworks and criteria for aural analysis of sound/music (Dillon 2001c, Pratt 1990).

When participating in non-Western music it is advisable to adopt a more flexible and culturally inclusive aural analysis framework. Examine the rules of thumb described above and consider adopting a sound in time and space model of aural analysis as described by (Vella 2000). This approach to the pedagogical analysis is culturally more appropriate and ethically more reverent to communities where music functions as cultural knowledge. Nevertheless, the concept suggested by Bruner and presented here is that we revisit fundamental understandings at progressively deeper levels and Indigenous knowledges are constructed to be encountered in this way too. Ethically though the understanding is guided by the relational knowledge and whether the participants in music making contexts can have access to this knowledge or should be given the opportunity to encounter knowledge through a "common ground" experience.

6. *Music is a part of life and community: Treat it as such in schools* (Burnaford, Aprill and Weiss 2004, Dillon 1999a, 2000, 2001c 2006f, Dillon and Chapman 2005, Dillon, Stewart, Brown, Arthurs, Dodge and Peacock 2004, Fiske 2000, Gardner 1993a, 1993b, Hallam 2001, Robinson 2001, Rusinek, Burnard, Evelein, Economidou-Stavrou and Sæther 2005).

Music is not just part of the curriculum but can be used as an effective learning tool in other subjects. More importantly, it can be used as a unifying cultural force within the school community and as a way of projecting the image of that community to the world beyond school/community. This aspect will be expanded upon in our discussion about the school as village. What is important in this understanding is that we need to consider the opportunities for music to have a living dynamic function within as school community. In the case study school there was a simple contract with the twenty-four ensembles at the school. Each ensemble committed to making music for their peers and for their community, and to push the boundaries of their art. This simple contract evolved into students leading musical direction and event design fro concerts, religious services, arts festivals and a myriad of audiovisual outputs for the community. This provided an opportunity for students as makers to work to briefs, deadlines and be active participants in the school community. Pedagogically this provided monumental educational growth, socially it built pride, resilience, spirit and personally, it fostered belonging, and self-esteem.

7. If students gain broad general music experiences in the classroom and they also learn to be reflective and self critical about music then this skill enables them to make sense and gain access to the meaning of music wherever they find it (Dillon 2001a, 2001c, Fiske 2000, Saatchi and Saatchi 2000, Schon 1984).

Within the relatively safe environment of school, we can experience a range of cultural and chronological experiences of music making. When a student makes music the way it is made in community and they have reflective practice and critical analysis built into guided reflective activity this naturally leads to an understanding of how music is made. .For example, a student who composes, produces, and advertising jingle gains an understanding of how music is used in advertising to be persuasive. Critical reflection of this process and product allows critical analysis of this pervasive musical form that floods our lives. This is a step in making our students able to be critical of aesthetic product wherever they encounter it. Similarly a student who has an embodied experience of cross cultural music has the potential for a more open relationship with "other" cultures and may have the beginnings of a common ground relationship with that culture that transcends language and decolonises their understanding.

8. Music is meaningful in personal, social and cultural ways: Students need access to all of these through the classroom and school environment if they are to make sense of the world they live in- a world where music plays an important role (Csikszentmihalyi 1994, Dewey 1989, Dillon 2001a, 2001c, Elliott 1995, Fiske 2000, Paynter and Aston 1970, Reimer 1989, Saatchi and Saatchi 2000, Swanwick 1994, Vella 2000).

These meanings have been discussed here at length and the meaningful engagement matrix introduced in Chapter 5 provides a tool for examining the presence of meaning in musical activity. Primarily you will need to examine the teaching methods, resource, curriculum design and policies that allow access to this kind of interaction. Focus perhaps first on a "real world scenario" that demonstrates the problem in practise then construct an approach and or policy that embeds all of these ideas drawn from the previous two steps and make sure that it includes a making, skill development and reflective/presentation stage that allows access to all three areas of meaning. Then re-use the notions of personal, social and cultural meaning as a checklist for the potential for your strategy/plan to deal with the problem.

What we can do

1. *Use all the data from the above to construct a personal rationale that begins by describing and stating the problem, describing your context succinctly.*

2. *Then examine the aspects of the context drawn from the context analysis diagram that will identify the constraints and positive aspects of the whole context and student's need.*

3. *Next, include the theoretical understanding drawn from the checklist above and perhaps look at readings drawn from this checklist.*

4. *Finally construct a solution in terms of an approach, which will include strategies, lesson and project plan ideas, policies and a teacher's stance, which describes the values inherent in the approach, i.e., attitude such as music is music or a focus on creative and imaginative product rather than technical perfection or an attitude of full and enthusiastic participation over technical perfection but with strategies to build skills.*

5. *Evaluate by describing how the approach addresses the personal social and cultural meaning issues. For example:*
    - *Personal meaning: from composing, creating, or achieving a challenging task.*

> - *Social meaning: the activity may be developed in a collaborative interactive group.*
> - *Cultural meaning: the activity has a presentation in a positive feedback environment i.e. concert, exhibition, or recording. The idea here is that the music conveys something to a community to which the community can respond by sharing and can value both the work and the maker.*

The student as maker: A definition

The concept of "student as maker" focuses upon three basic principles. First, music needs to be experienced and reflected upon through the musical processes of composition or creative making, performance and realisation, and active analysis of and listening to music. This process must contain reflection both in action and on action (Schon 1984, 1987). Second, music making needs to be done in both the classroom and in the school community. It needs to be both purely aesthetic and push the boundaries of the discipline and it must be functional and pragmatic and serve the community in a responsive, reverent and interactive way. Third, the selection of content should draw from a broad range of materials. This content should include multimedia and globalised repertoire and process—music from a variety of taste cultures—and such music needs to contribute clearly to musical knowledge through a revisiting of musical elements at progressively deeper levels.

The "student as maker" attempts to unify these ideas into curricula, co-curricular, cross-curricular and extra-curricular plans. It draws a philosophical basis from current theories of arts and music education and seeks to explore the effects of context and institution upon them. "Student as maker" incorporates within these ideas a notion of art life reintegration that constitutes recognition of arts education and schooling as significant contributors to individual students' formations of self—what Buber (1969) calls the education of character. I argue that there is a need to counterbalance the negative effects of the so-called post-modern condition (Lyotard 1984).

If, as described above, we are formed socially by our interactions with significant "others", and there is a growing proliferation of non-present and technologically mediated social experiences- then what kind of people are being formed? "Student as maker" highlights social interaction through present and uniquely expressive ways of communicating, advocating that these kinds of musical experiences might ground individuals in human relations that contribute to the constitution of self. "Student as maker" also values modes of interaction with technological means of production, as a means of demystifying the process of music making in the world today. It provides an opportunity for students to develop critical reflective skills about aesthetic product as it is found in commodities. Students who develop these skills through making music and reflecting upon both product and process will have had experiences with technological and globalised forms of music making and thinking. Through this, the processes of production will be demystified and less abstract. I suggest that, because of exposure to relevant experiences in music making, they will be more critical of art as it is found in commodities and the world today. In 1995, I wrote that the concept of "student as maker' is essentially a "tool for analysis for arts curricula" and outlined its central tenets as follows:

> The essence of "student as maker", is to recognise the integration which is occurring between life and art and give individuals access to critical values and an educated perceptual ability which can recognise and be critical of art in life, from within it as well as from a distance. The power of reflection in this way is the key to active participation in the postmodern world and beyond. Furthermore the ability to make or be creative with aesthetic materials, and I believe any materials, is the source of generic skills which will be invaluable to individuals in vocational, intellectual and social relationships. Through making we make ourselves – the process of creative making and reflecting causes a change not only in what we create but also in the makers themselves and surely this is education for life (Dillon 1995b, 70).

Added to these "instrumental aims" (Dewey 1970) is the essential integration of the development of critical reflective skills in relation to experience and a clear process of revisiting fundamental concepts of musical knowledge. I am suggesting that, as a result of this kind of approach to music learning, students will gain skills of critical analysis, self-development principles and an openness and willingness to participate in music making as a process of lifelong learning.

The concept of "student as maker" claims to facilitate outcomes through exposure to broad and deep experiences with the "spirit" of musical "taste cultures" (Gans 1975), which Walker (1990) calls a "pan-cultural" approach. These experiences should be representative of different cultures, times and places, as well as providing a solid grounding in Western European art music. Through this experiential process, both within the classroom and through an active and conscious participation of arts making within the school as community, "student as maker" seeks a kind of reintegration of art and life. In this philosophy, the school is considered to be like a "village" community, a community with its own ceremonies, rituals, beliefs, morals and values (Dillon 2000b).

Further, arts has a role to play in the unification, expression and formation of that community's image and "personality" as well as a significant role in how those things are projected to the wider community. The master's research I undertook addressed the question of music curriculum in the context of concerns about good education—concerns about student and changed forms of society. The research discussed a range of educational theorists who take seriously making and community as part of educational activity. This selection of literature spans philosophy, education, cultural theory, arts and uniquely music and arts education. In the section that follows, I would like to discuss each of the concepts put forward above that define the "student as maker" and highlight the literature that led to those insights.

Dewey and art as experience

John Dewey is without a doubt the most significant influence on the ideas presented in this book. I am continually astounded at the robustness of his thought. Within Dewey's thought lies the kernel of "student as maker", the ideas of child and curriculum and school and society (Dewey 1963). From Dewey, the "student as maker" draws several important insights. The first is the notion of art as experience (Dewey 1970). Dewey recognised and defined the experiential qualities of arts making as fundamental to its understanding. He highlights the duality of the perspectives of artist and product and that "the actual work of art is what the product does with and in experience" (Dewey 1970, 3). This viewpoint draws attention to the idea that an artist is engaged with the product directly as maker of art, within the process of making an art object and as an active perceiver of art. The artist is perceptive about the process and product and dynamically responds to both experience and reflection in practice. There is also recognition of the relationship between product and perceiver independent of the process of making.

Dewey explores these ideas in tandem through the concept of experiential learning. In this model, the student's understanding is enhanced through a process of engagement with meaningful arts making and reflective activity and through experiences that involve both the roles of perceiver and maker. This kind of experienced based activity has also been termed "discovery learning" (Bruner 1960) and was explored in practice throughout the 1970s in Australian education within the so-called "progressive and radical" education movement. These approaches to education have their roots in Socratic questioning and critical development through such ideas as Rousseau's Emile (Gardner 1993b). The research of "student as maker" was critical of the practices that surrounded the perceived failure of progressive student centred education and its failure to deal with the wider cultural and social contexts in which students operate. In that critique, I also drew attention to the lack of attention to the balance between experience and reflection and the modes of evaluation of what it was students gained from these activities.

The "student as maker" utilises experiential and discovery learning as models of critical development in approaches to music education. These concepts are developed in more recent educational ideas such as "constructionism" (Papert 1980, 1996). Papert's notions of "constructionism" in the teaching of mathematics adds further evidence to the ability of such methods to engage students with meaningful and deep knowledge through project based learning. These activities have relevance to how mathematics and art appear in life. Dewey and Bruner both highlight the importance of activities that reflect those that occur in the discipline or domain and their relevance. It is suggested that because these activities are "present" and concrete (Gardner 1993b, Papert 1980), even if the student is capable of Piaget's formal operations stage of abstract reasoning (Mussen, Conger and Kagan 1974), learning in this more direct and concrete way increases the depth and longevity of the knowledge.

There is universal support amongst music and arts educators for music as an experiential activity (Eisner 1985, 1991, Elliott 1995, Swanwick 1981, 1988, 1994, Vulliamy and Lee 1976, 1982, Walker 1990). All of these theorists advocate an experiential approach to music learning. They focus in some way upon critical reflection or listening and advocate that music education should be taught in a way that represents how music is made in society. It is the balance of these ideas of making and listening and the role and selection of suitable content which form the points of argument and discussion amongst these theorists.

The position argued in my earlier research is that the content and focus of activity in music making should consist of a broad selection of musical styles and periods. These activities should reflect popular culture so students may gain a critical perspective on the role of music in youth culture. Students also need to have access to experiences that provide them with skills that will enable them to be expressive within this culture rather than simply being passive consumers. The breadth of these experiences should include twentieth century art music and the associated innovations of form and technology. For example, a selection of activities would include music from Western art music, world music and music from other cultures.

The selection of materials needs to be based upon the ability of those materials to engage students with concepts of musical knowledge, at progressively deeper levels of understanding. Pratt's "elements of music" (Pratt 1990) are proposed as a checklist or basis for this universal concept of musical knowledge. Pratt's concepts were selected because the definitions are more clearly inclusive of non-Western and twentieth century musical ideas. Elements such as "space" (Pratt 1990), or where music is in relation to the listener, are increasingly important in listening to and composing music especially with electronic music and recording. This element is particularly important in acoustic phenomena (Walker 1996) that involve integration with movement and the relative position of participants in relation to sound. Dewey and Bruner suggest that revisiting the fundamental concepts of arts, science and humanities at progressively deeper levels forms the basis for experiential curriculum. In music learning, Swanwick (1981) highlights the activities of composing, performing and audition (his term for critical listening) as the basis for music education.

Dewey's notion of experiential learning has been reinvented to respond to contemporary contexts with such ideas as "domain projects" in the arts (Reimer and Smith 1992), "constructionism" (Papert 1980, 1996) and "knowledge by design" (Perkins 1986). These approaches utilise the same fundamental philosophy of immersion in experience and critical reflective activity, which simultaneously reflects community life, work and practice in the discipline. It is argued by Gardner that these kinds of approaches to teaching method are "intelligence fair" (Gardner 1993b) and more able to cater for students' individual differences. "Student as maker" seeks to draw these notions together as an approach to teaching method and to expand the influence of the experiences of music making beyond the classroom to the community of school and the wider social context. It is the role of arts in community and the recognition of a school as a community that informs the next part of the discussion of "student as maker".

"Student as maker": The student–teacher relationship and the environment

The "student as maker" explores the idea that effective communication of music experience and knowledge is dependent upon the total school environment, as "it is the whole environment both social and natural which educates the child" (D'Cruz and Hannah 1979, 63). Dewey suggested that the schools should be an "embryonic community life, active with the type of occupations that reflect the life of larger society" (Dewey 1963, 29). Within the understanding of that idea, we need to examine "the relationship between student and teacher and the environment, with reference to the community as a whole" (Dillon 1995b, 6). Bruner outlines the necessity of teachers "establishing a systematic and contingent interaction between tutor and learner" before intellectual development can occur (Bruner 1966, 6). These factors are awakened and projected by the teacher's "stance".

For Dewey and Bruner, the teacher is seen as a practitioner, someone who is actively engaged in the process of making or exploring art, science or humanities. The notion of a particular "stance" or position and relationship between student and teacher was explored in Dillon (1995) from the viewpoint of Martin Buber's philosophy of inclusion (1969). It is the idea of inclusion that forms the foundation of the student-teacher relationship in "student as maker". Student-centred learning conceived in this way involves not just awareness of cognitive processes, learning difficulties and approaches of the student but a consciousness and acknowledgement of the whole person, and "living through" the student's experiences. Buber describes it as being centred upon an extension of the teacher's own concreteness and a:

> fulfilling of one's own life situation in such a way that one experiences the complete presence of reality which one participates, living through the standpoint of the other without forfeiting anything of the felt reality of his or her own activity (1969, 28).

Dewey also was quite clear about the role and responsibilities of the teacher:

> To direct growth, to foster the student's appropriate skills and dispositions, so that the pupil will want to go on learning from experience. Increasing their capacity to live effectively in their environment, gaining also the capacity to change or reconstruct their environment in some measure by their own means (in D'Cruz and Hannah 1979, 131).

The concept of "student as maker" argues that, in arts education, the aspects of art that are less amenable to understanding in a cognitive sense or in language can be transmitted though the teacher's actions—the teacher's activity as an artist him or herself.

In relation to community, the relationship occurs on several levels. Within the classroom, a microcosm of activity needs to reflect the kinds of collaborative and social interactions and arts' making that occurs in life. Music making in the classroom consists of a series of long-term activities that revisit concepts and elements of music knowledge at progressively deeper levels. This is done through the activity of creating, improvising and composing, performance and realisation of products and active analysis, reflection and criticism of music product and process. Curricula from the United Kingdom, the United States and Australia agree that these kinds of activities are central to music learning (Abbs 1990, Curriculum Corporation of Victoria 1994a, 1994b, Elliott 1995, Reimer 1989, Reimer and Smith 1992, Swanwick 1981, Ministry of Education 1988a, 1988b, Victorian Certificate of Education 1991). What is more poignant, is the recognition that music learning extends beyond the classroom in instrumental studies, bands, orchestras and choirs, formal and informal performance and music making at home. I suggest that we need to recognise that classroom music should be the nucleus from which all these other activities radiate (Dillon 1995b).

The recognition of the multiple modes of musical engagement extends in two directions. First, in the classroom there is a need to simulate musical contexts through imaginative immersion in musical cultures. Second, an opportunity exists for music to become a significant part of the cultural life of a school. This allows for reflection of music making as it is in the wider community and a "real" interaction and function for music within the school community. There is a need to recognise that conscious and structured reflective activity needs to be part of the process of music learning in both contexts. It is this factor and attention to it in the classroom, during and after experiences and as a uniquely musical way of thinking about experience that provides an approach that will counterbalance the criticism of experiential learning. Self-directed development and reflective skills are the generic goals of "student as maker". This is critical not only in the reinvention of the process of art as experience but also in the light of living and making art in the twenty-first century. In "student as maker", I also argue that these kinds of critical skills and arts making experiences are a necessary counterbalance to the negative aspects of the post-modern condition (Lyotard 1984). In the next section, I will briefly summarise the generic implications of this approach to arts making and learning, its effects upon self-formation and the implications for contemporary curriculum.

The "student as maker" and the postmodern condition

"Student as maker" responds to the notion of the post-modern condition in several ways. There is not sufficient space here to enter an argument about the existence of a distinct post-modern or high modernist era. Rather, I acknowledge that "certain conditions exist that have significantly altered our way of life and that these conditions need to be addressed in education" (Dillon 1995b, 19). Such factors as the information revolution, globalisation, commoditisation of arts and aestheticisation of life have a profound effect upon how we teach and learn. These issues have implications for the development and interpretation of curriculum.

Schusterman (1992) discusses a kind of reintegration of art and life and this is apparent through a kind of realisation of the idea of a "global village" (McLuhan 1967). At the same time as this kind of reintegration of art with life, we are also redefining it and the kinds of relationships we have with the "other" through the proliferation of image (Hinkson 1992). This is done both directly and indirectly through extended forms of the social (Dillon 1995b). What is most clear is that the kinds of relationships we have are changing. There is a proliferation of "non present" interactions, such as telephone, television, radio, film, the Internet, video games. The question that arises from this is that if we are formed socially through our interactions with others, then what kinds of people are being formed in this process?

The concept of "student as maker" suggests that through a variety of interactions and experiences with music making, which includes globalised content and technological means of communication, we are placed in a position of being able to be critical of these forms. It is also suggested that, through the kinds of activities advocated, students are grounded in relationships of presence in an expressive and different way from that of language, while also being exposed to these forms of communication and interaction. It is argued that these experiences form a counterbalance to the negative effects of the post-modern condition. The foundation of this argument is based upon the recognition of the school as community and the development of critical multimedia thinking and reflective skills through prolonged engagement with arts activity. There is a need here to incorporate processes that educate perception through a variety of logics and media of communication. These logics should not be constrained by the linearity of language/literary traditions of curriculum construction and delivery (de Bono 1990).

With regard to commodification of arts and aestheticisation of life, it is a fact that "the role of arts in commodities is abundant and yet because of its abundance quite transparent" (Dillon 1995b, 26). Every commodity is in some way touched by art. "Student as maker" deals with this notion by including the functional and pragmatic role of arts within the content base of curricula. Music in advertising, film and video becomes a source of relevant artistic product for creation and critical analysis. It is used as an example of arts in society and as a way of revisiting concepts of music making through the production of relevant arts products. Most importantly, the idea of producing such music contributes two essential ideas to music education. Firstly, it allows students a critical perspective on what might previously have not been analysed and, secondly, it helps demystify what is often an abstract process.

When the curriculum is inclusive of a variety of "taste cultures" (Gans 1975), the idea of gaining diversity of experience and a critical perspectives on arts as commodities and the notion of commoditisation of aesthetic product become active parts of the curriculum and learning discourse and make it dynamically responsive to change. These outcomes offer ways of responding to important issues such as ethical and meaningful engagement with cross-cultural music and technologically mediated music making within contemporary music curriculum and practice.

The "student as maker" and culture

If we consider as proposed here that in making music, we effect change in ourselves and transformations of our consciousness then it stands to reason that diverse cultural experience can provide access to a broad range of expressive understandings as well as cultural ones. The "student as maker" suggests that the principle goal of music education is to become more expressive as a musician and to understand how music is expressive in other cultures which increases access to a wider range of expressive techniques and enables access to an embodied, non-verbal understanding of "other" cultural knowledge. While the "music is music" approach discussed by participants in this research has merit because it promoted openness to diverse musical and cultural experiences and understandings subsequent critiques of the musical element critical framework of these ideas suggests that this kind of cultural framing still lends itself to a colonial viewpoint of musical otherness. Vella's approaches to aural perception (2000) "asks simply what is happening with sound in time and space and what are the relationships to the context and culture that structures these sounds" (Dillon and Chapman 2005, 190). This potentially provides a more culturally and chronologically inclusive aural perception framework.

The implications of this for the student as maker of music is that while grounded in Western musical forms be they art music or popular forms the student has a framework which allows music to be experienced as embodied understanding through direct engagement with the musical ideas of other cultures. Teachers can facilitate simulated experiences also. At the case study school embodied understandings of Kenyan songs, movement and percussion were applied to an African reinterpretation of Sophocles Oedipus. While the songs and dances had been taught to students directly by a Kenyan teacher the music itself underwent a syncretic change facilitated by the difference in context and cultural understanding. In reflection, students reported gaining an understanding about how music is affected by environmental and cultural factors.

The cultural implications of "student as maker" are predicated upon access to simulated or realistic embodied understandings of how music is made in a dramatisation of a cultural context. This should where possible be delivered by a representative of the culture. The teacher's role in this is to act as a "cultural manager" (Dillon 2005a) and facilitate experience that enables embodied and directly musical understandings where possible. The teacher's role is also to stimulate reflective discourses to enable students to seek to make sense of their experiences and challenge their current worldviews. The experience will always be as a simulation it does have the capacity to give access to understandings about how human society expresses itself in sound. At the case study school, this resulted in students who participated in this kind of music experience to have more open and eclectic musical tastes than their peers.

The "student as maker" and technology

Dennis' story in Chapter 4 describes an example of the student as maker and its relationship with technology. Dennis' exemplifies Brown three metaphorical perspectives that describe usage of the computer as a tool, medium or instrument (Brown 2006). This description of the role of the computer in music making describes the changing role of computers in music making during the creative production process. For Dennis' it allowed him to use sampling and sequencing as tools for constructing complex polyphonic and polyrhythmic musical ideas. He was able to use the computer as a medium developing and previewing musical materials. His composition *Minimalisation*, was an electronic work developed on a 16-track sequencer using clavinet samples and bass drum which explored the compositional technique of minimalism. In live performance, Dennis' used the computer as an instrument when he "played" the sequence generator by selecting sequences by reading audience responses. His performance and selection of chunks of digital music which he processed using a Digital Signal Processor (DSP) to effect the timbrel qualities of each layer of sound. He performed large-scale transformations in the music as he shifted loops of music and smaller more subtle changes through timbrel transformation.

Dennis' experience of music making with music technologies suggests he had access to a different kind of musicianship and music making. Both he and the teacher clearly understood how the computer worked as a revelatory medium, functional tool and as an expressive instrument. As Brown suggests,

> When viewed as a tool, the computer is seen as a device to be controlled, when understood as a medium it becomes a vehicle for exploring musical possibilities and, when approached as an instrument, it can be a conduit for musical expression (2006, 6).

This shifts the role of the computer in music production. It allows us to observe the relationship between music technology and the creative process. This is important because it allows us to design experience and facilitate curriculum that recognises the capacity and role of the technology in the process of production of music.

Conclusion

I now want to summarise all that I have said about the concept "student as maker". The "student as maker":

1. Facilitates deeper, more easily assimilated and transferable learning while promoting higher levels of retention of knowledge;
2. Is "intelligence fair", and allows students of all intelligences (Gardner 1993b) and learning styles to learn easily. That is, it does not favour those who are logical/sequential and language based over those with other learning styles;
3. Teaches a process of lateral thinking, gives experience with making and reflecting and being creative with aesthetic materials;
4. Utilises multiple logic rather than being based upon text alone—"student as maker" is fundamentally structured on image, text and experience and the interplay between these modes of communication and thought in action and reflection;
5. Utilises the social context in a relevant and reverent community based approach and uses collaborative activity as well as individual effort to reach a shared and valued aesthetic goal;
6. Gives grounding in human activity, and is about human endeavour of individuals, groups and exemplars of excellence in human work. This functions as a counterbalance to the increasing profusion of "non-present" relationships, which abstract us from the social, and human;
7. Provides experiences with making and reflecting upon the art of self-peers-teachers-local community-specific culture-and other cultures from past and present contexts;
8. Experiences self in action–self in perception about action–self as critic of other work which leads to developing aesthetic understanding, and educating perception;
9. Provides education as a generic tool for criticism of artistic product as it appears in commodities or as a means of marketing commodities;
10. Provides an interactive multimedia environment where thought, action and reflection are expressed in a multiple mode of communication rather than just textually;
11. Includes popular culture and pan-cultural elements to give overall breadth thus signifying the fundamental aesthetic need in all humanity and creates openness to the new and unfamiliar; and,
12. Uses technology in an aesthetic application and demystifies the making process which may be obscured by high technology.

In relation to social formation of individuals as a goal of education, I propose that the goals of "student as maker" contribute to the aesthetic development of a student in the following ways:

1. *Expressive*: Through making and reflecting, students learn to be expressive about themselves and their culture.
2. *Creative*: Through making and reflecting and developing the "micro-aesthetic" "flow" state (Csikszentmihalyi 1994, 95) into artistic or aesthetic products the students learn to be creative with materials and may be able to facilitate a transfer of these skills to other idioms.
3. *Perceptive*: The student learns to be perceptive about art and grows in their ability to enter into dialogue about art, understanding progressively the vocabulary of words, ideologies and concepts, which refer to art through a continuous process of making and reflecting. The student revisits fundamental concepts at progressively deeper levels.
4. *Critical/reflective*: The student learns through making, reflecting and perceptive activity to be critical and develop skills of criticism in art and about artistic product as it is represented in life.
5. *Social*: Through interaction with making in groups/ensembles, and reflecting and perceiving, students learn structured and appropriate methods of questioning, criticism and communication which are directed towards a common and intrinsically satisfying goal.
6. *Communicative*: Through the processes of group creativity and reflective forum—verbal, demonstrative and written—students gain structures and encouragement about a variety of complex reflective tasks, developing understanding and using ideas and words for communication with others about art and its representation in culture.
7. *Adaptability and receptiveness to change*: "Student as maker" provides an approach which is open to difference, accepting of variance with our own culture or time and able to be analytical and critical from a fundamental musically sound in time and space aural perception framework, as well as able to identify the culturally selected factors which create the differences.

CHAPTER SEVEN

THE TEACHER AS BUILDER: THE MAKING OF MEANING

Introduction

In this discussion so far, I have focussed upon the meaning that students attach to music experience. I have suggested that the meaning is located in three primary areas of experience—the personal, social and cultural—and that meaning in music can be both "caught" and "taught" (Swanwick 1994). I have suggested the need to structure the environment in some way so that learning takes place. Intrinsically motivated activity is significant in the memory of those who participate in the activity and becomes meaningful if it has the capacity to provide challenge that engages and sustains interest. Music making in its myriad of forms has the capacity to offer such challenges of engagement and meaning.

In the interview transcripts presented earlier, students commented upon teachers and environments that facilitated their musical experience and contributed to the making of meaning and self. In this chapter, I will explore teacher and environment, viewing the teacher as a builder of music learning contexts. The evidence for this discussion is drawn from interviews with teachers and students as well as from field observations and document analysis. The approach to examining the teacher as facilitator of meaning involves data from a variety of sources. In student interviews, I asked students about environment and their relationships with teachers. I asked teachers similar questions and I observed and collected policy documents that outlined the physical and cultural aspects of the school environment.

These findings offer support to Swanwick's description of students' initiation into what he describes as music discourse (Swanwick 1994). One of the problems for music education lies in defining what he describes as a productive tension between the intuitive and analytical aspects of music learning (Swanwick 1994). The questions raised by this aspect of the research are: how do we teach the intuitive? How can we construct an environment so that intuitive understanding might be caught? Furthermore, how do we devise teaching methods so that the analytical becomes intrinsically motivated or at least palatable until it becomes meaningful? In this discussion, this means that we need to examine what kinds of approaches and relationships were perceived as successful in bringing about meaning and access to the layers of intuitive understanding (Swanwick 1994). What persons, places and things sustained continued involvement with the music discourse?

In a theoretical sense, what is at issue in relation to creating "flow" and analytical development is primarily a matter of complexity, that is, circumstances, environments and people create or present tasks, which can be made progressively more complex for the student. This complexity presents the opportunity for challenge and ultimately for a flow experience, which leads to meaning. In an analytic sense, this complexity is linear and progresses in relation to skill and technical achievement. These kinds of skills are motivated by achievement and are easily able to be translated into a logical pedagogy. The intuitive "complexities" and challenges are more intrinsically motivated and deal more with depth of aesthetic understanding. These are less able to be placed in an orderly pedagogical form but are facilitated by particular kinds of encounters with music making.

Teaching and embodied relationships in the instrumental studio

In the field study for this research, I spent 12 weeks in the school as a participant observer. During that time, I taught music classes, conducted ensembles and gave individual singing lessons to students. Some of my most intense encounters occurred in studio teaching; the act of continuously reflecting on these experiences through field notes alerted me to how I called upon embodied understandings of singing and how that understanding was applied to the deeply personal relationships formed in this kind of one-to-one music teaching:

> I wanted to use this [opportunity] as a way of getting a feel for the instrumental teacher's one-to-one perspective (Notes from Field Journal 1997, 12 August).

I taught three senior students at lunchtimes and in my spare lesson periods. The following vignette is a summary of my contact with one of those students in August 1997.

Phillip's story

I had known Phillip for around five years, having taught him in the classroom and worked with him as a vocal coach in school productions. We had a good relationship; it was relaxed and friendly. He knew me both as a teacher and singer/performer and had approached me and asked if I could teach him purely technical aspects of singing to improve his overall performance skills. The lesson structure over the eight weeks that I taught him was similar each week. We began by discussing how he felt about his sound and how he thought it was affected by exercise, then began a formal warm up of humming exercises, bubble exercises and tongue trills. Following this, we worked on physical breathing exercises, vowel sounds, tone and mouth shapes. The repetition was used to create a practice routine habit that would benefit his development after I had gone.

In the early lessons, I spoke to him about how I had used the "bubble exercises" and tongue trills as preparation for a recording session on the previous weekend and was surprised at the clarity of tone and ease of my upper register. Over the next few weeks he also reported an effect upon his sound. As we ran through these exercises the difference was notable and he commented that he could hear the change in his voice. We reflected upon each sound he made, listening carefully for strain and overproduction. If we heard evidence of this in his voice, my usual approach was to "feel" the sound that the student made through imitation, and then try to describe the position of mouth and tongue, which would correct the problem.

Phillip, like many students (including myself), had great difficulty rolling his "r's". This is a very unusual exercise used in the "speech level singing technique" that I was doing with him. The exercise can take up to three months to perfect and persistence is important. Throughout the time I worked with Phillip he never quite managed to perfect it but we kept trying and I continued to describe my own initial problems with it and encouraged the small changes that he achieved. Encouragement centred on hearing a nice sound in his voice—it was a "micro-aesthetic". We listened together to a single note or a scale on a vowel the focus was on sound rather than music in context. Phillip was enjoying the sound that he made and was immersed in a shared listening experience with me that focused upon his voice. At one point, he was able to run a bubble exercise up to C above middle C, which was a noticeable movement from the previous week. He was able to feel the speech level underproduction and acknowledged that he understood the change.

We ended each lesson with a review of practice routine and setting of goals for the next week. I felt the relationship we had developed was based on a trust in what I could do with his voice, and the relationship was predicated upon my assessment of his development- a little like a doctor diagnosing a patient. I was conscious of communicating experience and understanding, and feeling what the student feels to correct faults. Over the time Phillip made good progress and gained an understanding and formed a routine for practice, which contributed to him a gaining a leading role in a school musical production.

Keyboard teacher James similarly described how his own intuitive experiences were able to benefit his transfer to students:

> It allows me to talk experientially about music if you know what I mean rather than stuff you sort of know 'cause you've learnt it from a book or something like that. Obviously I feel much more relaxed and comfortable talking about things that I've experienced and areas I work well in. So when I'm looking at those kind of areas with students and dealing with trying to help them figure things out themselves I'm able to relate to them in a way, 'cause I've sort of done the same sort of things myself (James 1996, pers comm. with teacher, 28 October).

The vignette of my experience with Philip describes a studio-teaching situation with a talented senior student. I chose it because it outlines the closeness and minute focus of the studio lesson. The interview with James provides further evidence of the transfer of experiential and intuitive understanding in teaching music. Studio teaching deals on one side with the analytical and technical development of music skills and on the other with the interpretive and intuitive aspects of performance. Often the first is based in exercise and the later contextualised by its relationship to performed musical works. These are generally motivating while exercise is less so. This vignette focuses upon a student who has requested that the focus be upon technical work.

Several observations can be drawn from this vignette. First, as a teacher, I took an interest in the student's needs and valued what the student brought to the lesson. Second, my own experiential understanding was shared with the student informally as we discussed how we produced a nice tone and what affect the exercises had upon our sound. There was a sense of a shared discourse here, and a trust in the idea that a change would occur. Third, by "feeling" the student's problems through imitation, I was able to communicate quite abstract ideas and facilitate an understanding based upon listening, reflecting and experiencing the sound. Fourth, the student experienced a noticeable change in the sound and was encouraged both verbally by me and by the sound itself.

What was most unexpected about this interaction was that we both enjoyed and gained "flow" from the micro aesthetic of singing single notes or non-musical exercises. We gained a challenge from the subtlety of change. Before this experience, I had been of the opinion that music out of context was not intrinsically motivated, which made the analytical aspects of technical work less appealing to students. I am conscious though of my own enthusiasm for such sounds and believe that this may have been an influential factor in the student's enjoyment. Certainly intrinsic motivation occurred and Phillip was sufficiently motivated to practise at home. He showed an understanding of the problem and the work needed to correct it. There was in that a challenge and a clear pathway for meeting the challenge. The complexity of the challenge increased in levels of aesthetic subtlety.

Studio teaching and meaning

The encounter with Phillip as an instrumental student suggested to me quite strongly Buber's (1969) notion of inclusion, a kind of "living through" the teacher's experience with music making. The following themes arose from the interviews with students and teachers about studio music making experiences, which contributed to personal meaning:

- Self-containment
- Reflective practice
- Enhanced perception and openness to new musical experience
- Relaxation in private music making
- Teaching and learning the intuitive
- A change in the way we think
- Initiation into a personal discourse

Student participants used all of the above-mentioned terms to describe the meaning of music making in their studio experience. They are a direct result of one simple idea: that of the student "living through" the teacher's experience and eventually gaining entry to the discourse where they can move independently of the teacher.

The notion of self-containment is a habit of developing an analytical and critical evaluation of self in performance that involves discussion about the sound and how to improve it, facilitation of experience and reflection upon that. It is a development of a critical thinking and of a routine of development and problem solving. The kind of focus on critical listening to "micro-music" problems assists in developing and enhancing the overall perception of the music the students listen to. The idea of music as "relaxing" is attached to self-containment. The studio lesson encourages the routine of self-directed practice and playing and ultimately helps to develop the skills that give access to making music as a private and personal activity for relaxation or personal expression. It is where the student might experience the intra-personal aspects of music as a way of communicating with self and as autonomous expression.

Phillip's success with music experience gave him the ability to adopt a practice routine that was effective in gaining him a desired outcome. Achievement of this change in his voice had a profound affect upon his self-esteem and sense of self. The meaning for Phillip came from the effectiveness of the teaching and learning relationship. In a cognitive sense, Phillip gained a skill in critical listening and self-reflection, which affected his skills in aesthetic thinking. Intrinsic motivation and progress become a reciprocal arrangement. It also had a lot to do with the nature of his relationship with me. There was also a relaxed and open environment and the mutual initiation into the discourse—a kind of collaborative journey, which was pleasurable for us both.

Participants considered friendliness, openness and musical skill of the teacher important, but this was not enough for the students. They also placed a value upon progress. In this example, Colin, a multi-instrumentalist, discusses his motivation from progress/success and his relationship with his music teachers. Here he compares his piano and trumpet teachers:

> She was a great teacher [his piano teacher] but I just couldn't relate to her, like her room was very posh and I would walk in and I would do the lesson and I would walk out. I wouldn't stop and chat with her like I do with Matthew. With the trumpet it was a whole new thing, like we're good friends so it really helped keep my motivation there. I just sort of ran out of steam with the piano and so I decided to stop that whereas with the trumpet and bass, the bass even more, David I mean he's just like an old kid, he's very, very relaxed in his classes, the language that he uses is like the language that I use, I don't know it helps to have that sort of relationship with your teacher, it gives you motivation to keep going and when you start having successes it pushes you even further (Colin 1997, pers comm. with student, 13 March).

Colin is a highly competitive sports person and making progress in music was imperative to him. He sought challenge in all of his pursuits. In this transcript, however, he mentions the relationship and the language and feeling of sharing his musical experience. His description of the personal relationship outlines his need for more than professional congeniality but describes a need for a deeper relationship with his teachers. He eventually ceased learning the piano because the interpersonal relationship was absent. He played piano up to seventh grade Australian Music Examination Board standard, which constitutes a large commitment and a challenging repertoire but gave up learning from this teacher after completing the exam. The goal of reaching seventh grade was one negotiated with his parents. Colin's response is typical of comments from students about their teacher. From this, we can suggest that progress, friendliness and openness are very important in the student-teacher relationship and that absence of any of these qualities may discourage students' sustained involvement.

While the students describe the most effective teacher-student relationship as friendship teachers' view of the relationship is quite different. Teachers found progress and friendliness to be significant motivating factor in the learning relationship. In this extract, Simone, a string teacher, describes how she tries to treat her students fairly and equally despite her assessment of their ability and progress:

> I try to be very professional and not to let my feelings come through. The fact [is] that I really enjoy teaching certain students because they are musical, work hard and they're enjoying what they're doing as much as I'm enjoying teaching them. But I am always aware that they are my students. They don't have any other relationship to me but that of student (Simone 1997, pers comm. with teacher, 19 February).

Simone is also highlighting the power differential in the relationship they are her students not her friends, although she describes further how several ex students have become long-time associates and developed into friends. What is most important here, is that the student and the teacher perspective of the relationship differs. The student perceives the relationship as friendship, the teacher as a more professional relationship. Buber described this kind of inclusiveness as being "where the teacher stands at both ends of the bipolar relationship while the student experiences only one" (1969, 100).

Teachers and students alike highlight the importance of the teacher's ability to use multi-media approaches for teaching the intuitive aspects of music through demonstration, descriptive language, gesture and facilitation of experience. This kind of approach was described in the observation of Jane the instrumental conductor discussed in Chapter 7. The idea of "feeling" or internalising the student's problem and solving it was an important theme described by instrumental teachers. By doing this, the teacher shows a preparedness to recognise the individual needs of the student, and to tailor pedagogical development to suit. Students and teachers alike suggested that the most effective means of communicating musical knowledge was through facilitating experience through active making, listening and critical reflection.

Students commented that it was important that the teacher understood them and took them into their own lives as practising and reflective musicians while also being aware of the student's unique individual development. Senior students in particular were complimentary to teachers who had encouraged them to develop their "own style or sound". It is at this point that the student is most notably able to function independently within a musical discourse rather than as a passenger accompanied by an adult. When the student reaches the point where they become self contained and have gained reflective/problem-solving habits, that is when the meaning becomes truly their own, and not simply shared with their teacher.

In Csikszentmihalyi's (1994) terms, it is at this point that students becomes autotelic and creates or finds their own challenges and goals and sets about achieving them. Music making has within it an infinite set of unique individual challenges and these can be achieved both technically and aesthetically. In the case of the vignette described above, the challenge became a microanalysis of a sound, a vowel, a tone, raised to a high degree of aesthetic subtlety and intuitive complexity. The painter Henri Matisse once suggested that pure colour without form had the power to move imagination: in this case it is a single note or tone. So much of what is learned in music is gained from intuitive understanding, by immersion in the context.

The teacher facilitates technical challenges externally through curriculum and music pedagogy and exposes students to their own intuitive understanding of music by embodying and modelling behaviour. The meaning is gained from initiation into the music making discourse through the teacher's lived experience. It becomes a solo journey when the student has become self-contained, sets their own challenges and goals through action and critical reflection upon their music making. The instrument skills and personal meaning gained through their relationship with the discourse give them access to greater experiential understanding of music in other contexts such as classrooms or ensembles. This encounter forms the foundation of their access to other forms of music making and meanings.

Students in the study described a movement towards interdependence as a desirable and effective part of music education. Rather than describing the process of learning music as a linear process that moves from dependence towards independence and interdependence, teachers in the study were careful to include this process amongst the openness of the environment. Rather than being linear and progressive, these self-contained ideas were perceived as being cyclic—that is, the student could move freely between dependence and interdependence at any time or chronological age. This was perceived as being necessary because of the vast range of musical skills required. Part of initiation into the discourse suggests lifelong learning about music making and expressiveness within the domain.

Each encounter with music learning contains specific qualities that contribute to the musical development of a student and their access to meaningful music making. All of the contexts of music making offer particular aspects effectively and may be less fluent in their delivery of others. Too often, examinations of music learning have focussed solely upon parts of the continuum such as the classroom, studio or band rather than a broad representation of meaningful music experience. In an examination of what it is that studio teaching contributes to the student's access to meaning, we can extract what it is these experiences add to musical understanding. The studio experience is profoundly personal; its relationship is rooted in the mentor like tradition of teaching and learning though a "master". The focus in this case is on the very specific skills of expression and performance on a single instrument or voice and the ultimate development of an independent or personal sound or musical voice, unique to the student. These qualities are specific to this teaching environment and this intense and personal relationship with a teacher.

Classroom music

When I began the analysis of data concerned with classroom music, I was initially disappointed by some of the comments made by the students, and shocked by some of the negative circumstances I observed and recorded in my field notes. It seemed that classroom music was considered the "poor cousin" to the more challenging ensemble program. Students interviewed considered that it was less personal in its relationships with the teacher than studio learning and generally, as one student described, a "little light on" in respect to its depth of content and ability to provide challenge. This was particularly the case with compulsory classroom music but still prevalent in respect to elective classroom music lessons. Many teachers viewed classroom music as an introductory agency to studio learning and ensemble participation with a smattering of generic music education. In some respects, it encouraged the musically able and "filtered" out the less talented and less-able students, by restricting access to some music knowledge thus creating an elite group of students. As I have spent a large proportion of my life as a classroom teacher, the initial description that emerged of my professional focus was not encouraging.

A very different picture started to emerge when I began to probe further into the question of what was unique about classroom teaching. I examined what classroom music could offer to music learning that was not being offered by the more focussed experiences of studio and ensemble. It became clear that classroom music had contributed in a distinctive way to developing their music making more broadly, regardless of whether or not they compared the experience unfavourably to other music experiences, or they ranked it lower in importance or enjoyment. In the analysis of interview and field data themes emerged that described how classroom music had given access to ways of making sense of all of their music experiences. They valued being introduced to music from other cultures and times. Students described how they had been given the opportunity to safely taste a variety of musical experiences, instruments and ideas. Most often it was where they had had their first ensemble and instrument experiences. They commented favourably about how the classroom was where they were introduced to creative making both collaboratively and independently and learnt how to think critically and reflect upon music experiences in a variety of contexts. These aspects in particular are seldom represented in studio or ensemble programs, where the focus is upon the specific activity of making or recreating music. Modelling behaviour of reflection and perceptive thinking occurred in the studio teaching. This kind of reflective approach is outlined in the example of Phillip's singing lessons and in ensemble rehearsal such as the description of a rehearsal outlined in Chapter 7. This kind of activity is less common in these contexts and is seldom a goal, while the activity of "making music" takes priority in these contexts. What I was able to observe here is that students brought their experiences with music listening to the classroom and it is here that these making encounters were shared, valued, broadened and reflected upon.

Classroom music as a gateway

One of the roles of the general music program or classroom music program is to act as a "gateway" to instrumental music, ensemble experiences, making and presenting music and other musical styles from other cultures and periods– past and present contexts (Curriculum Corporation 1994a, 1994b). Jason, a 16 year old who plays trumpet, guitar and writes songs, talks about the effects of his classroom music experiences:

> It just opened up doors to different pathways, like we just tried different styles of music; we weren't too great at the instruments at the time but still. And they [classroom teachers] just showed us some concert band pieces that we attempted to play and, yeah, studied theory and stuff a bit. (Jason 1997, pers comm., 20 March).

Jason is commenting upon the variety of encounters he was exposed to in classroom music. He is describing the classroom music experience as a gateway to other experiences in music making, providing his first tastes of concert band ensembles, music from other cultures and instrumental music. A classroom teacher noticed his attraction to trumpet and guitar and encouraged him to join bands and take up studio lessons. In many cases, students reported beginning instruments through the classroom instrumental program of exposure to instruments. Students, who already played an instrument, often took up another instrument.

Classroom music as creative music (creating, making, presenting)

Classroom/general music also has a role to play in facilitating collaborative making activity and experiences with new instruments, new forms, styles and new media/technology. Edward, a 17-year-old guitarist and clarinet player, describes the opportunity for creative work in the classroom:

> I loved the creative activities. I always got excited when we were given a task to do that was creative. I remember once we were to make an answering machine jingle. That was one of my first experiences of making music for a purpose and that was really good fun. I love making my own music. I was glad that was part of the music syllabus (Edward 1997, pers comm. with student, 9 July).

In the case study, classroom creative activities revolved around the curriculum idea of domain projects, which are long-term or repeated projects involving issues central to the domain of music or art (Reimer & Smith 1992). Edward's description of "the answering machine jingle" was such a project, where he and a small group of students had been given a "brief" to compose and perform a jingle for a staff member's answering machine. Edward's comment that it was "one of my first experiences of making music for a purpose" (Edward 1997, pers comm. with student, 9 July) echoes other participants who described the classroom as the place where this kind of focused creative music had its beginnings.

The effects upon self-esteem of such activity are quite profound. Students felt a sense of ownership and pride in the product. Margaret, a 16-year-old piano player and composer, describes her experiences:

> Oh that was good, [creative projects]. I liked that. I remember doing something with James in a keyboard group and I still remember that it was good because we were making it up as we were going along, it was better, it was, you made it, and it sounds good (Margaret 1997, pers comm. with student, 21 March).

For Margaret, it was the moment that her interest in composing was recognized by a classroom teacher. She was later directed towards learning composition as a principal studio study. She was also introduced in this activity to the "new media" of synthesizer performance and computer music. What is being described here is not only classroom music as an introductory agency but the role of teacher as "animateur". The teacher is recognising student interest and directing them to ways of extending and building upon that interest. The phrase [the classroom teacher] "started it all off for me" (Phillip 1997, pers comm. with student, 5 June) was common amongst participants reporting first experiences with creating music and providing the first instrumental and ensemble experiences.

Classroom as a place for reflection

I was particularly surprised by interview data collected from teachers and students that suggested that the classroom was the ideal place for teaching and learning musicology, research, aesthetics and criticism. From Csikszentmihalyi I note "activity and reflection should ideally complement and support each other. Action by itself is blind, and reflection impotent" (1994, 226). This kind of response is supported by the empirical data. In this extract, James outlines his understanding of the role of classroom music:

> I think the classroom aims to develop an aesthetic sense of music—like basically be able to respond, to music to have some sort of response, that appears to be the aim and, just expose students to music as an experiential thing rather than a something that they're passive, that they just listen to. So I like the way they're introduced to certain elements of music making and encouraged to try those elements out for themselves (James 1996, pers comm. with teacher, 28 October).

James articulates here his perception of the role of classroom teaching at the school as aesthetic and experiential. He sees the teacher facilitating a response to that experience through reflection on it. He is describing both the generic aesthetic function of classroom music and its role as introductory agency, but also the critical aspect of response, of focusing attention on experiencing music making and responding through critical thought and reflection. Students, such as Edward, also valued the aesthetic dimensions and the opportunity to reflect upon what they experienced in the classroom and spoke about how that influenced their present thinking:

> It [was] just good to have the ear to pick up on that kind of stuff and to be able to talk about it and know what's happening and that's definitely what the discussions have brought along. It's really interesting to see how all these do fit into what I do today (Edward 1997, pers comm. with student, 9 July).

It becomes a valuable analytical skill and improves the process of listening and self-criticism. Edward continues:

> I sit down and listen to music and practically tear it apart to find the tiniest little sounds and usually I have a friend with me and we just discuss it, we discuss it for hours. That's what we like doing, it's a favourite pastime. It's given me a key to that kind of a world (Edward 1997, pers comm. with student, 9 July).

In the Chapter 5, students commented on how they had gained enhanced listening skills that they had derived from their musical experiences. They also spoke of listening to a broader range of music than their non-musically experienced peers. The origin of this enhanced perception and broad listening base was described unanimously by participants as being drawn from classroom reflection and critical activities and classroom domain projects that involved music from other cultures, styles and periods.

Meaning and classroom music

The evidence presented here suggests that the classroom program can assist in the gaining of reflective skills, access to a range of music styles, and critical thinking and listening. The creative experiences contribute to an understanding of how art is made and the structure of music. These are skills of self-containment that allow students enhanced expressive capacity that makes their engagement with music making more meaningful in a personal way. In the social context, it provides collaborative creative activity and often constitutes the "first tastes" of music making experiences in large and small ensembles. It offers the development of skills of working with a diverse group of variously able others—teaching tolerance, understanding and patience. The musically able students, who were critical of the "un-musicality" of their peers and the lower quality of classroom music making, spoke of how it developed their patience and described how they benefited even from unsuccessful music making through reflection on it:

> We had a few stuff ups that didn't sound that good. It still just helps you develop your own creativity (Wendy 1997, pers comm. with student, 31 July).

> There's always been non-talented people who either don't want to be there, or can't play that well. Like in those things we did in Year 8 and Year 7. But you can't always have great situations. It's just another one of those things that's a learning experience, playing with people no matter how bad they are. I mean I've always learnt stuff from being in classroom situations, especially like in the later years (Jack 1997, pers comm. with student, 10 July).

When classroom music leads to meaningful reflection, even unsuccessful music making may become worthwhile learning.

Cultural meaning is a more complex idea in the classroom and it is linked to the notion that it is the teacher who designs and creates the music making and learning environment. The classroom is a small and controlled environment. It has been criticised as being unlike real music making, artificial or simulated. It is this quality of control, which makes the elements of psychological and physical environment able to provide a "safe environment" for presentation of music making, for students to take creative risks and to talk reflectively and openly about music experience. It can be a place that values students making as unique and expressive and where music meaning is both caught as well as taught. It is like a microcosm of the real world. Unlike the world it simulates, it can be a safe place to experience meaningful music making as the following students attest:

> It gives you the confidence, cause if you can play in front of a classroom [you can play anywhere] (Janet 1997, pers comm. with student, 17 April).

> It was the first place I ever played a solo. That's where I first thought, "I can do whatever kind of music I like" (Linda 1997, pers comm. with student, 5 March).

> Oh it was good, just for the different experiences and there was always a pretty comfortable environment. There was never any pressure if people didn't like the music we made or anything] (Wendy 1997, pers comm. with student, 31 July).

The students here are describing a "safe place" to make music to an audience of peers. For that to occur though, the teacher needs to create an atmosphere in the classroom that is open, friendly and relaxed—one that is accepting and encouraging of music making and a safe place to make and reflect upon music. Students interviewed recollected just such environments in their memories of classroom music experiences. In a sense, the classroom attempts to control or simulate meaningful experience, and in this case the idea of cultural meaning is experienced within the "micro world" of the classroom. In this way, the teacher can recreate the access to aspects of a reciprocal cultural meaning in a safe and encouraging way. While educating the performers, the teacher in this situation is simultaneously educating their responses as an audience. Students learn to be both performers and critical reflective audiences.

A fragile psychological environment

What emerged from interviews and observations was how dependent the classroom was upon the teacher as the builder of that environment. The teacher needed to provide:

- intrinsically motivating music activities that were challenging yet achievable for all;
- an environment that was open to "music as music" where style and form from a variety of cultures and periods could be sampled, experienced and valued for what they contributed to an understanding of music overall;

- an environment in which it was "safe" to take creative risks and talk about intuitive ideas and expression.

The characteristics of the teacher most valued by interviewees was made up of the following actions and character:

- the teacher must be a maker, animateur, and a builder of psychological environment and creator of atmosphere and attitude;
- they must be personally encouraging, open and have an interest in what the children bring to the relationship and value their interest in music; and, most importantly,
- they must facilitate experience through imaginative curriculum.

The classroom teacher as builder of meaning

The classroom emerges in this analysis as having a unique and pivotal role in providing access to meaningful experience and an opportunity to make sense of the other experiences that form the range of musical encounters. Dewey suggests that in many respects his "art as experience" brought a new focus in arts education upon the intrinsically motivated joys of arts making experience. What was misinterpreted in many adoptions of his ideology was the absolute necessity of reflection to make sense of these experiences. Music is meaningful in itself personally, socially and in a wider cultural sense, but experience with this meaning—although significant—is made more complex by its exposure to developing skills of reflection and aesthetic criticism. In the studio, this is closely focussed and modelled behaviour, which is sometimes not conscious but felt and transferred. In the ensemble, this is also the case when directed by a conductor and becomes a necessity when the ensemble works collaboratively. It is in the classroom where all of these experiences have the opportunity to be reified by conscious and detailed reflection and critical thinking.

In 1995, I argued (Dillon 1995b) that it was this immersion in activity and experience without sufficient focus upon conscious reflection, which contributed to the perceived failure of progressive education in the creative arts. The broad and unified access to meaning in music education is dependent upon the classroom being "the hub" of the music-learning wheel. It is from this hub that access to experiences radiates, and when combined with reflection it forms a strong basis for gaining skills that enable the layers of understanding to be formed. The classroom experience, then, should actuate the access to meaning and give tastes of music making in a sheltered and safe environment. Criticism of the classroom as being "watered down" or irrelevant to "real" music making are turned upon themselves. It is necessary that the classroom be a controlled environment so the teacher can safely and successfully facilitates meaningful experience to participants. It is not so much a "watering down" of the experience but a conceptualised simulation of a "real encounter" that enables students to gain the "spirit" of the experience. The meaning of music changes in relation to the context so the focus of the school experience is not so much cultural authenticity but what the experience contributes to musical knowledge. This applies as readily to experiences with other cultures and times as it does with understanding our own rapidly changing culture.

For many of the students interviewed, the classroom experience was perceived as being "a little light on" or not quite as exciting an experience as their instrumental, ensemble or performance encounters. What I have attempted to do in this section is to determine what an ideal and specific contribution might be. The "glory" in music teaching will always go to the conductor/director of the successful ensemble or the teacher of a genius child protégé. The classroom teacher will have to be content with defining their role more clearly—hence the definition of the role as gateway, the introduction of creative and diverse music styles and cultures and most importantly the teaching of the meta-cognitive skills of reflection. The intention is to give clarity to the role and propose that the potential for this function is to act as a unifying force uniting experience in other contexts through its direct influence upon aesthetic thinking.

The ensemble

In the interviews and observations for this study, the ensemble was mentioned most often as the most memorable and personally rewarding experience for students. It is where a different but nonetheless important relationship with a director or conductor is forged, and where the social and cultural meanings are often gained. Participants saw the ensemble as the "real music making". It is the context where analytic and intuitive understandings are expressed musically, where experience is gained and social and technical instrument skills are challenged and developed. Students made quite strong distinctions between their large and small ensemble experience saying that the positive aspects of the large ensemble were its ability to absorb a variety of skill levels. They commented upon the largeness of the ensemble as a physically moving experience, which gave them a sense of belonging. The small ensemble provided a more intimate social setting for playing and learning music, and one in which the responsibility of "one person, one part" provided interest and challenge. This was particularly the case with student-directed ensembles such as rock bands and chamber groups. Students interviewed suggested that, at different times in their musical learning, each kind of ensemble contributed to their musical development in a unique way.

What I would like to determine here is what the characteristics of ensemble music making are, and in what ways they contribute to the making of meaning. In this analysis, I will focus upon three types of ensembles that I observed during field observations. The first provides a different perspective on the large ensemble/wind ensemble described in the last chapter, looking more succinctly at the relationship between teacher/conductor and students. The second recalls a rehearsal of the more innovative small ensemble, which formed the basis for the pilot study. Finally, I will examine a rehearsal of a small self-directed all-female rock band. The focus of this analysis is upon the specific qualities of each ensemble to provide opportunity for complexity and to seek links of the experience to meaning.

The wind ensemble

During my observations of a rehearsal at a music camp, I recorded the following description of a conductor interacting with a large ensemble. She demonstrated a strong connection with her students despite the "tyranny" of large numbers. In my research journal, I recorded my observation of her in the following way:

> She has great control, a command of respect through the necessity of control, but a benevolent approach where she outlines and explains and shows her feeling and love for the music. The overall culture of attentiveness, questioning and relaxed interaction while focussed on the music is present here. It is a sharing partnership, the size of the ensemble not inhibiting the personal input. They work together but are led inclusively and with a consciousness of the education, telling why and how and facilitating experience to give understanding. She uses description and sings constantly to communicate, encourages verbally and understands the problems. She teaches many of them their instrument or as a classroom teacher- she was probably instrumental in their being involved in playing the instrument in the first place. This is a very strong relationship (Notes from Field Journal 1997, 12 August).

The large directed ensemble

Large ensembles in the form of concert bands and orchestras are often the "flagship" of a school music program, the public face and the measure of the large involvement and quality of a school's music program. Students interviewed for this study suggest that this was their least favourite music experience but one that had given them useful organisational knowledge and discipline. The social experiences of such ensembles are undeniable, but what are the musical and educational values and what does it contribute to meaning for the student?

The wind ensemble talked about above was a fifty-piece concert band. It accommodates a broad range of skills from the early learners (post training band) through to the very able. It was a compulsory ensemble and all wind and percussion players at the school were required to play in the band. This in itself made it unpopular. The music it plays at this stage of its development was generally large-scale works, which are complex formally in terms of linear structure and instrumentally complex in the vertical structure of the instrumental arrangement. The works are highly notated and strictly directed and interpreted by a conductor. In many cases, this is not an ideal learning situation, with the conductor/teacher taking a very mimetic approach to the direction.

The field notes above describe a far more inclusive relationship, despite the size of the ensemble. The complexity of such experiences lies in the formal structure of the pieces and the organisation required to achieve a performance of the works. The conductor described above was adding an educative quality to the experience by inviting students to participate in being perceptive about their sound. She used the same methods utilised by studio teachers to encourage and facilitate understanding through experience and perception about the music. Her use of metaphor and descriptive language, clapping, singing and visual demonstration show the diverse means required to communicate. Her goal was to involve the students in the process of music making, asking them to be perceptive and being reflective with them. By both doing and being, she shared her understanding—she was creating an environment where music might both be taught and caught.

Students and teachers interviewed spoke of the large ensemble as being a "safe place" to begin playing and where they first experienced music making social relations. The vertical age structure of such an ensemble certainly provides the social opportunity to mix with a variety of age groups. The school psychologist supported the important role of this kind of ensemble as a structured place where social interactions were less dependent upon personality than what the student was able to contribute to the whole:

> Being part of the band has been a really safe connection for them. I can actually think of quite a number of students who have taken friendships away from being part of a band as it has been a really safe vehicle for them to exercise those skills (Barbara 1997, pers comm. with teacher, 4 June).

When asked to comment on what created this effect, Barbara said, "I guess how it's run. There is an acceptance for who you are" (Barbara 1997, pers comm. with teacher, 4 June).

The school minister made similar remarks about this aspect of ensembles: "What seems to gel with kids at this school is the fact that they belong to something a production an ensemble a small music group which has had the effect of raising their own awareness of who they are" (Mark 1996, pers comm. with teacher, 14 October). These ensembles have a variety of simple and complex parts; the chances of success at a variety of levels are high. Hence, the complexity is mainly inherent in the largeness of musical and social structure.

What this means is that this kind of ensemble may offer an experience with complex music, and it offers a safe first experience with music making. Furthermore, the large ensemble also offers a unique social experience, which is accentuated by the impact of performance. Potentially, such an experience could contribute to personal meaning through the complexity of form and notation. It adds an aesthetic dimension through the collaborative achievement of a "sound" and ability to interpret conducting nuance. Consequently, there is potential for personal, social and cultural meaning.

The cultural meaning is derived from the great value that a school community, parents and teachers place in the large ensemble as representative of them. This was very evident when this wind ensemble went for an overseas tour. Alternatively, the musical material might not be challenging enough, the social encounters shallow and over-structured and concerts soul destroying. The responsibility for all of this lies with the conductor's ability to organise the ensemble so that it succeeds and to choose material that is sufficiently complex to challenge aesthetically and analytically. The strengths of such an experience lie in its inclusiveness and the complexity of the music performed. The skills gained are those of large-scale collaborative work.

The synthesizer ensemble

The synthesizer ensemble/art ensemble was a small, directed ensemble. The responsibility for formal structure and individual parts (one person per part) was upon the individual. The music was negotiated with the director. The process becomes participatory, the social structure more intimate and dealing with interchanges of an aesthetic nature. The analytic complexity of this encounter is gained through technical skill and the responsibility of "one person one part". The individuals depended upon each other musically. The aesthetic complexity of this ensemble was drawn from its attention to detail in "feel" or the unity of the rhythmic and tonal qualities of the interpretation. This is about depth of understanding. It is not simply playing the music but doing it in a particularly moving way. In some cases, this ensemble improvised so the structure of the music was "moment dependent". Students and teachers interviewed suggested that this was the most educative of the ensemble experiences. This comment from James the keyboard teacher and synthesizer ensemble director reflects clearly the value of the small ensemble as education:

> I think small ensembles probably are the most musical ensembles in that the idea of a small ensemble or chamber ensemble where there is not as much duplication of parts so there's more—each player has to take more of an initiative for themselves, whereas that is not to say there is no initiative in a large ensemble but its a different. In the small ensemble, basically there's one part per player and all the other parts rely on that player to make a meaningful cooperative, musical contribution if you know what I mean, and there's not as much, perhaps there is less room for superfluous parts in a small ensemble. If you take a rock band for example—bass, guitar, drums and singer and if any one of those members doesn't pull their weight musically the whole sound suffers 'cause there's not much room for - you know, how many people can decide they don't want to play in any particular song and all that sort of stuff because of how they sound. The audio spectrum is the bass has got the bottom, the guitars have got the middle and the drums have got something else and people have to have lots of initiative as players so that they say can fulfil that role musically. So I think that the idea of small ensembles or chamber music ensembles is a very musical context for people to play in and I think that there's a chance for them to learn a real lot because they have to initiate a lot of the learning themselves (James 1996, pers comm. with teacher, 28 October).

Teresa reinforces this view from the student's perspective:

> Because we're small we can be flexible and that's just such a good thing and everyone has a really positive enthusiastic attitude, which really is infectious. I mean I've always been very driven when it comes to music too. The other thing with access to equipment and stuff I mean I don't play anything which requires a lot of equipment apart from the wind controller (Electronic MIDI synthesizer controller which is blown like a Sax or Clarinet and has a full range of "synth" sounds and a 6 octave range). That was fun taking that home and learning all about that (Teresa 1996, pers comm. with student, 26 October).

Teresa is also describing the new skills she gained through the technological encounter of a "classical flute player" with an electronic MIDI wind controller. These kinds of encounters facilitate meaningful experiences in the personal through complexity of both analytic/skill and aesthetic/intuitive expression and socially, through the intimate aesthetic discussion, collaborative reflection and group experience.

The cultural meaning is gained by the public pride in this "higher level" of complexity of "form and feel" presented. The students also felt that they were contributing to the development of the domain itself, contributing to musical values. Once more, the role of the director in choice in terms of music and the way in which the director involved the students in their own love of music was seen to be critical in the success of this kind of ensemble. Indeed the jazz ensemble observed they "swung" like their teacher —that is they were able to present a sophisticated rhythmic feeling in the jazz idiom. Their director transferred the intuitive understanding of this concept to his students through demonstration, clapping, playing, singing, metaphor and descriptive language. The teacher as builder of these environments is again critical in the success and educative qualities of the experience.

The rock band experience

During preparations for a large concert, I observed four girls in an all-female rock band. The depth and closeness of their relationship provided an opportunity to observe what students described in interviews as a "deeper way of knowing" which students suggested they experienced in small ensembles. After watching the girls rehearse for a concert, I noted in my research journal that

> The switching between humour and genuine encouragement is interesting to observe. The girls are very caring for each other and sensitive to moods. They are able to have really "bitchy" jokes and "have a go" at each other but not be offensive. Amongst these girls, there are some very fragile self-esteems and they are very conscious of being supportive of each other (Notes from Field Journal 1997, 13 August).

The rock bands I observed were the least structured in terms of their rehearsals. At first, it appeared that the music was not complex and presented little opportunity for challenge. A closer examination of students and teachers' interviews revealed that the complexity of this encounter lay in the aesthetic of "feel" or playing consistently and accurately. The complexity of rock music is often in its production—that is, its timbrel choice and tone, balance and overall sensibility. Significantly, the small self-directed ensemble is complex socially. It is intimate and participants referred to a "deeper way of knowing" each other that they gained from this kind of encounter.

This focuses upon the personal aspects of achieving the challenge of aesthetic and technical difficulty. The participants also gained a direct personal meaning from the expressive aspects of composing and arranging music themselves, as well as organising and running rehearsals. They also demonstrated a great commitment to making music in this way. The social meaning is hinged upon the deep and intimate relationships gained through this kind of experience. From my research journal excerpt presented above, it is possible to see the high level of cooperative interaction, which took place at the rehearsal.

The cultural meaning in this case is a serious issue—what is being projected by this kind of ensemble is intensely personal. The members of the group decided for themselves what to play and how to perform. The response from the public was important acknowledgement of the group members' choices. Nevertheless, this kind of relationship and group presents a very self-contained attitude—one where self-criticism and self-support are most apparently developed.

Certainly public affirmation is important, but in some cases, negative response can also have a profound effect upon the group's development. The group observed was an all-female rock band. They experienced a great deal of male opposition to their music when they first began to play. It was almost as if the loud rock/grunge music they performed was exclusively a male domain. In a sense, this appears to be a contradictory idea to that presented as cultural meaning and its importance to the music maker or artists. It is the tension between affirmation and acceptance and the self-contained passion of expressive music making that makes ultimate acceptance and affirmation even more valuable. History is full of examples of artists who made meaningful and expressive art without the acceptance of the community but continued to make art buoyed by their self-contained perception of what was meaningful to them. It is sometimes sustained by their membership within their particular artistic discourse or domain. It is a pathway that innovators in a domain often face and gives the domain the means of its own growth. In the case of our "all female" rock band, they suggested that this negative peer response to them actually made them a stronger and more determined group. The negative response helped them to shape their sound and make their ultimate success an even more meaningful experience for them because this had further assisted them to mould their music in a creative and innovative way that contributed to the development of the domain.

Each of these encounters provides different opportunities for music learning and the facilitation of meaning. The large ensemble provides complexity of social conditions and of musical works. It offers safe experiences for novice players in the personal, social and cultural sense. Small-directed ensembles provide a good educative basis for learning music, which is challenging and can contribute aesthetically to the domain. The difficulty of such ensembles is that they require a high level of skill to cope with the responsibility of "one person, one part". The intimate social aspect is also a strong contributor to meaning and learning. The small self-directed rock band seemed to have the least complex musical structure in terms of analytic complexity but a demanding social requirement and responsibility. Participants considered this to be the most personally expressive of the ensembles with groups being particularly proud of their "own" style, their own compositions and their unique sound. The responsibility gives this kind of ensemble the broadest aesthetic depth but the least analytic complexity. The educative qualities lie in the use of music as a creative expressive vehicle rather than simply a re-creative one. The cultural meaning in such an ensemble is more referential and is directly personal. The outcomes are development of self-directed team skills, self- containment and realisation of collaborative creative work.

When we examine the ensembles in these terms, it is easy to see that each has unique educational applications. Some more are appropriate for early learning, others more relevant to later development. Each encounter has qualities that touch on social and musical skills in quite a different way, moving from the dependence of the large ensemble upon structure and strict direction through the independence of the small-directed ensemble to the interdependent nature of the self-directed ensemble.

Performance

In this section, I would like to examine the role of performance as part of music education. There are fundamentally two areas in which performance or making of music occurs beyond the classroom and an ensemble rehearsal. The first is the aesthetic presentations to display student progress and promote musical development for its own "artistic" sake. Second, there is the role of music performance, making and presenting in a ceremonial and pragmatic sense. School speech nights, assemblies, church services, remembrance days—there are a multitude of areas in which music is made and performed as a part of a school or community ceremony rather than as a central focus. In this discussion, I will examine what effect participation in both of these contexts has upon musical development and the meaning that students attach to these events.

In terms of the meaning described in this study, performance of any kind relates most strongly to the notion of cultural meaning. It is primarily about the presentation of artistic product to the community and the response and value that the community attaches to that work. The community attaches meaning to the art object. Added to this is the notion that the makers, too, present themselves as an expressive character that the community responds to. I am suggesting that the making of art affects and educates the character of the maker and that the community responds to this projection of person independent of product. Cultural meaning is about the reciprocal exchange of meaning between the maker and the community. In this analysis, I separate the person and the product as Dewey outlined in *Art as experience* (Dewey 1989). This is so that we can make a distinction between the aesthetic relationship of making and the relationship that perceivers have with the product independent of the process.

Performance is a prime goal of music making. It adds complexity to it and provides another dimension to the challenges it is able to present to the maker. Presentation of the product is an important factor in reassuring and affirming the relevance and value of music made. Despite the strong suggestion of participants that most music makers were self-critical and self-contained in their understanding of the product of music making, performance still figured as an important part of music making experience. At the case study school, performance/presentation of student music making occurred actively in both the ceremonial and pragmatic aspects of school life as well as music for the sake of purely aesthetic purposes. In short, music was made to contribute aesthetically to the domain as well as for practical ceremonial purposes where the focus was upon the event rather than the music.

Community response to music making as a whole, and within subcultures in the community is an important aspect of motivation, reassurance and affirmation. As the English and drama teacher Jessica said, "That what you love to do is worth doing" (Jessica 1998, pers comm. with teacher, 22 January). This may occur as part of the whole school community in ceremony, as part of youth subculture and as an aesthetic contribution to the domain. The affirmation and feeling of belonging and recognition is in this way multi-levelled. Interestingly, students saw little difference between a pragmatic/ceremonial presentation and a purely aesthetic performance. Teachers interviewed supported the conscious integration of art and ceremonial activity as an increase in the range and possibilities for performance and one that reflects the kinds of performances required in the "real world". In this respect, they considered the approach to be relevant to life. Students interviewed echoed the teacher response, in this regard.

What I would like to examine here then are the characteristics of environment that encourage, support successful performance, and then consider what each encounter contributes to meaning. First, let us consider some comments made by the school minister/counsellor about his perception of the role music plays in ceremonial events and in particular music that was made by students specifically for the events:

> It's generated a feeling of not only acceptance but of owning…I think what it said to me was that the cultural symbols that we use in a number of places, if music is at the centre of it, it resonates more than just the visual. We are a culture that listens to music, but to hear our own music is almost breathtaking…Yeah I think there is what I would call a democratisation of the process that the students,

its a grass roots thing in a sense. It hasn't been imposed by a tradition in the school which says you must do this it says what can you offer what is your gift and that is far more rich in people's ability to respond than something which has just been handed down from generation and its been imposed as part of the folk lore of the place, and this is for me a very special indicator that this is a healthy community and not waiting for something to be passed on from on high. They are actually searching inside for their particular gift to offer (Mark 1996, pers comm. with teacher, 14 October).

What Mark is describing here is that through making music for a ceremonial purpose, the students play a participatory rather than passive role in the ceremony. This in turn sets up a reciprocal arrangement where the community values and feels a pride in both the product and music makers. This short extract in itself embodies the idea of a cultural meaning. Certainly, a student gains a sense of personal meaning from music making that is self-contained, and that, which is made in fruitful collaboration with others, but this reciprocal arrangement adds a whole other aspect to meaning. It is where music product moves into a wider cultural dimension.

Cultural meaning is possible when music product meets the community. The complexity that this adds to the process of making is that it must communicate something to the community and simultaneously represent the community. In the ceremonial context, this means that the music making must fit the requirements of the ceremony. In the above extracts, the minister is suggesting that those who make the music gain a sense of belonging and recognition. The non-musicians who participate in the ceremony feel a unity and inclusiveness because one of has made "for them" and the music their "own". Doing this task for the music maker is a form of focussed and complex music making that is different to self-contained activity and adds the wild card of the community response.

Experiences with performance to community can be positive, affirming, like the situation described by Mark, or soul destroying, and negative as experienced by the all-female rock group. The difference in this case comes from how the environment has been "arranged". It is possible to provide an environment where performance is an encouraging experience and where negative response leads to correction of the music and learning from the mistakes rather than personal rejection. I discussed earlier that being part of an audience is as much a learned response as preparation for performance and learning how to be an audience is one of the valuable skills gained from classroom music. Outside the classroom, and in the school community, music made for a purpose is also a potentially safe and useful educative experience. The focus of pragmatic music making is often less upon the technical and analytical aspects of music making and more upon the referential aspects of the music to provide mood for a particular context. It is the appropriateness of the music as a socially unifying force that is the focus rather than the skill of the performer or the quality of the composition. This kind of music making is potentially a safe environment for gaining access to cultural meaning if the teacher constructs and prepares the event carefully.

Music making for school ceremonies and purely aesthetic performances was common at the case study school. Performance of any kind adds another dimension of complexity and challenge to music making. What was different in the two contexts was the focus. In aesthetic music performance, we encounter the notion of judgement by the domain of music itself rather than just the audience. These kinds of performances often focus upon technical analytic perfection as well as aesthetic/intuitive expression. This kind of music making has a greater link to pedagogical development of graded music, music that has been designed or composed to increase in complexity or challenge in a progressive manner. The response to performance has two dimensions—firstly that of the audience, and secondly the self-criticism and "informed" criticism of others who are in the discourse. On the other hand, pragmatic performance is more clearly linked to more emotive music/mood invoking music. The judgement of it is in terms of its appropriateness to the occasion and ability to express or enhance the emotive qualities of the ceremony.

What is important about both contexts is that they need to be constructed so that the environment is encouraging as well as challenging. It is here that we can see that the "teacher as builder" of environments for learning has the most impact. It is here also that the links between the contexts of studio, classroom and various ensemble rehearsals become clearer. It is in the microcosm of the classroom that the environment may be controlled so students can learn to be an encouraging audience, perceptive listeners as well as participants. It is in the ensemble rehearsal that students learn about the difficulty of collaborative performance and it is in the studio that they gain the technical and focussed instrumental skills to negotiate musical form. Not only is it important that the student has learnt to be a musician, but that, they have also learnt behaviours that encourage and are supportive of performance. I observed a culture of such support and encouragement in the case study school. Most significant in these observations was an underlying attitude and environment of openness that was shared amongst the music teachers. A student commented about the school in this way: "[The school is] different in terms of that openness but different in terms of taking risks having synthesizers in an ensemble and rock bands and things like classical and jazz it's good to have a diverse background" (Jack 1997, pers comm. with student, 10 July). James, the keyboard teacher's, comments are also representative of the teacher's view of openness within the school environment and its effects on student learning:

> Here the music teachers are open to all styles of music from free form jazz through classical and into rock and roll and rap. I think that has a good effect on the students. I have found that rather than imposing stuff on them that they come to us to ask about jazz or electronic music or about rock musicians (James, 1996, pers comm. with teacher, 28 October).

There was a strong element of constructing an environment both physically and psychologically on a whole-school scale as well as in smaller contexts. Once more the degrees of control of the environment emanates from the structure and preparation facilitated by teachers as builders of environments.

Building a performance environment: The skills of teachers

What, then, are the skills required by a teacher to prepare or build such an environment? The skills of assessment, choice of appropriate materials, preparation and reflective practice are inherent to all music making and perhaps learning contexts. Teachers need to show an awareness of the abilities of the students involved, knowing what was needed pedagogically to develop and facilitate meaningful activity and to provide sufficient complexity to provide challenge and still to be achievable. In aesthetic focussed performance, this normally requires the selection of works that are both entertaining and complex technically. Interestingly in the case study, in works that displayed innovation or student composition or improvisation, it was originality and successful form that they valued most highly. This had the effect of encouraging creative risk-taking. Surprisingly, this kind of creative music making was more apparent in ceremonial music making such as church services where the music was functional and expressive of a mood. Mark, the school minister, described the dual affect of the music maker's feelings of belonging and affirmation. He described the "breathtaking" feeling that the music was made by "one of their own" (Mark 1996, pers comm. with teacher, 14 October) as a powerful description of the cultural meaning gained through pragmatic music making. This aspect of music making levels criticism at Reimer's (1989) notion that functional music making was not music because it takes away from the expressive qualities of the music. I think a more accurate interpretation of this notion is to suggest that pragmatic/functional music making can also contain aesthetic and expressive qualities, but that it may be more simply structured and focussed by the function.

Students and teachers interviewed suggested that the value of both forms of performance were:

- *Aesthetic*: To provide a challenge, to gain responses from community—affirmation and criticism, to experience the communicative and expressive qualities of music making.
- *Pragmatic*: To increase the opportunity to perform in a varied context; to provide a challenge, to experience music as a functional expressive communication, to participate in the community as a musician—offering self as a music maker, to gain affirmation from the community.

Access to cultural meaning is enhanced by exposure to music making which is pragmatic or functional and aesthetic and contributes to the domain. Students saw both as performance. Teachers saw both as an increased opportunity for students to perform and as a dual context that reflected music making in the "real world", where musicians perform for purely aesthetic purposes and as commissioned works or "hired" performers. The point this raises is that performance opportunities in both contexts facilitate meaning and musical development for the participants. At the case study school, there were student rock music festivals for rock bands, chamber music concerts and soirees, multimedia church services and formal speech nights and theatre productions. All ensemble rehearsals were directed towards a performance or a number of performances in these contexts. Directors of ensembles and instrumental teachers either used or created performance opportunities as goals to direct their activities and primarily to add the challenge of performance to the students' learning.

Solo performances were also directed similarly towards performances and to examination performances where the teacher and student prepared pedagogically designed material for formal graded performance examinations. While this kind of solo performance preparation provided a challenge for many students, teachers often described the process as a negative one for some students. This kind of performance is often a particularly stressful one for students. What I feel emerged from analysis of this kind of performance experience was that the ability of the teacher to gauge the readiness and ability for the student to gain from the experience was most important in all aspects of performance. Csikszentmihalyi (1994, 74) suggests that "flow" can be gained when the challenge intersects with the ability to achieve it. What this suggests is that the teacher needs to be able to gauge and judge the student's capacity and the appropriate level of challenge as well as have some control over the environment, which enables the experience to be successful. If the experience is not, then the teacher needs to be sufficiently in touch with the student to turn reflection upon a negative experience into an educative one.

Building context, embodying understanding

Two main ideas emerge in this analysis of music education as a continuum, and as a system of varied contexts for learning—first, that each context contributes complimentary access to meaningful experience; and second, the importance of the teacher as builder of environments. In themselves, these are not unique insights, but what is different about them is the description of them and the ideas that emerge to link them. What is evident from this case study is Swanwick's (1994) notion of music education as initiation into a discourse—it is the experience of music making in a variety of contexts that contributes to the development of student's musical knowledge. What this research contributes to this understanding is that the teacher's ability to structure the environment, model musical behaviour and teach critical reflective skills unifies this understanding for the student. Csikszentmihalyi's (1994) concept of "flow" as a state of engagement that is autotelic and which adds to the complexity of consciousness is evident within numerous data reconstructions presented here.

This research dissects the nature of the challenge and presents in Swanwick's terms a clearer distinction between the analytical and intuitive understandings gained through music experience. The proposition here is that, through a teacher's construction of environment and their sensitivity to students' needs, an environment can be constructed where musical knowledge might be "taught" and "caught" (Swanwick 1994). Evident also are the importance of the teacher-student relationship and the idea of the teacher's embodiment of curriculum, modelling of musical thinking and action and the sensitivity of the inclusive relationship (Buber 1969).

It is not always possible or desirable for all music learning to take place in a school setting. Much of the literature that deals with music education is philosophical rather than practical and these discussions fragment the experiences of music making rather than examining them as activity in social context. What is missing is a dynamic relationship between theory and practice where each enhances and expands the other. The result of such fragmentation of music learning into self-contained and often unrelated encounters has been that each context perceives that it is responsible for the student's entire music education. Alternatively, each teacher may hope that the aspects they have no time for in their particular area are being attended to in other experiences.

In a curriculum and education sense, this is a very haphazard approach. What I have attempted to emphasise is the potential role of the classroom in music education. Far from being a "poor cousin" or lightweight variety of music education, this research has suggested that the role of the classroom may be highly significant in allowing access to aesthetic experience to all. In this sense, classroom music's perceived lack of relation to "real music" making is actually amplified. In a classroom, we are able to provide simulated experiences, which attempt to guide students towards a worthwhile experience in a form that is both achievable and broad. It becomes a taste of music making which invites participants to participate in the more fully focussed experiences of music performance and learning in the studio, ensemble or as a solo performer.

The role of gateway or introductory experience has long been a part of the classroom curriculum. Classroom music approaches such Kodaly, Orff and others have often been criticised as being unrealistic and having no relevance to music outside the classroom. I would argue that this is not a valid criticism. It is the knowledge, which is gained from the experience that is transferable to the wider discourse of music and this knowledge and understanding, is what is relevant and meaningful for the student. Music experiences are made meaningful when students are given the opportunity to reflect upon their music encounters in this controlled environment. This is the key to understanding the pivotal role of classroom music in the continuum. It was in the classroom that students interviewed often had their first instrumental and ensemble experience. Often classroom teachers directed them to the more focussed ensemble and studio lessons. The prime role of the classroom is to provide diversity of experience in music culture from different times and places, to give access to creative music making experience and, most importantly, to provide the opportunity for students to think critically about aesthetic experience. Students' recollection of this role was considered by them to be the most valuable memory of their classroom experiences.

These ideas are prominent features of state and national curriculum documents, such as the Victorian Curriculum Standards Frameworks (*The arts framework: P-10* 1988), *A statement on the arts for Australian schools* (Curriculum Corporation 1994a), and *The arts: A curriculum profile for Australian schools* (Curriculum Corporation 1994b). Many curricula, in practice, do not pay enough attention to the reflective aspects of aesthetics and criticism or to the possibility that music exists beyond the classroom or that they could have any influence over musical knowledge acquired outside the classroom. As suggested by Dewey (1989) and myself (Dillon 1995b), attention within the school curriculum is given to the making of art and not to reifying the knowledge gained through reflection. What emerges from the analysis of data from this case study is that there is a real need to recognise the role of the classroom as the place where music experience may safely be sampled. More importantly, it needs to be recognised as a place where students learn to be perceptive about music experiences in a number of contexts and are encouraged to reflect upon it in language and writing.

The role of the classroom in introducing students to creative activity should also not be underestimated. Indeed, the best understanding of the structure of music comes from experience with creating musical form and reflecting upon it. The experiences with music making that may not be given by the ensemble or the studio are most important. The Victorian Curriculum Standards Frameworks (1988) refers to "past and present contexts" when describing experience with music from other cultures and times, non-traditional performance approaches, music technology and musicological research and sociology. These experiences are all uniquely part of the generic education expected of classroom music.

The success of such a generic approach to classroom music and its role as the hub of the discourse that radiates outwards to the other more focussed musical experiences are wholly dependent upon the teacher. It is the teacher as builder of environments and facilitator of generic experience who is entrusted with a great feat of perception and creation. Both teacher and student interviewees emphasised that the teacher needs to be able to be in touch with the students' needs and interests as well as with the materials available that will be both challenging and achievable for those students. The analysis suggests that the teacher must also be aware of the other opportunities for music making that may be available in a school or community that will best facilitate extended challenge and interest for those who need it. This is the role of teacher as animateur. It is one, which is particularly necessary for classroom teachers but also is a valuable asset for studio and ensemble directors.

Essentially, this is a matter of recognising an interest in or a profound engagement with a musical encounter, and facilitating access to a more complex and challenging experience in the form of studio learning, ensemble participation and performance opportunity. If classroom music is the only music education for some students then it fulfils the role of a generic aesthetic education for all. More importantly, though, it should give access to all aspects of music meaning in the personal, social and cultural sense through the structure of its curriculum and the teachers' taking of the students into their own love of musical experiences. It must also project an environment of openness and train students to be perceptive and constructively critical of music making.

Once we consider the potential for classroom music to act as a hub of the musical discourse, which radiates outwards to more complex and challenging analytic and aesthetic experiences, the role of studio and ensemble music become more easily defined. The studio is where focussed instrumental skills are learned through a close relationship with a teacher. The studio is where personal meaning and self-containment in music learning are established and where they grow. The ensemble is where social meaning is gained. The kinds of ensembles and their degree of independence and challenge are determined by the size and input of the members. Each kind of ensemble suggests different kinds of learning experiences, which can become valuable at different stages of development or suit particular individual personalities. What is important about this observation is that a focus upon one particular kind of ensemble experience or the exclusion of any of them reduces access to meaningful experience and growth and diversity of the challenge presented by ensemble participation. Participants in this case study highly valued the access to different ensemble experiences and highlighted the access that it gave them to different musical styles. This aspect of ensembles is largely due to the openness of teachers and the school to diversity of musical forms and styles. As suggested by the drama teacher, Jessica, it is not necessary to like the music the students bring but value their interest in it.

The cultural meaning gained from the reciprocal interchange of music making, music makers and community is a powerful aspect of music meaning and motivation to participate in music learning. The analysis presented here supports the idea that it is necessary for music making to be both pragmatic and aesthetic. Firstly, this increases the amount and varies the context of performances. Secondly, as Jane suggests, "It's imperative, it's got to be there, it involves the community in the aesthetic experience; it involves the aesthetic experience in the community" (Jane 1997, pers comm. with teacher, 13 February). To focus purely upon the aesthetic and "art for art's sake" performance creates elitism and tends to exclude those not inducted into the discourse. Alternatively, a pure focus upon ceremonial or functional music making reduces the possibility that music makers might contribute creatively to the development of the domain. Exploration of both values each experience and increases the access to cultural meaning.

What this analysis is primarily attempting to reinforce is that each encounter of the student within the discourse of music making contributes distinctive aspects to music education. Access to a broad variety of music experiences can only strengthen the understanding and skill level of music students. These experiences may not be connected by curriculum or even experienced in the same school or place, but reflection has the potential to draw all of these experiences together. If the understanding gained through this process is able to radiate outwards and bring unity to the discourse, then this increases the challenge and complexity of all musical experiences. There is then more chance that the learning will become meaningful. In terms of the process of music making, this suggests that there is a need for awareness of the inter-connection of music experiences and the strengths of each encounter to deliver challenge and meaning. Most importantly, there is an implicit need to recognise the potential for the classroom learning experience to facilitating generic experience and reflective practice. Once this role is embraced, classroom teaching acts as the thread that draws together the other encounters of the discourse. It assists in making sense of them as well as acting as a gateway to deeper more complex experiences with music making.

Teacher as builder and the concept of culture

How do we build environments that provide access to ethical syncretic cultural experience? To answer this question I will describe the structures and practices of the central case study school. This case employed philosophical principles that potentially encouraged cultural diversity and ethically appropriate experience. Nevertheless, while the approach showed evidence of a positive effect on the development of openness to diverse cultural experience for students as we will see in retrospect that we can comment on the analytical framing of this thinking.

Music is music

The "music is music" approach seems to affect adolescents even with quite strong one band or style approaches. As suggested by the keyboard teacher James, openness to musical style, genre and culture was a well-established principle at the case study school: "They can see that it is OK to like music that might not fit their peer group's ideas, but through playing a variety of stuff and that open attitude they tend to develop a broader listening base (James 1996, pers comm. with teacher, 28 October). Educationally this notion can be found in Bruner's theory that suggests that there are fundamental concepts of knowledge that we can revisit at progressively deeper and deeper levels. At the case study school these concepts were built around an adaptation and application of Pratt's (1990) extended aural perception framework. This approach to aural analysis utilises a process of considering the "effect" of music on the listener and then examining the "effectors" that caused this. Within a Western Art music framework, Pratt's elements are re-extended to include placing in space and an extended concept of pitch-organisation. This approach when coupled with an approach to reflective practice involving *Arts Propel* music journals and verbal reflection allowed students to experience music making and reflect critically on music using the aural perception framework as a language for aural analysis. Coupled with this approach the concept of "repertoire" in the case study site was based upon the principle that all music contains musical knowledge and that some genres, styles and cultures value or extend the expressiveness of some elements over others. Hence, the idea for example that complexity of rhythm could be found in African music's, complexity of harmony and form in classical, complexity of timbre and space in popular culture. Students at the case study site had access to music making experience in three locations. I will examine how cultural materials were presented in each location.

The instrumental studio

In the studio in small groups or one to one lessons students access to diverse cultural materials were not mandated but the notion of repertoire was expanded to include non-notated genres. Studio teacher's were encouraged to act on students' interest in music and the needs of ensemble that the students were a part of. Consequently, teachers either did aural transcriptions, created tablature or taught aurally pieces of music, which did not have notated representation. Secondly, improvisation was included as an activity in these lessons and as practice for students. This kind of approach provided a skill base for rock and jazz musicians and contemporary classical performers. While cross-cultural music experiences were not mandated in the instrumental studio lessons those that participated in ensembles that performed cross cultural music had the opportunity to work with a teacher on their part.

The ensemble

The case study site had a large number of diverse ensembles. Each ensemble had a contract to do three things:

1. A performance or production for their peers;
2. a performance or production for their school community; and,
3. something that pushed the boundaries of their art.

The ensembles were not conventional in instrumentation and so repertoire and arrangements could often not be found in printed form. The solution to this was that ensemble leaders/directors and the students themselves were responsible for selecting and arranging and composing their repertoire. These conditions set the scene for diverse musical performances. To add to this, cross-cultural musicians were invited to give workshops at the school, which provided a basis for new repertoire based on these experiences.

An example of this in practice involved a group of improvising musicians working with a Papua New Guinean musician preparing a piece for the opening of an Indigenous education conference. Students worked with the principles of music from Papua New Guinean using rhythms and timbrel materials from Australian Indigenous and European musical forms and using instruments from across those cultures. The resulting piece provided an interesting cross-cultural setting for the event at which they performed.

Expressing the idea of syncretism sonically

The concept of syncretism describes the coming together of different religious or philosophical beliefs. When ideology moves in time and space and is relocated to another country, interpreted by different people or encounters new ideas that have the potential to be blended together, syncretism occurs. It is an important concept to describe what happens when musical practices and values move locations or are reinterpreted in different times and places by new performers. We see this kind of reinterpretation, re-purposing and appropriation of musical ideas in popular music all the time. Continuously we are faced with new styles, genres and associated sub cultures. Of course, musical ideas have moved around the world, been traded, appropriated colonised and blended for thousands of years. In today's environment, syncretism raises many complex issues associated with ethical appropriation of musical knowledge and of course, the notions of intellectual property and copyright present other layers of legal complexity to the blending of sonic ideas. New technologies also present ways of appropriation that allow music to be purchased instantly. While these issues need to be considered for classroom music, the focus in section is about how the age-old process of syncretism can be used as a pedagogical tool to create experiences that simulate syncretic processes so that students gain an understanding of how music grows, changes and responds to environment, values, ideology and resources.

The classroom

The classroom provided the most formal introduction to cross cultural music experience. The focus was upon African music and its attachment to hybrid forms. Consequently, Latin American, West Indian and South African music formed a large part of cross-cultural experience. The reason for this selection was to provide an understanding of the origins of youth music such as rock music and other popular forms such as jazz and blues, which were also taught in earlier years. In later years, the selected focus was upon long form music meaning music, which has structures that are more complex. This also focused upon twentieth century styles such as minimalism, serialism, Musique Concrete and electronic music. The logic behind the selection of genres was to challenge elemental constructions of what music is and relate these understandings to the popular culture that formed a basis of most students' lives or extended those who were single focused.

Furthermore, music in the classroom utilised *Harvard Project Zero Arts Propel* (Davidson 1992) approaches through domain projects and portfolio assessment. Projects were contextual and in most cases replicated or simulated a real world environment to provide a context for the music, which had a relationship to its origin. Pedagogically each domain project followed Swanwick's (1981) "CLASP" approach providing a range of creative production and performance experiences. Built in to every class were critical reflective sessions (Schon 1984) led by the classroom teacher using a student reflective diary (Brown and Dillon 2001). As James describes, it put forward a "music is music" focus (James 1996, pers comm. with teacher, 28 October).

While Western Art music and European folk music was common, the focus in the classroom among ensembles was on a deep understanding of the twentieth century, and how composers and performers interpret a variety of musical genres, periods and cultures. The logic here was that as Bruner (1966) suggested in a *Theory of instruction* which refocused education from content to concept basis, it is impossible to teach the entire history of music across all cultures in a few years of school. There is simply too much information. We therefore need to select the material, which will provide complex experiences with a diverse range of musical elements (Bruner 1966). This is how the case study school framed the concept of revisiting fundamental concepts at progressively deeper levels.

Connecting experiences

The role of classroom music in music education at the school was to provide a gateway to deeper experiences in studio and ensemble contexts but primarily its function was to give access to creative experience, diverse cultural experience and to provide analytical and reflective frameworks for students to make sense of music wherever they found it. There was evidence that this kind of openness was apparent. While this approach was considered at the time to be a positive outcome, I would like now to criticise this model and propose some solutions that perhaps are more ethical and culturally appropriate.

Analytical frameworks

While the basic premise of the approach described above has merit, the fundamental flaw is the analytical framework. While the framework for aural perception was an expanded one and this is a useful tool for analysis and provides a language for discussion about music it is however a Western framing of how music is perceived. What I have found recently is that when we apply a sound in time and space model of aural perception while this approach is also drawn from Western philosophical thought it does not presuppose a system of values nor presume a connection with a body of excellent works. It is more able to examine notions of embodied understanding such as rhythmic "groove" and constructions of aural perception that are more about volume, timbre and intensity of activity. Chapman and I (2005) suggested that this approach, as described by Vella (2000), provided an opportunity for music making to be perceived in a more culturally inclusive way. Further to this notion, we suggested the following principles when approaching culture and context in the study of Indigenous cultures:

- Place the understanding of Murri and Koori music in a context of world issues and perspectives including colonialism, post colonialism and post modernism
- Address the music from an indigenous worldview rather than/ or at least as well as a Western worldview—focus on meaning rather than sound
- Enrol the students in the issues around the music and identity in the country but personalising their perspective
- Have the Indigenous music delivered by Indigenous Australians
(Dillon and Chapman 2005, 192).

These ideas provide a more politically active approach to cultural materials. While the above-mentioned principles were developed specifically for engaging with Indigenous Australian cultures, they provide an ethical framework for approaching all non-Western cultures. What is critical here is that when approaching cultural materials we need to provide an open aural perception framework that is culturally inclusive and engage with the context as a political act that enacts the relationship we have with music and the music has with wider issues and perspectives.

Teacher as builder and technology

How do we build environments that integrate and show an understanding of the intrinsic qualities of music technology? I will continue to draw upon and construct a description of the case study schools' approach to music technology in practice in the three locations of music experienced outlined above.

The instrumental studio

In the instrumental program at the school, composition was taught privately using music technology. Synthesizer was taught as a solo instrument a study that went beyond physical activity to include programming and timbrel manipulation and creation. Teachers on all instruments were encouraged to use sequenced backings for practice tapes. They also used notation programs to develop print materials and arrangements.

The ensemble

As well as the hybrid, electro acoustic combinations of ensembles such as jazz bands with an electric piano player the school had a dedicated electronic ensemble and several experimental electro acoustic ensembles. For example an electronic ensemble utilised wind controller, electronic drum and percussion pads, an electric violin and cello that used digital signal processors and a trio of synthesizers. As well as composing and arranging their own works this ensemble played "classic" electronic works by Reich, Jarre and Riley. Furthermore, they facilitated electro acoustic performances with percussion ensembles and choirs.

The classroom

The classroom sported a single Apple computer with sequencing and notation software plus algorithmic programs like M and Band in a Box. Three synthesisers with onboard 8-track sequencers were in the classroom as workstations for composition. There was also an early Yamaha 4-track recorder and two drum machines. The classroom resources were such that groups of students could work on compositions and arrangements around a workstation consisting of a keyboard with sequencer and an amplifier. With a curriculum focus upon twentieth century music both popular and art music this rich technological environment enabled access to creative collaborations and experimentation, recording for reflection and criticism and the production of real world products. The flexibility of the environment, as it was set up with workstations, allowed a variety of teaching and learning contexts ranging from small group work to large ensemble performance.

Technology in this setting was present as an Instrument in its own right allowing pedagogical development of synthesiser and computer. It enabled technology to be a medium through which music could be represented and communicated. It could also be a tool enabling complex musical transformations to occur effortlessly when using sequencers, Algorithmic software and recording devices. What is also apparent in this description is that the teachers also engage with technology as part of their practice as musicians. Furthermore, technology is integrated with production of music within a real or simulated context. In relation to the teacher as builder, there are three factors of importance here: firstly, that the teachers model technological use; secondly, a pedagogy for development of the technology is put into place; and, thirdly that the philosophy that forms the environment values technology as a means of expanded musical expression. What this suggests is that there is a need for a reinterpretation of what musicianship means in the light of technological use. As well we need to know about the qualities of teaching which lead to this kind of creative tool use.

What we can do

Here are some ideas for what we as music educators can do as teacher builders:

- *Understand that you are the principal instrument of the teaching experience and need to model the values and attitudes that you expect from students. Much of this is embodied and intuitive knowledge so you need to play, create and sing to and with students at every opportunity and talk your reflections and analysis out loud so they can see that this is a continuous process.*

- *Remember that planning lessons as teacher as builder involves creating a clear context where the parameters of the task become the goal of the lesson or unit sequence. Just as a film producer provides a clear brief for a film score the teacher as builder provides a clear brief that contains the musical knowledge and materials to be used in the creation or performance of the music. The selection of repertoire or the definition of creative tasks parameters is the lesson plan.*

- *Keep in mind that the student should encounter an environment constructed by the teacher that contains the musical knowledge which he or she then engages with through making presenting and reflecting on experience.*

- *Each lesson and each unit needs reflective activity built in so that it becomes a continuous discourse about how to make the music we are making more expressive.*

- *Treat assessment as a continuous and democratic activity that extends upon performance and presentation of music and its analysis. It should include both process and product and be negotiated against curriculum outcomes and student expectations and established by the student, peers and teacher.*

Part III

Practical

CHAPTER EIGHT

MEANINGFUL ENGAGEMENT WITH MUSIC AND PERSONAL MEANING

Introduction

In my work with jam2jam, a program that generates rhythmic and melodic pop song grooves in real time, I have been continuously amazed at how engaged I am after five years of research and use of the program to still sit for hours sometimes—shifting sliders up and down to generate new grooves and play around with the creative production components of the instrument. The program is aimed at four to eight year olds and yet I lose myself in playing with the instrument. This is an intensely personal relationship with composing or improvising which has a long history of being able to engage me. This says something about my own relationship with music making, what pushes my buttons, what engages me about musical structures and activities. It is a personally meaningful experience.

This kind of "personal meaning" refers to the relationship we have with music making. This relationship is amplified here through reference to case study materials to illustrate the qualities of teacher and the architecture of music experience that provides access to meaningful and engaging music making experiences. The values expressed in this discussion seek to build upon what many see as natural aesthetic responses of children (Aronoff 1969) or perhaps more simply the playfulness of humans with sound. I would like to frame these responses in such a way as to facilitate access to meaningful activity which is engaging and leads to a transformation of consciousness. Participants in the case study describe the particular relationship between student and teacher. They outline the kinds of characteristics that provide for learning which builds upon natural aesthetic response as well as that which facilitates engagement that leads to gaining personal meaning. It highlights the ability to self actuate an ongoing personal relationship with music making that enables it to be used as a means of relaxation and personal expression as well as a means of understanding how human culture chooses to organise sound expressively.

Defining personal meaning

Luke, a 17-year-old rock guitarist, described what music meant to him when he said, "I don't think it has to be good to get a kick out of it. And, I don't think other people have to hear it for you to get a kick out of it either" (Luke 1997, pers comm. with student, 4 June). I define "personal meaning" here as the meaning gained by an individual engaged in making music privately. Luke is describing a self-contained attitude, one where music making is personal and not judged externally. He is not suggesting that quality is unnecessary in this context, but that the standard and the pleasure gained from making music privately is self-determined. He is talking about the pleasure gained from his personal experiences with music making. His definition of what is considered 'good' in music making is the quantifiable technical and analytic aspects of music making. Several interview participants spoke of a deeply personal encounter with music making.

Two further aspects of this idea are provided by Colin, a 16-year-old multi-instrumentalist, He describes his personal satisfaction and self-drive in the following way: "You've got to get your enjoyment out of it, of what comes from inside you, not from what other people say to you (Colin 1997, pers comm. with student, 13 March). Margaret, a 16-year-old composer, spoke about her musical pieces in this way: "I like that, [composing] because you are in your own little world, having an experience that no one else can have" (Margaret 1997, pers comm. with student, 21 March).

What both Colin and Margaret are saying is that this is a realm of personal satisfaction, "flow" gained from a personal encounter with music making. Some participants described a need to express themselves in this way; others saw it as integrated with self and something they would always do a kind of intra-pers comm. with self. Most powerfully, the data gave a sense of the effect of the encounter that provided a change in consciousness, which led to making the self more complex through the interaction. This suggests that the personal experience is significant and meaningful. The goals in this context are self actuated and self-determined. The challenge provided by the encounter can be technical and analytic or intuitive and aesthetic or both simultaneously. Within the intimacy of this self-contained activity of making music in the personal domain of experience, the students spoke of the emotional affect of the encounter.

The idea that music making experience can provide a self-motivated and personal experience is an important one. Students who are experienced at self directed activity which affects their personal mental health and even as described above autotelic behaviour that allows a control over mood and sense of self that can be influenced by self actuated activity in music making. It is obvious that people make music or have a relationship with music in personal ways can achieve a state of happiness from this encounter but what is exciting to observe here is how students use it in self actuated ways to both gain personal pleasure and deepen their relationship to their self. Indeed several students interviewed talked about music making as a form of expressive relaxation.

Within the notion of self-contained music making, participants reported a pleasure in the solitude of making music. They used the terms "relaxed" and "relaxing" frequently in discussion of their private music making experiences. In contrast, they described music making as an "energising" activity. Edward, an 18-year-old rock guitarist and band clarinet player, describes this feeling after a "great performance"—"I come off stage with an amazing amount of energy. I want to run around the oval [playing field] twenty-five times" (Edward 1997, pers comm. with student, 9 July). Despite this tremendously high-energy description of performance success, less successful performances were not considered a negative experience. On the contrary, it was this aspect of music making which showed that participants seemed to be self-contained and self-critical they valued their own judgement on success rather than taking the audience response alone or external critical response. Edward's comments on a poor performance highlight this idea: "I've noticed a bad performance doesn't affect me too much. I just get off stage and think well that wasn't too good we'll have to work on that" (Edward 1997, pers comm. with student, 9 July). The idea of self-containment in the realm of personal experiences is amplified and given flexibility by the focus upon autotelic problem finding and solving (Csikszentmihalyi 1994). The idea of "bad performance" as educative is a mature process of thinking, and this suggests an ability to reflect critically on action for the purpose of improvement. This suggests that, through the process of Edward's music education, he has gained the habit of critical listening, experience and reflection.

The movement towards self-containment is an interesting issue in itself. In interviews about early music experiences students recalled social meaning as most important. It appears that at this stage they gained personal meaning "through" or with their teachers as a kind of shared or family response. As they mature and their relationships with both teacher and the discourse broaden, they gain "flow" from the experience itself, which gives then access to personal meaning of their own. The social meaning, which I will discuss in more detail in the next chapter, is at the same time extended and deepened through the continuation and diversity of social musical encounters. This notion of sharing in personal meaning through a practicing musician/teacher was common in the data. It also suggests strongly the importance of embodiment (Bresler 2004) and modelled behaviour in music learning and teaching.

Sharing meaning

What is apparent here is the issue of having a meaningful music making experience as a student, or sharing in or experiencing one "through" a teacher. Either way, this encounter involves experience, and reflection. It is guided reflective activity and perception about the music making process and the music made that reifies the intuitive experience and introduces layers of understanding, making it educative. The manner and approach of teachers in ensembles, studio and classroom interactions with students, was one example, which demonstrated or rather "lived" the self-critical and reflective music maker. During the field study, I observed a 40-piece wind ensemble "section rehearsal". Although this experience refers more specifically to what might be classified as a social music making experience, the focus in the following excerpt from my research journal, is upon the student's imitation of the teacher's behaviour:

> I had observed the conductor for over an hour while she rehearsed her band. She was very animated and excited about the music and the sound, being conscious to solve problems that arose quickly so that the sounds made by students were pleasant and motivating. She sang, clapped used metaphor and analogy, explained clearly why and what she was doing and made sure that each adjustment resulted in a noticeable change. She facilitated experiences for students who played through parts and all the time, all forty students were invited and involved in the collective activity of making a good sound.
> She divided the ensemble into sections, led by advanced and senior students. What took place when I wandered these smaller units rehearsing was that each of the sections ran their rehearsals in the same manner. Using metaphor, clapping, singing through parts solving technical problems through reference to their understanding of fixing the problem. Fundamentally, all groups observed were imitating the reflective problem finding and problem solving behaviour of the conductor. (Notes from Field Journal 1997, 12 August).

The students observed above, were "imitating" and adopting the approach to self-criticism, problem solving and analysis used by their conductor/teacher. They used the same "multi-media" approach to communication, one that involves singing, clapping, demonstration and verbal analogy. This kind of transfer of "reflective practice" from teacher to student was often observed in ensemble rehearsals and studio lessons, and within classrooms. The meaning gained by students in the above example has its roots in the social as well as personal, but what I am looking at here is individual demonstration of self-critical/reflective practice. This suggests a developmental process where the senior students move towards interdependent educative and reflective behaviour while junior students experience the change through others. What is evident is the development of a habit of critical listening, problem finding and problem solving and the self-contained reflection that gives access to personal understanding and meaning. In a very real sense, this skill not has been "taught" but "caught" (Swanwick 1994) by the students and modelled by the teacher.

Teaching the intuitive

The teachers interviewed supported the idea that they needed to be able to transfer their intuitive knowledge to students through a variety of media and experience. Intuition is defined in this research in Swanwick's (1994) terms as being personal or acquaintance knowledge. The kind of understanding gained through direct engagement with music making. Teachers in this study suggested that their own experiences as musicians and people added credibility to their words, while the ability to demonstrate conveyed intuitive understandings and embodied knowledge. In an interview with the school counsellor, he suggested that music and drama teachers were able to reveal something of themselves to students, to expose a vulnerability that perhaps was less present in other more formal subjects and teaching relationships. As a classroom music teacher Peter describes this:

> Yeah, they get to know you as a person and as a musician. You expose yourself in a way, by writing songs for them and with them and playing with them, and performing for them, singing to them. You're exposing your inner most feelings and expression to them (Peter 1998, pers comm. with teacher, 10 January).

What teachers said about the acquisition of personal meaning was that they were aware of the power of their own attitudes and being as influence upon student behaviour. They were conscious of the need to transfer the intuitive through their own experience as musicians and were prepared to expose a vulnerability of self to students to do this. How much each was prepared to do this was dependent upon personality and relationship. What was universal for teachers interviewed was the need to demonstrate through performing on their instrument themselves. This is a primary factor in teaching "intuitive" concepts of musical knowledge.

All my friends are musicians

An interesting dichotomy arose from further examination of this analysis, which distinguished the so-called "musical" students, and students with only youth culture association with rock music listening. Here Edward describes the difference between his own understanding and that of his perception of his girlfriend's response to music:

> Me and my girlfriend listen to music and we both hear completely different things and music has definitely trained my way of thinking in regards that I can hear a completely different side of the music than what people who aren't trained in music can hear. It was interesting one day we had an interesting discussion about it. To her it was just sound coming out of speakers. It seemed to me, I got the impression, that it was a very two dimensional kind of thing, the sound that hit her and if it was an exciting sound you can move to it and soul sounds and stuff I would say that I would look at it as a more three dimensional aspect I can take it apart and I look for different things it's hard to explain (Edward 1997, pers comm. with student, 9 July).

Like Edward, students who were musically experienced spoke of having enhanced aural perception. They reported openness to a broader range of music listening and experience. They compared their ability to listen to music with those who did not have access to their experience and understanding as being like the difference between two-and three-dimensional perceptions. They claimed an enhanced perspective through their intuitive understanding with experience and the analytical reflective skills. On the other hand, students with "no musical interests" except their attachment to youth culture expressed their understanding of the music they listened to in a youth culture or referential way and with a purely and culturally subjective understanding and responses. Their comments about music were limited by their vocabulary to talk about the structure of music.

Students interviewed and asked for comment during observations both verbally and in writing about music commented using colloquial language "this is shit" or "this is cool", which implies even more strongly the subjective response of subculture attachment. The language is perhaps "not appropriate for school" being the only available descriptive terms to articulate their personal responses. Nevertheless, I observed that these students also received a social meaning through the cultural reference to membership of youth subculture and personal meaning through an attachment to these experiences and their own feelings/aesthetic understanding. The differences lay in the ability to articulate their response, to express themselves within the media of music and to effectively "think musically" within the aesthetic form. They too were attracted to its personal, social and cultural meanings, but their responses were more subjective and integrated with the cultural reference.

It should be understood here that I am not denigrating this response, as I believe that it is fundamental and a human one. I am simply drawing a comparison to the responses of the musically experienced students. The same meanings seem to be in place; the differences lie in the potential for gaining understanding. Experience with making and reflection provides access to an analytic understanding for "musical" students. This deepens their ability to listen and experience music outside of the youth culture and that broadens their access to other music, allowing them to "transcend local cultural practices" (Swanwick 1999, 28).

Diversity of musical style separated musical and non-musically experienced peers, "Musical" students participated and listened to a greater range of musical styles (jazz, classical, world music, rock) and demonstrated openness to new musical experience and listening. Each of the meanings of music described in this study exists in the non-musically experienced. The personal, being drawn from their referential experience, the social through peer association and youth subculture and the cultural through what that musical style projects about a person and how that interacts reciprocally with cultural values. What is clear when the students are compared is that, although the non-musically experienced students display similar access to musical meaning, the access to increased complexity required to provide flow experiences is limited.

I am not denying that this kind of experience does not provide flow; rather, that the opportunity for increased complexity and challenge becomes an incremental experience. Flow may emanate from dancing or from the social interaction but not directly from participating in the music making or perception experience. Musically experienced students spoke of the enhanced perception gained from experience and listening/reflection. They described a profound difference in their ability to hear music "more deeply" than their non-musically experienced peers. They reported that this was because of their experience and analytical/ critical thinking. What follows are several examples of what students saw as the effects of such experience upon their musical thinking:

> *Edward*: I would look at it as a more three-dimensional aspect I can take it apart and I look for different things. (Edward 1997, pers comm. with student, 9 July).
>
> *Brian*: It kind of makes me think in different areas. I listen to more classical music, than I did before, which I don't know whether that's directly, related but I seem to have broadened a bit, got into jazz and things like that, rather than more straight down the line rock, hard rock. (Brian 1996, pers comm. with student, 23 October).
>
> *Bronwyn*: I think I listen to a wider-variety of music now (Bronwyn 1996, pers comm. with student, 22 October).
>
> *Colin*: Well doing each style has broadened my musicality (Colin 1997, pers comm. with student, 13 March).

In each quote presented here, the student reports a change in self, a broadening of their openness to style and a deepening of their ability to listen in a multi-layered and analytical way. In this way, listening provides a flow experience for them, through the gaining of deeper understanding and a personal meaning, which adds to the induction into the discourse. For students to benefit from such an experience, both the environment and the teachers who create the psychological musical culture must project openness.

The teachers' attitude to creating an open environment

The teacher's attitude to musical style has a strong influence on how the students respond to musical differences and openness. In schools, there is great polarisation of stylistic and methodological differences and approaches. Within youth culture, the "tribal-like" divisions of musical tastes are a significant factor in the lives of both teachers and students. Teachers interviewed in this study emphasised that openness to a variety of musical styles was a vehicle for learning more about music. Despite their own personal taste, they advocated this broad approach rather than focusing unduly upon one, such as Western art music/classical music, rock music jazz, etc. Teachers and students in this study treated style as an opportunity to revisit the elements of music and expression. Keyboard teacher James comments on this idea:

> The "music is music" approach seems to affect adolescents even with quite strong one band or style approaches. They can see that it is OK to like music that might not fit their peer group's ideas, but through playing a variety of stuff and that open attitude they tend to develop a broader listening base (James 1996, pers comm. with teacher, 28 October).

The "music is music" approach, which values all styles, periods and locations for what they contribute to the knowledge of musical elements and human culture, creates an environment of openness that allows students to safely move beyond the confines of youth culture to experience music in a much broader context. It gives access to generic skills of criticism that are useful in understanding and appreciating any music. Within this kind of "open approach" the teacher needs to acknowledge the child's intrinsic interest in this music and consider "what the child brings" to the teaching/learning relationship. Jessica, a singer, drama and English teacher, puts this idea very eloquently:

> Even if they [the teacher] don't value the music but value the child's interest in that music, that's what it's all about. As long as you are open, and say that that's

not something that I'm particularly interested in, but if you are interested in this then why don't you...And still do the facilitating and advising that you normally would do (Jessica 1998, pers comm. with teacher, 22 January).

Classroom music teacher Peter highlights further the importance of the teacher-student relationship and the creation of an open psychological environment:

> Yes, it's the environment that is important. As you say psychologically but also in your relationship with those kids, that's the key, that's the important factor. I think that is a philosophy of teaching I've developed over the years. It doesn't really matter what you are teaching. It's the way that you treat those kids, the way that you respect them as human beings that they are going to remember and then anything that you do teach them becomes a lot more effective and they become more effective learners in an environment of respect (Peter 1998, pers comm. with teacher, 10 January).

The teacher's comments are about creating an environment of openness that facilitates and gives access to this aspect of personal meaning and leads to the process of listening and reflecting upon music to become a self-contained interdependent one.

A change in the way we think

> I think listening to music has a big effect on the way I think (Luke 1997, pers comm. with student, 4 June).

Participants spoke of a change in the way they think, or a development of their appreciation of divergent forms of thought, that they attributed to their involvement with music making. Students also talked about the satisfaction gained when exercising the creative side of their personality. Ex-students who had moved away from making music on a regular basis after leaving school described this concept as a "need" and these students felt a renewal when they returned to music making activities. Michael, a 20-year-old ex-student and composer, describes the affect upon his thinking:

> Yes it has its given me more of an idea about the proximity of what I can do because I know what is possible...It's made me a more rational or more open thinker...Because you are creative you can see what is possible. Where other people, won't break the rules, you can say "bullshit this is a different way, this is how you can do it, let's do it this way" (Michael 1997, pers comm. with ex-student, 22 December).

This suggests a development of self in a way that might have a generic application, a confidence in different ways of thinking. This is what participants described as developments of self that added to their character or intellectual abilities, which might be transferred to other domains or act as a balance to other modes of thinking.

Participants spoke of "exercising their imagination" with creative work, thinking in different areas' with a variety of musical styles. This was a most surprising outcome as those interviewed in an earlier study (Dillon 2001c) indicated that these kinds of assertions could not be drawn from their music experience alone. Jack, a 16-year-old drummer, comments on how the process of reflecting on intuitive experiences in music has affected his understanding of other creative activities:

> To a certain extent, the way I think and often the way I speak is often about being able to talk about the music. It gives you skills, and social skills, learning how to express. You can just play something that is hard to describe verbally what you are actually doing and that's always helped it's always a good thing to do, a lot of things I say, a lot of adjectives, I'll think "ah" that's a music term (Jack 1997, pers comm. with student, 10 July).

What Jack is describing is the word or phrase attached to abstract and intuitive experience having meaning when applied to similarly difficult-to-describe circumstances in creative work. He is suggesting that what he has gained from his musical experience is what Perkins (1988) describes as a "far transfer" of a concept or mode of thinking. This implies a movement of a process of thinking from one domain to another where it is meaningful.

Music as a personal discourse

The musical encounters described above are not isolated incidences but multi-faceted layers that contribute to the significance and meaning of musical experience. These layers of understanding are fused through their ability to initiate students into the musical discourse. As Margaret suggests, "I'm into it because it gives me inspiration and it has meaning" (Margaret 1997, pers comm. with student, 21 March). I have mentioned previously the idea that a growth or transformation of self is gained from the increased complexity of engagement with "flow" activity. If we consider music as a personal discourse, we are examining the opportunity for "flow" experiences. The music discourse provides an endless set of aesthetic challenges for individuals to find engagement and pleasure. In particular, they provide opportunity for challenge and complexity, which becomes meaningful through "discerning the limits of personal potential" (Csikszentmihalyi 1994, 222). Access to an environment with diverse opportunities for involvement with music making activities is the key to large-scale student involvement in the discourse. It is the engagement with the discourse and self that yields personal meaning.

Success in this encounter is self-evaluated and self-actuated—"goal directed actions that provide shape and meaning to an individual's life" (Csikszentmihalyi 1994, 230). This focus upon self-containment takes on far greater meaning when the student is actually able to contribute to the development of the domain. Students talked about introducing audiences to new ideas, and educating them. They saw themselves as able to play with creative materials and take them to audiences as an educative rather than a critical perspective. This idea was particularly notable when students spoke about new music played as part of a ceremony like a church service or school ceremonial function where "new music" underscored the event. The affirmation from the community that they received for being innovative was an important part of their perceived role in the discourse - to advance it was the aim.

Personal meaning is a powerful motivating force to be involved in making and perceiving expressive music. It is a critical determining factor in continued involvement in music making and understanding for any individual within a culture. From the narratives presented above and from others that inform this book, we should be able to draw some essential elements or the qualities of the teacher, the teacher's relationship with the student, and the qualities of the approach and context that provide access to meaningful personal engagement with music making and understanding.

What is a music teacher?

What has become an interesting issue in this study has been the mere description of what a music teacher is and perhaps does. Furthermore, the variety of experiences and types of teaching that fall under the heading music teaching is quite broad. A student may have studio or private instrumental instruction on their instrument or voice or private one to one or small group instruction in composition, improvisation, music theory or aural perception. Students may participate in large or small ensembles, which are directed or conducted by a more experienced musician or teacher. More commonly in the UK and Australasia classroom music teaching may be the student's only music experiences.

With so many different kinds of specialist skills attached to music making and learning there are a range of activities and often several "teachers" who may have different values and opinions about what constitutes music learning. The students and teachers interviewed in this study were studio, instrumental directors and classroom teachers. Naturally, as the number of students to teacher ratio increased, different styles of relationship became apparent. However, there were qualities that all of the participants seemed to share and both teachers and students described the importance of what Buber (1969, 164-165) describes as an "inclusive" relationship, where the student is taken into a selection of the teachers life as a musician and human being. Each of the descriptions drawn from narratives presented earlier by both teachers and students described similar qualities.

In the case study, classroom creative activities revolved around the curriculum idea of domain projects, which are long-term or repeated projects involving issues central to the domain of music or art (Gardner 1993b). Edward's description of "the answering machine jingle" was such a project, where he and a small group of students had been given a "brief" to compose and perform a jingle for a staff member's answering machine. Edward's comment that it was "one of my first experiences of making music for a purpose" (Edward 1997, pers comm. with student, 9 July). echoes other participants who described the classroom as the place where this kind of focused creative music had its beginnings. The effects upon self-esteem of such activity are quite profound. Students felt a sense of ownership and pride in the product as Margaret, a 16 year old piano player and composer, described her experiences:

What is important about both the nature of the relationship between student and teacher and the construction of an environment which gives access to personal meaning and engagement in music learning is perhaps the acknowledgement that the teacher is often the single critical factor in whether a child participates in music making or not. In education, notions of student centred learning are well documented but while the student needs to be the centre of the learning activity it is the quality of the whole relationship between student and teacher in context, which is really at issue here. "Inclusion" involves firstly an acknowledgement by the teacher that particular institutional and pedagogical values and constraints influence the decisions they make about what and how music is encountered, while different community and school context and student needs and differences will need to be researched to construct a meaningful environment and experience. So it is most important that students share in the values of parents and teacher's in relation to their music learning experiences as it is a reflection of the values the student gains through their association and immersion in the environment constructed by these value systems.

The qualities of the teacher

In an interview with Linda who began playing violin at age four, she mentions that her experiences of the violin on television included the idea that "it sounded so good". However, the comment about how it sounded is not as strong in her retelling of the story as her comment about what she saw happening there: a vision of a violinist, "the standing ovation", this one "vision". As interviewer, my follow-up question tried to probe further about what was important here, "Was it the whole thing?" Her answer does not refer to the aesthetic experience of sound at all, but to social and personal meanings. Even more importantly, she describes how doing "something that you had a talent for" would place you in relationships with other people and the community. This kind of inspiration is common amongst young children and I was moved to ask why this instance is different. Why does Linda move beyond an image of herself playing to a reality? The answer may lie in her parent's response and the quality of interaction she had with her first teacher. What was outlined here might be seen as an exemplification of what Aronoff (1969) has pointed to as a music experience needing to build upon the natural aesthetic responses.

In conversation with me Linda described her teacher in the following way:

Linda: I had a very good violin teacher. She was incredibly patient but she was always pushing me to be better but without pushing me too hard. And I had lessons with her for six years. And she saw me all the way through... like she was so incredibly positive about everything that I did that it gave me the basis, do you know what I mean?

Steve: The foundation for your talent for music?

Linda: Yeah.

Steve: Was she a particular kind of teacher? Was she a Suzuki teacher or were you at Steiner school at the time?

Linda: Yeah she was a Suzuki teacher and I was at Steiner but she taught me privately, outside of the school thing. But she encouraged me to be in things at school like the school orchestra.

Steve: So, what was so special about her? How did she teach you? Did she make it fun? Was she firm and fun? So, what was the character that this teacher had that made you really enjoy it for those six years?

Linda: Well because it was so long ago that when someone says "Lana", I just get this picture of her. She was always smiling. She was never, "No, that's wrong" [affected voice]. She was never, she was always positive. No matter how badly I played; she could always pick out the positive things. And she was never in a bad mood, never had a bad day.

Steve: Did she play for you?

Linda: Yes and she accompanied me. Because that's what I wanted to be, I wanted to be the solo person. And so from five years old I was playing with an accompanist and being the one in charge, and going, look, this is how it goes. And she was always (pause) like, she'd point out the things that I did wrong, but she wouldn't dwell on them.

[When asked about her teaching style]

Linda: I just had a connection with her. I just thought...it was just awe, I just thought, every time she picked up a violin my mouth would just drop open. And it was having such a great respect for how good she was. And how good she thought I was.

Steve: She made you feel confident?

Linda: Yeah, that I could be as good as her or as good as the guy I saw on TV. And she'd always make a connection between what I was doing at the time and what someone else did in front of ten thousand people (Linda 1997, pers comm. with student, 5 March).

Building on natural aesthetic responses

Linda's story displays what appears to be an effective building upon her natural responses. In her recollection, the teacher appears to have understood her attraction to the violin and built upon it. She took the child into her own life as a musician and provided the child with experiences and "tastes" of realising her ambitions. She made Linda feel that she "could be as good as her or as good as the guy [she] saw on TV". Presented here is a strong emphasis upon Linda sharing in the teacher's love of music, experiencing through her as well as having an experience of her own. This kind of music interaction is intimate and intense.

Apparent in all the interviews, is an attraction to music as an image. There was a very strong association with the sound made by the teacher or parent playing. The student's felt they could make sounds like that and they were attracted by their own achievement toward those ends. There is a sense of personal satisfaction in music making, an attraction to making music collaboratively and a conscious awareness of how music making is received and responded to by family, friends and community.

Personal meaning and culture

Personal meaning in the way described above is both affirming of culture and a sense of belonging within a cultural framework and can lead to confident engagement with "other cultures through musical experience. While experience of "other" cultures is never "authentic" it can provide an opportunity for non-verbal and embodied understanding of how music might be expressed in different ways to the native culture. Concerning musical knowledge, this has great potential for expanding the expressive range of a musician and can provide other frameworks for aural perception. If the purpose of music education is to be more expressive as a musician and producer of music tomorrow than we are today, then experience with music from across cultures and periods of history offers this opportunity. There is an educational opportunity for growth and transformation. Nevertheless the quality of the interaction and it ethical considerations need to be addressed for this kind of experience to be more than an affirmation of the dominance of European culture. Singing notated versions of North American Indian songs or playing saxophone transcriptions of Japanese koto works does supply a source of differently organised melodies and language but the technology of common practice notation as a tool for communication and representation and the decontextualisation of the music raises ethical issues as well as filtering meaning.

For a student to experience music making from across cultures there is a need for contextualisation of the experience. The presenter needs to either have a clear connection with the culture through embodied experience or facilitate experiences through a representative of the community. A personal experience of otherness is an important experience for students to have as it challenges the student's worldview and has the potential to decolonise their ways of thinking about others. It is however, a risky and dangerous approach in the classroom because of the discomfort and challenges it may bring to a student's sense of self, identity and being. I believe it is important to have this experience often to arrive at openness to musical experience, which engenders confidence in participating in new music.

As I have experienced in tertiary curriculum classes, decolonising or culturally challenging experiences affect our perceptions of musical values and these in themselves have been identity forming. It has taken me several years to notice that the kinds of experiences I constructed for students to experience otherness through cross-cultural experience were threatening to the student's very sense of self and how they constructed themselves socially. Nevertheless, I found that teachers who had gone through this process were more able to be effective in multi-cultural music classrooms. In the music classroom, it is important to be aware of these issues when expecting students to enter into this kind of culturally challenging activity. However, just because they are challenging experiences we should not avoid them—these are valuable experiences which enable embodied understandings of "otherness" and the values and expressiveness of cultures other than our own. Personal meaning involves the concept of a dialogue with self, identity and self-formation and awareness of culture and our place in it locally, nationally and globally needs to be part of music learning.

Personal meaning is about our relationship with music. Through participating in music making from other cultures we also have the potential to gain non-verbal and embodied understandings about other cultures. These kinds of experiences when coupled with reflective questioning and discussions about how context and sound interact can provide wider cultural understanding not based on words so much as an understanding of how human society responds and experiences music. This enables an expansion of musical expressiveness and can provide common ground for both cultures to negotiate syncretic outcomes in ethical ways.

This understanding should also include the notion that in many cultures music does not exist in the way that we perceive it in Western societies. Music in many cultures is linked to cultural knowledge and shaped by its function as a communicator, container and cognitive amplifier for cultural knowledge. This is a quantum leap for our thoughts about what music is, what it can do and why we make it. While in Australia we may not escape our historical connections to our "mother" culture we can visit other cultures and return enriched by the experience if we are able to remain open to the experience and accept it on face value, sometimes without reflection and sometimes with This is perhaps a self-serving activity where Westerners appropriate musical experience because they have the power and privilege to be able to do so. However a more inquiring and humble approach to such activity which considers and engages with ethical ways of interacting between cultures which engender respect and understanding and call upon the spirit of creating productive relationships has potential to deliver positive outcomes. It is important to consider that the benefits of experiencing culture through music making is beneficial to personal growth as a more expressive being and potentially beneficial to our personal growth in human relationships and understanding of how societies value music and construct meaning from it. There are significant implications for gaining this kind of personal growth for teaching, experience/curriculum design and philosophy and this too will need to be discussed in more detail so that the experience of musical cultures is ethically grounded in an understanding of appropriation and misappropriation of cultural materials.

Personal meaning and technology

Technology has expanded what is possible for individual musicians to make alone. The twenty-first century musician is no longer a composer or a recording engineer or an instrumentalist alone they are a producer who draws upon technological tools to analyse, create and generate, edit, record, manipulate, polish and distribute. As an example of the new possibilities, working with generative algorithmic technology enables five year olds to move from their first introduction to software to producing a compact disc recording of relatively high quality within an hour. The immediacy of the intrinsic pleasure of a young child simply hitting a drum and gaining personal pleasure and meaning from the timbre and volume of the sound has become even more complex. The child can experience detailed musical forms and immediately hear the shift in musical intensity, timbre, rhythm and form. Personal meaning and music technology is about invigorating the opportunity for intrinsic engagement with music making. This requires examining the affordances of technology to establish their capacity to provide personal meaningful engagement.

In music technology there is a clear division between music education technology that is analytically focused and those that enable intuitive exploration and discovery of music. Drill and practice music technology is seldom personally meaningful in a musical sense because it is focused in developing skills. It could however be flow producing because of its ability to challenge the user. On the other hand much sequencing and notation software provides an opportunity for self contained creative activity that is engaging and meaningful.

What needs to be ascertained from the pedagogical perspective for this software and the student's relationship to it is the kind of musicianship and expressive foci of the software. In loop-based sample software like Acid musicianship and musical knowledge is focused on chunks of sound pre assembled so musical knowledge is not at the level of the note it moves to the phrase level. Issues about the synchronisation of time and tuning of layers become the focus of musical knowledge as well as the structure of the piece in time. The critiquing of quality of production of final product also becomes an important generic consideration that provides an opportunity to learn about critiquing professional recordings. Because music technology can be engaging and meaningful on a totally personal level it also has the potential to simply be a child-minding device. This can occur when teachers do not attend to gaining an understanding of how the technology affects musicianship and how the experience leads to musical knowledge.

In constructing environments which give access to personal meaning with music technology the teacher needs to consider these two things: first, the kind of musicianship which is being required by the technologically mediated experience; and second, whether the technology affords analytical understanding which enhances skills and intuitive understanding. Effective uses of technology are based on a competitive challenge or intuitive production, which engages in intrinsically, motivated ways. To combat the use of technology as a child-minding device, every lesson should include a reflective session where the music made is exhibited to peers. This reflection should also include a verbal reflection or in the case of analytically focused material a drawing out of the musical knowledge encountered and a discussion about how the skill can be applied to creative production and performance so that the student can see the relevance.

Conclusion

The goal of teaching and learning in this approach is enabling a student to become a self-actuated expressive music maker who is open to music experiences from a broad range of cultural and chronological contexts. Music education is in this sense is about becoming more personally able to be expressive with sound in time and space and gain from the understanding drawn critically reflecting on music experiences we perceive made by others. In turn, each experience of making and perceiving should lead to us becoming more expressive as musicians. The goals of achieving personal engagement and meaning from music making need to be oriented towards the student being able to express them selves personally in sound in a cultural context, be open to a variety of cultural experiences and able to critically evaluate and reflect on their expressive qualities. Most importantly, the idea of moving towards self actuating or autotelic music making activity provides the opportunity for a student to move beyond school and teachers to manage their own lifelong music learning and have access to private music making for relaxation or personal expression.

What we can do

Here is a list of ideas drawn from students and teachers for music educators about the qualities of meaningful and engaging music learning:

- *The teaching relationship is friendly and provides an encouraging and open psychological environment.*
- *The teacher enables learning intuitive ideas through demonstration and playing through the teacher's experience.*
- *The teacher enables learning analytical/technical knowledge by relating these skills and understandings clearly to the expressive qualities that control over these provides.*
- *Students "live through" the teacher's experience of music making.*
- *Teachers and students create an environment which enhances perception and openness to new musical experience.*
- *The teaching and learning relationship moves toward self-containment in expressive music making and understanding.*
- *The teacher enacts and encourages reflective practice.*
- *The teaching context enables private music making as a form of relaxation.*
- *The teaching context enables private music making as a form of private expression of self*
- *The teaching context enables a change in the way we think making our consciousness more complex.*
- *The teaching context initiates the learner into a personal discourse with music making as a lifelong pursuit.*

CHAPTER NINE

SOCIAL MEANING AND MEANINGFUL ENGAGEMENT WITH MUSIC

Introduction

Music making as a means of communion with others, as a wordless way of knowing others is a powerful idea for self-formation and promoting social inclusion. Music making in congregations, bands and ensembles provides a vehicle for social interaction based on a musical discourse and construction of self. It is about connections between people and how they respond collectively to context, shared values and how sound might be used to express something about a collective identity. It is about relational knowledge and ways of knowing that are not dependent upon words and language. Consistently both students and teachers interviewed reported that music making provided them with a broader social contact with musicians from a variety of social contexts. They met and worked creatively with people of different genders, ages and cultural backgrounds. The relationship they described with others in ensembles was warmly outlined as a "deeper way of knowing". Participants described the process as getting to know other members of the ensemble through the music, through their expression, the commonality of the musical experience and the challenge of the task rather than words alone. It provided a cultural framing for awkward adolescent social interaction and a way of knowing others in multi aged groups in community music activities that transcended age gender and ethnic barriers.

Relational knowledge and common ground

At the Caboolture Country music festival in 2006 I had a conversation with Indigenous artist, dancer and educator Myarah Dreise who described her understanding about concepts of relational knowledge, knowing who you are in relation to others, the relationship with context or country, her perspectives on country music, and why it was used as an expressive form by many Indigenous people. I came away from that encounter thinking there was much I could learn about the social and relational aspects of music making. Further on in this discussion I also realised that music has the potential to provide a common ground (Dreise 2006, pers comm., 6 May). Myarah described to me how she felt being away from her country and how she would sometimes go to a place where she was allowed to practice her dances and how this practice opened up a connection with her country. She further suggested that it would be a wonderful act to provide physical spaces where people who were dislocated could do this, that is, open up a connection with their culture through making art on common ground. Sometime later it dawned on me that music itself had the potential to be a metaphorical common ground where people could meet to open up connections both with their own country and to open a way between cultures.

In this construction of the role of music in community the act of making music together and sharing it in a group provides embodied physical synchrony through the rhythm and sonic communication through the shared experience of timbre. While culture provides a framing for the interpretation of these signs the common ground is at the intersection or the borderlands of the shared musical experience (Dillon 2006e, Nakata 2002). In contemporary indigenous culture we can see this demonstrated in Australian context when we see Aboriginal elders who value musical expression through country music because it speaks about country and the relationship between people and with land and the tension with youths need to express themselves with hip hop music. The values in hip hop are potentially negative but elders recognise the importance of youth's need to express their social condition in this way and encourage the music making as common ground.

Music as a social discourse

Essentially, what is being explored here is the idea of music as a social discourse. It is a discourse that widens both the teachers and students perceptions of cultural understanding. Teachers have to be prepared to move outside their own cultural comfort zones but not become an "other" or even an expert on other musical values. What a teacher must be able to do in this context is to manage the experiences so that it builds on the students intrinsic motivations and challenges them. As said in the previous chapter a teacher does have to like the music that the students do, just value their interest in it (Jessica 1998, pers comm. with teacher, 22 January). Furthermore, they need not be experts in cross-cultural music but can function as a cultural manager in interesting, ethical and creative ways.

Four themes emerged from my analysis of social meaning as described by participants. First, they talked about the way they associate with other musicians as a "deeper way of knowing". Second, they talked about the breadth of social contact. Third, they discussed the pleasure of collaborative making, and finally, they referred to a sense of unity gained from the encounters. All of these themes are social meaning outcomes, which may be independent of musical experience and transferable to social skills in general. Certainly, they are not new ideas and communities have always used music with these purposes in mind to unify, bond and teach collaborative skills. What is important here is that we are able to examine the context in which these are seen and the interactions that occur within a music education setting and discern how these might be transferable to a broader educational environment.

Music as a deeper way of knowing

Participants spoke lucidly about the deep and wordless relationship experienced in small and large ensembles. They highlighted the shared understanding of intuitive experience, the sharing of collaborative problem-solving experience and a strong feeling of understanding gained through the group experience. Dennis, an 18-year-old synthesizer player, describes why he thinks playing in an ensemble is a different relationship:

> I think it is rather than knowing about them from what they tell you about themselves and what you ask them. You actually get to know them, through the music, and how they play and so on, and what they like to play. It sort of shows you a different side to people as well (Dennis 1996, pers comm. with student, 28 October).

What Dennis is describing is that the activity reveals something else about the personality of others in the way that they work collaboratively and express themselves creatively to solve aesthetic problems. He expands on this further when describing improvisation in ensembles, seeing it as a "conversation" and synergy of collaborative making: "You get to see the different creative processes that everyone contributes and so on. I also think it makes a better track" (Dennis 1996, pers comm. with student, 28 October).

Students who were already friends highlight this idea even further, and this is amplified when the community responds to or affirms their work. Fiona, a 17-year-old singer, talks about this issue with her "all girl" rock band:

> Yes. I think it has actually made the friendship between us all closer, spend a lot more time with each other. I think it is a good way of getting out your anger, writing lyrics. It has made me a lot more confident in myself, having people tell me that they enjoy our music or they think I have a good voice, or whatever. I think it has helped the rest of the band in their self-confidence as well (Fiona 1997, pers comm. with student, 12 March).

The teacher's perspective

The teachers also describe this deeper way of knowing from both personal experience and observation. Here Jane, the conductor of the wind ensemble, describes her understanding:

> I think it's a deeper way [of knowing]. You can get a certain experience from playing by yourself, but its nothing to what you get in a small ensemble an enormous experience, but in a sixty-piece ensemble whose souls are intertwined, making a sound, my God that's a pretty big thing. Something out of this world, when you feel like you're going to burst into tears. It's that feeling, and you can't create that you can only create the situation that makes it possible (Jane 1997, pers comm. with teacher, 13 February).

She is describing a transcendent experience brought about by collaborative effort that may in itself be an example of flow. Interestingly, she is dividing the kinds of experience by the size of the group. For her, the large ensemble experience was powerful and meaningful, but rare. What was most important in her statement was the acknowledgement that the experience could be facilitated. This aspect of facilitating meaning will be examined in more detail through a focus upon the notion of "teacher as builder".

Jessica, a singer and teacher of drama and English, highlights the power of collaborative experiences as memorable and significant:

> I don't think anything comes near to it, I really don't. Nothing else in your school life even academic achievement. But I think people will say that some of the greatest pleasure of their school days, where their best friendships were made, were the sorts of group activities of productions and performances, music and so on (Jessica 1998, pers comm. with teacher, 22 January).

What is most evident in these transcripts is not only the observation of students gaining a socially significant experience from collaborative making, but the teachers' identification of that experience and understanding of it. Talk of facilitating the experience was most clearly put by Jane while also articulating the pleasure of her own encounters. The sharing of experience, initiation into the discourse and involving the child in the teacher's life as a music maker are all aspects of theory, which find expression in these interview extracts.

Experiencing a broader social contact

Students and teachers also remarked upon the exposure to broader social contact experience from music making activities:

> You get to know people who aren't particularly in your friendship group but who you come to appreciate for themselves, for who they are and I think it's just a general understanding of people in general that improves (Jessica 1998, pers comm. with teacher, 22 January).

The idea that the groups are vertical (a variety of ages) is also an important issue. Ensembles are often multi-aged, contain both genders and may contain very different kinds of people to those the students normally form associations with. It broadens their associations and social contacts and provides a structured and focussed social experience. The school psychologist expands on this from her observations:

> The biggest things I see are the social connections that it provides, and there is a sense of no hierarchy and they are accepted for who they are and the instrument that they play. Being part of the band has been a really safe connection for them. I can actually think of quite a number of students who have taken friendships away from being part of a band as it has been a really safe vehicle for them to exercise those skills and I could never have taught them that (Barbara 1997, pers comm. with teacher, 4 June).

Her description proposes the "safety" of the environment and the sense of non-competitive collaboration that such ensembles provide. David, a mathematics and pastoral care teacher, adds to the idea of social breadth and a deeper way of knowing with this brief statement, "I think it's everybody working for a common good. They also get to know other sides of students they wouldn't normally see" (David 1998, pers comm. with teacher, 22 January). Teachers and students saw these as being particularly desirable outcomes. They spoke of it serving as a "therapeutic" device for shy and socially awkward students. They described it as a way of developing social skills in a "safe" and non-competitive environment for many students.

Gaining of skills as a collaborative problem-solver and team worker

Interview participants suggested that their skills of team working and group problem solving had been greatly enhanced by their experiences with ensembles and that this had taught them the value of, and enhanced the quality of, collaborative making. This was most apparent in observations of student-directed ensembles and creative classroom activity. In both of these experiences the responsibility for creative making becomes distributed amongst the group there is little room for superfluous parts and the intrinsic nature of the task becomes the directing force. While this observation and comment for participants had strong support, what were most important in the success of these activities were the two ideas mentioned by the school psychologist: safe environment and the sense of no hierarchy, with the task providing the challenge and success being self-evaluated.

Building of a sense of unity

It was a combination of all of the abovementioned interactions that led me to examine the idea of music as a discourse and its cultural meaning. It is appropriate here to examine the idea of social meaning as a building block for culture and this is most apparent in community rituals and ceremonies where music plays a significant part. Descriptions of participation in ceremonial events and community performance were perceived by interviewees as contributing to a sense of well-being and belonging and a consciousness that the group experience was unified by the common goal of music making. This aspect was described most eloquently by the case study Mark the school minister/counsellor, in his description of ceremonial events:

> It's generated a feeling of not only acceptance but of owning…I think what it said to me was that the cultural symbols that we use in a number of places, if music is at the centre of it, it resonates more than just the visual. We are a culture that listens to music, but to hear our own music is almost breathtaking (Mark 1996, pers comm. with teacher, 14 October).

In the data examined that was concerned with music making and the school community, there was a tremendous sense of pride in music that has been made for the occasion by students and teachers within the community. Jessica and David comment further on the effects of functional music making from a community perspective:

> Like going to those church services, even if you are not a believer, is that sense of identity and group oneness is very enlightening (Jessica 1998, pers comm. with teacher, 22 January).

> It gave the music students at the time a sense of importance (David 1998, pers comm. with teacher, 22 January).

What is being outlined here is the idea that music has been used for centuries to make ideology accessible and as a means of social control (Metcalf in Abbs 1990) as well as building a sense of unity. In this case study, the difference lies in the conscious application of this idea as part of extra-curricular activity rather than one that is institutionally imposed by the community.

Students interviewed saw pragmatic music making as being of benefit to their personal and social experiences and valued the challenge of making music for a purpose. The purpose often led them to experience style and form that they had not encountered in the past, which added to the breadth of their musical understanding. Most importantly, they were aware of the communication and resonance of music on these occasions. They described a sense of pride in their involvement and felt the power of music to "move people", which enhanced their understanding of music beyond their own personal and social experiences.

Discussion of this idea is linked more clearly with the "reciprocal meaning" associated with what I have termed cultural meaning. In the analysis of this idea, I was most conscious of the significance gained, being located in the individual and community. With this in mind, the evidence for this idea of unity, or what Csikszentmihalyi (1994) terms "reflective individualism" is about a sense of self within community and a community within self. It is about the community's valuing of individuals as a part of how their "civilisation" is perceived by other communities or generations. This concept will be discussed in the next chapter. What I will draw out now is the qualities of teacher practice, classroom and approach and how to apply these in practice with a community or school.

Teacher qualities, organisational principles and processes

Teachers in this context and subsequent interviewees displayed surprisingly similar characteristics. Regardless of their focus—be it classroom, community, ensemble direction or studio teaching—teachers were aware of the importance of the ensemble in connecting students with their musical expressiveness and with each other. The wind ensemble director whose student section leaders imitated her teaching style knew the value of small group ensemble experience as a way of communicating and managing large children of multiple aged and abilities alongside the motivational aspects peer interaction. Indeed students who learned piano expressed the most disconnection from their instrument reported the isolation from ensemble playing or social interaction as a significant detriment to their continued engagement. The teachers also participated in ensembles themselves—not to boost the quality alone but to model the approach and behaviour of musicians. Indeed Music teachers in the case study school rehearsed their own ensembles at the school and practiced using school studios so that students were able to be around musical behaviour.

Applying these in a classroom or studio

The principle observed here was that in every lesson students had some kind of ensemble experience. In the studio it might be a duet with the teacher or small group ensemble, in the classroom a presentation of composition or performance, in the ensemble rehearsal a mock performance. The qualities of teaching required were universally those of teacher modelling and participation and the structuring of some kind of ensemble presentation in every lesson. To gain meaning from music experience social interaction is essential. Music is a means of expressive communication in a symbolic form and postponing performance or ensemble participation to an annual concert is like asking a child to learn language by speaking only to itself for a year.

Social meaning and culture

Music is inherently social. It provides a basis and medium for social interaction. Music can be a means of social control. After all our police and armed forces seldom practice dance and visual arts but military and police bands abound in western culture. National anthems signify and present our national origins in instantly recognisable forms. Music in schools and across western European cultures has been used as a way of controlling children and adults alike. We march to rhythms in synchrony we sing in choirs with one voice, we frighten our enemies with the power of our unity with marching bands. Anthropologists suggest that human society began to sing collectively before it learned to speak in language. I recall tales of my mother singing in air raid shelters in World War Two. Perhaps as profound an experience of connection with others in the dark as can be had by humanity in fear for their lives.

It is this wordless connection that was spoken about by participants in this research, which is most poignant for us in relation to understanding the social implications of music making and its meaning. Music educators need to move beyond the fallacious idea of music as a universal language. It is neither a language presenting precise information nor is it universal. Indeed the word music is not common to many cultures any more than the western delineation of arts practice from cultural practice and ceremony.

What is possible with music is the opportunity to experience embodied understandings of music making in a social communication that is not based on language but could involve using language from the culture as part of the experience. This kind of syncretic experience where we encounter new musical materials through a collaborative experience of new music has potential to be educationally beneficial. It has the potential also to contribute to the expansion of musical knowledge and expressiveness. Once more however I must caution that this kind of experience needs to be introduced in a culturally ethical way. This means that the experience needs to have an understanding of the context and relationships, which shape the music and must provide an opportunity for the philosophy of the culture to be presented. The common ground approach described in the next chapter provides a syncretic approach to this kind of study that acknowledges ethical considerations.

In Indigenous Australian cultures for example song is relational as well as contextual. Songs, the embedded knowledge and their understanding are dependent upon gender, age, family origin and country (see for example Barwick 2005, Bradley and Mackinlay 2000, Ellis 1985, Marett 2006). Any form of de-contextualisation removes all meaning from these songs. Indigenous songs are even more social that Westerners experience. They can tell us who we are, who we are in relation to others, where we are from and the history of that place. A song will reveal new knowledge as the member of the culture grows and matures. While we cannot experience this kind of relational understanding of song and cultural knowledge, we can have experiences where this kind of understanding is revealed to us in a simulated way. For example, a simulation involving composing and performing song lines which tell us about relationships to each other and place might reveal an understanding about the complexity of this aspect of social meaning and music making. The power of music is in its ability to connect people socially. This power is intrinsically motivated and as such, we need to activate that intrinsicality through design, which harnesses this power in ethical and engaging ways.

Social meaning and music technology

Music technology is for the most part a socially isolating experience. The same immersive engagement that drives personal meaning for students' relationship with computers also makes it socially quite barren. Certainly when technology is used as an instrument, it has the same collaborative value as any instrument but with computers the usage is often a solo activity which does not afford social interaction. Collaborative production perhaps affords potential for social meaning. This is where several students gather around a computer and the computer mediates collaborative creative production. In the professional electronic music world laptop performances are becoming common, as too is live coding where musicians write computer code in real time to affect musical change in a collaborative way (Brown 2006, Brown and Dillon 2007). All of these occurrences of collaborative production and performance challenge our traditional notions of what musicianship is. We often doubt the authenticity of the music or the performance because our traditional understanding of musicianship does not allow us to value what a DJ does in live performance for example.

There are indicators about this idea in the data presented here about social meaning. A student who discussed how isolated from social experience he felt in piano lessons hints at the idea that a wonderful technology like the piano which can provide self contained polyphonic, polyrhythmic and dynamic performance in an expressive way and act as a way of creating and auditioning composition suggests to us that technology and isolation are not strangers.

The affordance of social meaning with technology is linked to an understanding of how the technology might be used in a way that allows social interaction in some of the ways described above that allow genuine musical communication. As educators, we need to evaluate what the capacity is for the technology to provide social experience and then create pedagogical frameworks, which encourage social interaction.

In networked improvisation (Brown 2006, Brown and Dillon 2007) which involves a virtual experience with generative music making this kind of interaction is built into the design of the software so students can play and perform live and in real time. This however still raises the issue of the authenticity of the experience. To facilitate a socially meaningful experience with music technology we need to do two things. First, we need to consider the kind of musicianship and expressive qualities that the technology enables. Knowing this enables the establishment of a focus for musical knowledge. Second, we need to construct environments that compensate for the lack of social interaction of the technology in our experience design. Music is ephemeral but audio technology enables us to recall it, revisit it and even discuss it with the sound present in the conversation. The power of technology to remove the ephemerality and abstraction from music is inherent in this capacity. To evoke the power of social meaning from our relationship with technology we need to construct social environments and take advantage of the potential of technology to provide social experience in meaningful and engaging ways.

 *What we can do*

- *Recognise that music is an intrinsically motivated activity (Abbs 1990, Aronoff 1969, Dewey 1989).*

- *Ensure that every music activity involve some kind of discussion or reflective process even if only briefly. It needs to be a habit of mind to discuss music with music present in the process so that it is no longer abstract but real and present.*

- *Ensure that music lessons have activities that involve performing or a presentation aspect and listening/audition/analytic response.*

- *With Western art music revisit the concepts of musical elements in increasingly deeper and more complex ways that build on understanding of music.*

- *In a non-Western framework adopt a more flexible and culturally inclusive aural analysis framework.*

CHAPTER TEN

MEANINGFUL ENGAGEMENT WITH MUSIC AND CULTURAL MEANING

Introduction

Cultural meaning is the most complex area of meaning explored in this research and yet it is the most apparent form in communities. It is a particularly powerful meaning. It is influential in the sense of self, the sense of self and others and reflects personal and community character. It is about expressiveness and the reciprocal interaction that both the artistic product and the maker have with the community. On the individual level, it is about the effect of music making upon self-esteem, and the sense of well-being. It is here that we begin to see that the personal and social meanings change us or educate our character, and further that this "changed" or continuously evolving being projects those experiences on the community they inhabit. The music teacher, Peter, spoke freely of the effects of music on his self-image and the affect of achievement upon the making of self. Edward outlined the reciprocity of that self and the affirmation of community. Linda warmly described her sense of belonging through music making. In early music learning, it is localised. It begins with the response of family then grows to teacher, school and wider community. The experience of learning music was described as an immersion in the values of parents and community and these values have cultural implications as keyboard teacher James noted his parents viewed music as "worth something".

A projection of self

In the non-musically experienced participants, music taste was observed as a projection of self, which contributed to defining self. In particular, membership of youth subculture was partially defined by music. Membership of youth subculture through this association with music is a factor that contributed to students' sense of belonging to a group. For the musically experienced access to this form of meaning brought with it a significant sense of affirmation of self and artistic product. Within the cultural group, this existed as a group acknowledgment of the presence of creative persons and of expressive product.

Both of these are valued by the culture and contribute to its definition. This in turn projects a reflection of a collective character. It says something about the culture. Contribution of innovation and achievement in the domain was also highly valued by participants. There is a duality here of pragmatic contribution to the culture which amplifies the feelings of usefulness in the community and the contribution to art or aesthetic development that provides challenge and pride in one's own work.

There is a strong feeling in the analysis of this area of meaning of the sense of unity associated with music making in the social sense and the personal association with music as a discourse. Even in a negative response from a community, togetherness and challenge emerge. An "all-girl band" observed in the case study experienced defiance at the lack of acceptance in their early career. They experienced sexist and often-hostile reactions from adolescent males who saw the brand of grunge rock these girls performed as male domain. The girls spoke of this making them closer as a band; eventually leading to elation at their acceptance and the community pride they gained through the challenge of seeking to express themselves within the community (Fiona 1997, pers comm. with student, 12 March).

Interestingly it was some three years after they had gained the acceptance of the adolescent males at the school when they won a district battle of the bands and experienced similar hostility from males from other districts. This in itself apart from commenting on the gender and identification qualities of youth music also suggests that a community can evolve its' character to over come its prejudices and present a healthier more tolerant cultural image. It says too that music can reveal cultural values and that these values can evolve and play a part in giving a community a means to its own cultural growth through embracing creative diversity. It can also reveal the negative aspects of a community and reinforce its intolerance.

The power of music in cultural identity

The school minister Mark (1996, pers comm. with teacher, 14 October), talked lucidly in interviews of "not only acceptance but ownership" gained through music making in the community and a sense of identity and pride in self and community. He saw this area of meaning as a collective expression of the community. Making music is about selecting and organising sound to express something that is us. In much the same way, communities select musicians and music that express and represent a collective culture. The English and drama teacher Jessica, described the effects upon individuals most eloquently as "an affirmation that what the students love to do is worth doing and which gave them pleasure and became a life skill" (Jessica 1998, pers comm. with teacher, 22 January), She further described the affects upon community as "a genuine reflection of what is going on in the place and an extension of the many things that are going on". These thoughts describe the projected image of a community through its artistic expression. Robert, a guitar teacher expanded upon this idea even further, saying that it expressed a positive image of the school community and flowed back into the school. He called it "a positive spiral" (Robert 1997, pers comm. with teacher, 20 February).

These notions combine to describe a meaning that is a complex but necessary part of culture. Access to it forms a most powerful determinant of student involvement with music making. So much so, that after a profoundly poor or bad experience with music making in schools, students who experience one powerful experience with this cultural meaning may remember it. Too many music programs and teachers survive on one good concert a year; whilst all that leads up to it is meaningless and boring to the child. Cultural meaning, and indeed each of the meanings described can be pleasurable in themselves and they can be intrinsically motivated, but they are most influential upon total musical development and learning if they are progressive and increasingly challenging and interlinked. The argument raised by this research is that the process of music education must provide access to all forms of music meaning.

Case study

Rather than isolate cultural meaning at this point I will draw upon the reconstruction of a single student's experience of meaning making through music education. While this represents a single case study, it should be remembered that the questions of meaning and access to meaningful music education were examined empirically in a participant-observation case study and examined in conjunction with an ongoing body of theorising about music education. As narratives about "musical lives" is central to the theories raised in this research I have constructed a brief story of one student's experiences with music making in that context to illustrate the idea of music, meaning and transformative experience for this child.

Dennis' story

Dennis was a Year 10 secondary student, he had learnt violin for about a week when he was 8 years old at another school but was so turned-off by the sound he made that he gave up quickly. At about age 12 he inherited his grandparent's piano that was put in his room. His parents enrolled him in piano lessons at his school but he also found this uninspiring whilst at home his dual interests developed, enjoying computer programming and improvising on his piano. His parents continued to encourage his interest and enrolled him in private "five C's piano methods" lessons (a method based upon a kind of kinaesthetic programming principle). From this method he began to use his fingers much more creatively in his improvisation and also turned his new found skills to MIDI sequencing on his Commodore Omega computer, even exchanging MOD files (Modifying files and exchanging them with each participant developing the work collaboratively) with other enthusiasts in other states by email. He struggled to remain interested in any other aspect of school life and his parents brought him to my school's speech night and he was immediately impressed by several of the school ensembles—an electro acoustic ensemble, a punk band and a soul band.

His parents transferred him to the school and once at the school as a Year 8 student, he enjoyed the classroom music focus on domain projects in rhythm and blues performance and composing. His classroom teacher noticed his love of composition, improvisation and computing and directed him to have private synthesiser lessons involving sound programming, sequencing and composing techniques. He also joined the electro acoustic ensemble and the soul band where he had the opportunity to not only develop his skills but also apply what he had learnt in his private lessons.

I should note here that the policy for school ensembles suggested that they do something for their school, something for their peers and something that pushed the boundaries of their art form. This made for a vibrant and energetic musical community where students composed or arranged music for school ceremonies and church services, ran outdoor rock concerts for charity or performed to promote the school at the city musicians club, at a school fair or a shopping mall or on an interstate or overseas tour.

Dennis could perhaps be described as the shy "computer nerd" adolescent. His social skills had been hampered by his low self-esteem and shyness. In this environment, he grew in confidence. This was promoted by the personal sense of achievement and intrinsic motivation. Classroom and extra curricular ensembles enhanced his social skills, whilst his performances at informal and formal concerts changed the way that the wider school culture viewed him. His nickname was the "Wildman" because when he got excited during an improvised synthesiser solo he bit his bottom lip. Nicknames and understatement based upon opposites seem to be an Australian tradition.

Amongst his classroom musical experiences, he explored African, West Indian, South American, jazz and rock styles. In Year 10 he participated in an elective that explored 20th Century Art Music styles such as serialism, minimalism, expressionism, nationalism, electronic and Musique Concrete not from a historical perspective but through engaging with making music using these compositional processes and examining how composers have used them effectively. The aim of the project was simply to compose an eight-minute piece utilising any of the selected "isms" or combinations. The focus here is on keeping the listener engaged over a greater time than a 3-4 minute pop song and developing creative processes to do this.

Dennis' final eight-minute piece was an electronic work that used samples taken exclusively from another Year 10 boy's body noises (you can imagine what some of them were). This work was one of the funniest and well-constructed pieces I have heard and the entire class was in stiches during its presentation. In terms of its expressive production values it showed incredible skill and control in capturing and synthesising samples as well as interesting structural development a very funky rhythmic groove, a good understanding of harmony, voice leading and arrangement. Dennis continued to involve himself in ensembles throughout his life at the school and now works in communication design and sound and has released several commercial recordings with the punk band he joined shortly before leaving school.

Over the past three chapters I have described three areas of meaning: personal (communication between self and music making), social (a broader social contact with musicians from a variety of social contexts), and cultural (expressiveness and the reciprocal interaction that both the artistic product and the maker have with the community). If we apply these to Dennis' story, we can see that:

1. His personal relationship with music was provided by his parents valuing of music in his life and the recognition of his engagement with it. This was further encouraged and nurtured by his classroom teacher, studio teacher and ensemble directors who recognised his engagement and encouraged and facilitated further experiences.
2. The ensemble and collaborative project work in classroom and co-curricular ensembles gave him opportunity for social meaning through his interaction with peers, older students, girls and staff.
3. Both in classroom performance and in the many performances for school functions, tours and public appearances Dennis had access to safe and encouraging performance opportunities that were a genuine contribution and expression of the community, cultural and youth sub-cultural values.

What does Dennis' story mean in a school? It means that we need to be able to provide:

- a psychological environment that values and encourages expressive music making of all kinds;
- access to instrumental experience;
- access to ensemble experiences; and,
- access to meaningful sharing of musical expressiveness for the school and wider community.

For the school policy that nurtures and facilitates access to meaningful musical experiences, it means the need to develop a school philosophy that integrates classroom, instrumental and ensemble programs with school ceremonies and events so that curriculum provides the opportunity to make music for a school community and its staff and students. The idea is to emulate a village where all participants can express themselves artistically across the arts learning areas.

In the case study school it was this kind of policy that led to the kind of diverse and integrated performances and roles of music as: an electro acoustic ensemble composing and performing a "stations of the cross" multi-media work at an Easter service, techno pieces at a lunchtime dance party, and performances of works by Reich, Jarre and Japanese electronica as part of a chamber music series. Further, we cannot underestimate the role of the teacher in this process—it is both the teacher's values and the context built by the teacher that gives the child access to personal, social and cultural meaning.

What are the characteristics of the teacher?

Swanwick suggests that analytical musical knowledge can be "taught" but intuitive knowledge can only be "caught" from someone who knows (Swanwick 1994). Dennis was "taught" and acquired skill through the desire to be more expressive. He also encountered experiences and policies that led to him "catch" musical knowledge too and this is involves "the teacher as builder of music learning contexts" and requires a teacher to create an environment where the student will encounter the learning that you prepare for them. The characteristics of the teacher most valued by interviewees were made up of the following actions and character—the teacher must be a maker, animateur, and a builder of psychological environment and creator of atmosphere and attitude; they must be personally encouraging, open and have an interest in what the children bring to the relationship and value their interest in music; and most importantly they must facilitate experience through imaginative curriculum.

What is the teacher's role?

From analysis of Dennis' experience, we can see that his teacher provided a safe and encouraging environment where music making and reflection was valued. The evidence of reflective practice was most apparent in interviews with students whose articulate descriptions of musical experiences far outstripped any that I have even seen in tertiary studies. The encouragement to talk about, talk to, describe, and analyse musical expression with music present showed a maturity of understanding that enabled then to clearly to be part of a musical discourse.

Dennis' teacher also acted as a gateway to deeper musical experiences in the school and wider community. His membership of school ensembles, his performances and commissioned compositions were actuated by his teacher's interaction with the community on his behalf. The effects of this on his personal and social development were profound.

Dennis' teacher and the philosophy of the school to promote musical styles equally as "music is music" enabled participation in a broad variety of active music making experiences across times and places that lead to an understanding of the diversity of how human societies interact with sound in expressive ways.

Dennis' understanding of how music is constructed, refined and produced in the real world provided him with critical thinking tools to be able to be critical of music wherever he found it as aesthetic product and as a commodity. This approach gives students the generic skills of reflecting on and making sense of music in their lives.

Applying these in a classroom or studio

Cultural meaning is linked to the nature of music making. It is fundamental to a sound community. It speaks of who we are—our relationship to others and our relationship to our community. In a classroom access to cultural meaning means sharing the beginnings of compositions or performance pieces so that collectively students can reflect on its expressive qualities and analyse its potential for increased expressiveness. Or it may simply involve the class singing or playing together and recording the outcome and discussing it. In the instrumental studio, it is Suzuki who recognised the significance of social and cultural meaning to learning development. Small group ensembles and family concerts and private mini performances in safe but critical environments nurtures cultural meaning building a sense of musical community and initiating students into a shared discourse. The studio performance can be as simple as a teacher student mini concert or a gathering of students to play for each other.

Ensemble directors/conductors exploit the value of concerts extremely well but often not as part of a discourse but as advocacy alone. Like the ensemble director described previously who had students imitate her teaching and learning behaviour. She had created a discourse where music was played and reflected upon. "Show and tell" amongst sections and between them abounded in her teaching approach. Peers taught younger students. Older students were part of the discourse created by and through the conductor/director.

I have seen music lessons in Europe where music history is taught and even in this non-participatory environment, experiencing all musical meanings is possible. The fundamental principle is that music is made or played or listened to and people are connected through a shared discourse where the music itself provides a common ground for discussion. Music is present in the discourse of making and perceiving music. We are able to share in the cultural values embedded in it, deconstruct the expressive processes and engage with personal, social and cultural meanings. In this way even at the most basic level of listening we can share meaning and gain an understanding of cultural constructions of sound and the values embedded in it and perceive these with some understanding of context.

With my own experience of Indigenous Australian music, while I can never experience native meaning, I can understand the role of music as a container and communicator of important contextual, cultural and relational knowledge. In country music I can understand how music speaks about country and expresses that connection. I can experience something of how music is used in this way in a way that is reverent to the community of origin. Understanding the cultural meaning of music allows us to understand how societies and sub cultures project themselves and their character. It allows us to perceive the importance of humanly organised sound to each community and understand how music both speaks of the community and transforms the individuals within it.

Cultural meaning and "other" cultures

Cultural values frame how we perceive "otherness". Within our cultural identity we have values which condition how we interact with other cultures. Colonial constructions of intercultural relationships impose particular ways of interpreting meaning on others. In Australia, which is a former British colony, there have been more than two hundred years of these colonial values imposed upon what is now a culturally diverse society. Waves of immigration and refugees have questioned the appropriateness of our European values or interpreted distorted versions of them into our culture. Even more dramatic in its effect on culture is context. Colours that work aesthetically under European light look garish and odd in the Australian sun. Similarly, sounds that signify cultural identity in Europe concert halls are lost in the vast spaces of our country. So colonial are we that the natural aesthetic resources of our country are too often ignored. The Indigenous peoples of Australia use music to store, communicate and process important cultural knowledge and this is largely ignored or misunderstood by mainstream Australia, which problematises the relationship between cultural meaning and context. It delineates understanding of music that serves a function for knowledge transfer from music, which simply expresses something about culture. Indeed the nature of aesthetic constructions of music seems to forbid its functionality even though much classic music was originally functional.

When home is exotic

I would like to recount here a brief story about my own realisations of my relationship to native Australian culture and context. A little while ago I sat down to a meal at a fashionable restaurant in my hometown of Brisbane, which specialised in serving indigenous and native Australian cuisine. Despite my familiarity with a broad multi cultural range of tastes and flavours from around the globe it was the most exotic meal I had ever tasted and yet all the food: meat, fish, vegetables and fruit were indigenous to Australia. I have found that this experience is a fitting metaphor for our taste cultures in regard to music and culture. The food at the restaurant might be called syncretic. They used Indigenous resources and a French chef prepared these ingredients. Certainly, the ingredients were appropriated and reconceived, filtered though a European construction of what food should look and taste like but the power of the experience for me was that the flavour of my own home was strange and unfamiliar to me. The influence of context and the resources are so powerful that even when appropriated and reconceived the flavour pervades the production of cultural artefacts and our response to them.

It is important here to understand the difference between music that is syncretic or responds to changes in culture and environment; traditional constructions of music where it acts as a repository for humanities important information; and, as a means of communication of these ideas to successive generations. Story, design gesture in dance and song are seldom separated from the ceremony or event that these ideas are part of. Music is seldom separate from the context or the ritual.

A vignette

In respect to the understanding of cultural meaning in music making these concepts need to be clearly understood. When we make music, which is syncretic we are in fact trying to experience the flavours of another culture within a framing that we understand. Syncretic music offers us a common ground or intersection of cultures. For music education simulations of syncretic flavours through hybrid styles and experiential activity can present opportunities for understanding. For example, in the case study school Year 9 students learned South African songs though an aural/oral transmission process alongside some dance movements in an outdoor location. After each class, they reflected on their singing and movements and where their bodies were positioned against the pulse. Once the songs and movements became well known to the students, the class was moved to several different locations with either familiar or unfamiliar instruments or sound sources.

The students were given a task to reinterpret the materials they had learnt in the song and movement in relation to the location and a new set of musical values each time. The teacher had carefully created a simple location, selected resources, and constructed a value set for each location based on what might have been available in various African influenced music. The result was not an authentic understanding of South African vocal music but an understanding of how embodied ideas of music are affected by context, resources and what a cultural considers to be expressive of its condition.

All reinterpretations of other cultures music are appropriation. Most are syncretic. What needs to be determined is how can this kind of understanding be done in ethical ways? Certainly human society has traded musical ideas and instruments for centuries and this has enriched our understanding of each other. What is unethical is appropriation of cultural knowledge with out permission or deconstextualisng it so that it is devalued as knowledge. Embracing diversity enhances cultural meaning and this potentially increases our expressive range in music education. Cultural meaning is also valuable when it acts as a conduit for an understanding of culture and how human society organises sound for its own purposes. We need to seek common ground, intersection points that engage with the tensions between cultures and the ethical issues of syncretic music. We can engage with the flavours of traditional music if we do so within a simulated context and provide the opportunity for reflection about the relationship between sound, society, context and knowledge systems. Engaging with culture is inherently political, dangerous and ambiguous but ignoring it or not engaging with it for fear of offence denies us the opportunity for growth and understanding.

A way forward

To engage with music and culture we first need to identify our own constructions and experiences of musical cultures identifying how it relates to context. Many of us come from a Western and Christian framework and philosophy; I do not seek to judge any position in cultural values nor favour one interpretation but seek to present an opportunity for multiple worldviews, which I hope, will strengthen an understanding of humanity as a whole. As the Torres Strait Islander scholar Martin Nakata says, our approach needs to allow us to engage with the tensions at the interfaces or intersections between culture (Nakata 2002:1). It is here that we will find understanding and identify misunderstandings, here that we hope to know the syncretic qualities of music which grow and change with contact with new expressive sounds and also identify the importance and meaning of why some music is traditional and needs to remain so and remain outside our world of understanding and for us to respect that sacred and unknowable quality. Some music can be known by invitation into the discourse and some and others only by right of ethnicity, birth, age, gender or location.

One thing I have learnt in this process is that understanding cannot be reached through a single lens or worldview nor can it be reached by not engaging with the tension at the interface between cultures. If there is no tension, there is no challenge to our worldview and a single worldview either colonises or subjugates "others" when this happens. We only hear in mono and see through one distorted world. What is needed is to open up a dialogue between and identification of your own construction of what music and culture is and those of others. If we enter into a meaningful relationship with music in personal, social and cultural ways this will lead to a transformation of self such that we grow in our understanding of self, others and cultures through musical rather than verbal/textual and intellectual experience.

Cultural meaning and technology

Human culture is inherently technological. Humans are tool users and tool creators. Technology mediates our relationships with most creative activities. Cultural meaning is about identifying how culture has affected our musical values and structured our production. We need to understand how technologies afford unique expressiveness that signifies cultural identity. Brown's approach to dividing the use of technology into tool, medium and instrument is useful in understanding the relationship the creative process has with technology and the role both the technology and the musician has in the creative process (Brown 2006). The relationship that musical tools have to cultural meaning is that they extend the capacity for expressiveness or expressive understanding. Most music technology is inherently isolating rather than socially or culturally unifying.

Music education software as described earlier in the discussion of technology and social meaning is rarely able to encourage social connection or project cultural identity. Music technology functions more effectively for cultural meaning when it is a medium for storing and communicating musical knowledge and sonic product. A technology such as Common Practice Notation not only serves as a medium for storing musical knowledge but also frames how music is constructed and perceived. So too does contemporary digital recording. Technology as a container for cultural artefacts contributes vigorously to cultural meaning.

The computer as a medium can dilute cultural values through the appropriation of sound and its re-contextualisation. Technology does facilitate social and cultural interaction when it is used in as an instrument in an ensemble performance for example. The kind of reconstitution of what musicianship is and the location of performance is necessary when viewing cultural meaning and technology s instrument. The solution to this conceptual problem of authenticity of musicianship is simple. In the real world DJ's use turntables as instruments (in fact more turntables were sold in 2005 than flutes). Computer musicians use laptops in performance, so too do electro acoustic performers and chamber group as well as popular music makers.

The key to facilitating cultural meaning with technology is to examine its capacity for facilitating cultural interaction and building community. This is different to social meaning, which is more about the relationship between musicians in that it involves a relationship with the wider community of values and practices. We need to identify the technologies affordances as a tool, medium and instrument and how these can be interpreted so that the technology and student relationship is enhanced. The creation of a community of music makers is promoted by networked technology such as MSN, Chat and more recently sites like Myspace and YouTube. They provide both the capacity to store unique cultural and sub cultural values but to project and distribute these values widely. Networked Improvisation as discussed earlier also provides a virtual sonic context where communities can be built based upon collaborative music making across a network, Networked software works well because they are engaging and dynamic. This intrinsicality is predicated on the capacity of the technology to reliably facilitate musical relationships and build the capacity of communities.

What we can do

- *Explore and reflect upon your own cultural relationship with music.*

- *Consider what aspects of cultural music making that give you "flow".*

- *What is your current understanding of the relationship between music and culture?*

- *How can teachers and coaches create environments which provide understanding about cultures and music? Discuss what this means in the instrumental studio, the classroom and the ensemble context.*

- *What factors determine success in cultural learning?*

- *Create an approach for music teacher in each context (classroom, ensemble, instrumental studio) can include cultural experience within every lesson.*

CHAPTER ELEVEN
THE SCHOOL AS VILLAGE

Introduction

As a music teacher in a school that shares a religious ideology, music teachers are required to be musical directors of church ceremony. Every school also has their own rituals: speech nights, graduations, celebrations of times and events that are significant in the school community. Many music teachers perceive this as a little unfair after all the mathematics teacher did not have to spend hours preparing music for a liturgy arranging for ensembles, accompanying and rehearsing choirs with ancient and often poor quality music chosen at the last minute by the religious instruction coordinator or Parish priest. Music directors in schools regardless of their religious affiliation are constantly called upon to represent the school by placing bands in the local shopping centre or any one of a dozen obligations that seem to be about using music to represent the character of the school or to celebrate it internally.

It was perhaps in a moment of desperation in a busy music teacher's life to think one year to address these kinds of extra curricular musical events as part of a greater understanding of how the school saw itself as a community which led to discussions and planning sessions with the Principal, religious education coordinators, curriculum advisors and school council. Bringing these together led to the idea that to have ownership and build community we needed to allow the students to create the music and structure the events in partnership with the community. It was this that led to the insight about the possibility that a school is very much like a village with its own values, economy, practices and rituals and how music might play a role in shaping and projecting that identity.

This chapter seeks to understand the potential of school music in the making of meaning. The focus of the book so far has been on the meaning of music to young people and the processes that provide access to that meaning. Now I would like to turn attention to description of a theoretical "ideal environment" for meaningful engagement with music. The concept of the school as village predicates on the idea that a school has an identity, rituals, values and a unique contexts, which can shape how it is perceived by others. Furthermore, it builds on the idea of classroom domain projects and simulations and extends their influence to the world outside the classroom. It also links the two.

The idea here is that needs for music to be produced that come from the school community such as speech nigh fanfares and music for liturgy be commissioned by the school to be produced by the students. It draws on ancient principles and very recent real world contexts for music to be made. Put simply, it replicates how Bach worked in his community or how a composer is commissioned to make work for a film or ceremony. The teacher's role in facilitating this as integrated and often interdisciplinary curriculum is essential and a description of the kinds of qualities of teachers in this context and their roles and responsibilities and the structure of the classroom in this change environment is necessary.

I will begin here by describing systematically the qualities of the teachers and the structure of classroom, studio and school community that nurture access to meaning and growth of musical knowledge and understanding. The focus of this description is upon the teacher as builder and interpreter of contexts and examines the "controllable" and educational aspects of curriculum, method and human interaction. This description begins with the understanding that the school is not perceived as an artificial construction of reality but a real community that has rituals, values, constraints and potential like any place where people gather as a community. What is artificial is that the reason for community is education. In this case study, there is a conscious attempt in curriculum and school community to reintegrate music with life. It is presupposed that the environment reflects the wider community whilst having the capacity to provide access to meaning through experience, reflection and understanding. The artificial aspects of school life are actually advantageous. Within the confines of school we can encounter simulations that have safety constraints that have dangers eliminated or controlled. We can experience a simulation of experiences which focus us pedagogically on issues of education and life long learning. We can reflect on experience and share it. With the concept of school as village, the whole environment is important. For music learning in the case study, school music was experienced in many locations: the instrumental studio, the classroom, the ensemble, at home, in a garage with a band, at church or at a youth club.

Before we recognised the potential to connect these experiences through reflective practice and attention to the school as a community to be engaged with as a whole all of these experiences were disconnected. In many schools instrumental and classroom programs seldom even talk to each other and more often compete for limited funds. The student's experiences in multiple environments are also disconnected and often contradictory. To come out of school music with any kind of unified connection with music is more due to luck than planning. Yet these notions have a basis in philosophy and certainly there are countless models from life and history where we can observe how communities make music in the real world. The school as village seeks to replicate this with a pedagogical framework which seeks to unify and connect musical experiences through reflective practice and to provide a clear "real world" basis for music making that allows the student to see the relevance of music making in the world today, across cultures and times.

A philosophical basis for the school as village

I began this research not by asking what is the meaning of music to young people but where it was located. In doing so, I was able to observe the phenomenon of meaning in context. In the review of literature, I undertook an analysis of the "meaning" of music that sought to draw together the particular emphasis of each of the parts of music learning experience. Reimer (1989) was seen to focus on the expressive qualities of music. Elliott (1995) emphasised the importance of making music and reflecting on it. Walker (1990) highlighted the importance of embedding the "acoustic phenomenon" in cultural context and its relevance to the way music is made in the world today. Swanwick sought to examine more succinctly how children gain meaning in school music. I also presented the so-called "deviant" views (Reimer and Wright 1992, 280) of John Cage (1961), who argues for an integration of life and art. Through this analysis, I was able to identify the differentiation between the meaning of music as an objectified art form or product, its value in a culture and its personal referential qualities. While this provided useful background knowledge, I found that it was necessary for me to locate meaning in context rather than abstract it and examine it as an art object.

In music composition, we often discuss the idea of "effectors and effects" (Pratt 1990). In simple terms, what this means is that music has an intuitive or aesthetic affect on listeners—the craft of music involves understanding the ways in which musical elements and culture combine to cause those effects. In a sense, this is what I have attempted to do with this research. We know that music is meaningful; otherwise, it would not have been so much a part of human life for so long. My idea here has been to examine both the "effector and the effect" (Pratt 1990), the analytical and the intuitive, as Swanwick would put it (Swanwick 1994).

My reading suggests that meaning, values and significance are all closely tied together. If an experience is significant or valuable to the individual, then it is very likely that it would be meaningful. What is important for educational processes is that, if things are valuable, significant and meaningful, then they are also intrinsic and memorable—both of which make the teacher's job of educating easier and the student's task of learning more pleasurable.

Csikszentmihalyi's (1994) study of "flow" has provided me with an important understanding of the intrinsic qualities of music making. He identified that people who are challenged and have the capacity to meet that challenge feel flow. He identified arts and sporting activities as activities that most likely provided these kinds of challenges and flow. People who experience "flow" find it significant, valuable and meaningful. "Flow" is about that feeling of spontaneous oneness with the task, a merging of maker and product. As a musician, I know this feeling well; as a teacher, I have seen it in the faces of students and peers. If we experience flow, there is no doubt that the activity is meaningful. Meaningful experience is a reason for participating in music making and I believe that the kinds of meaningful experience or micro aesthetic experiences vary widely amongst individuals. In a sense, I could say that this study replicates Csikszentmihalyi's research in a new context. I now want to explore the kinds of environments we can create as teachers to illustrate how music making that is connected to the way that music is made in the "real world" can lead to transformative pedagogical and social outcomes.

The physical environment

The structure of the physical environment is one that is partially controllable and partially interpretable. The structure of a building is not alterable, but a teacher can manipulate the use and contents so that it is functional and invites engagement with music making. Just as a classroom full of desks in neat rows structures a particular kind of experience, a large open room with a drum kit, amplifiers and a variety of instruments in it provides a completely different dynamic. The teacher's role is to build and interpret a physical environment so that it is able to give access to meaning. The physical environment needs to be one that has the flexibility to involve students in encounters that can provide personal meaning through interaction with music making, either alone or through a teacher. This is related more to access or institutional permission to be in the space. This is largely about the psychological and institutional environment, but the space has to be constructed so that it can provide this access in the first place.

Flexibility is the key. Physical environments for music-making need to able to accommodate music making by individuals and groups and often several groups working at the same time. With this aspect, noise is a consideration: the room and the teaching space need to be able to provide an environment where groups are able to hear themselves without too much distraction from others. The room needs to provide a large enough space so that sharing of music making can evoke a sense of cultural meaning gained through interaction with peers. The teacher would need to take into account the use of external venues such as school halls and concert venues. The teacher should also be aware of access to music making within the local community such as concerts, community music and arts projects, composers and artists in residence—these provide a resource for extending music beyond the limitations of the school and classroom.

These seem like obvious descriptions, but the comments from students and teachers interviewed, and also my observations, suggest that they are crucial to access to meaning. In the case study site, when the music department moved locations the approach to teaching and the kinds of activities altered radically, with the size of the rooms and proximity to the school hall affecting the kinds of group work in classroom music, sizes of ensembles that could rehearse and the volumes of rehearsals. Interpretation of physical environment is critical to what can be taught. We only need to ask what kind of music lesson might be taught in a room full of desks in neat rows to know the impact of physical environment upon music learning.

The social environment

The social environment is a multi-levelled construct. The social environment includes the student-teacher relationship, the classroom, the year level, the campus, the school and the community. The teacher can both build and interpret these so that they provide access to meaning. The themes described by those interviewed in this study were openness and friendliness. Students described their relationship with effective music teachers as "friendly" but also valued the effectiveness of the learning as a motivating factor. Teachers used the word "professional" to describe their relationship with students. Friendliness was taken as a matter of course. The teachers' description of the relationship between themselves and students is reminiscent of Buber's (1969) notion of "inclusion". They conceded that in some cases the inclusive relationship might become friendship in later years.

The dimensions of this relationship are made clearer when we discuss the perception of the relationship from both the student's and the teacher's viewpoint. The idea of openness was most valued. Students' perception of friendliness was largely due to the interest that the teacher took in the student's life and the ability of the teacher to share their own feelings and musical life with the student. There is a sense of intimacy in what the music teacher Peter described as sharing his innermost feelings with students through his performing and composing with them. There is a revealing of one's intuitive self and "feelingfulness" that music making provides. This is necessary as education and is perceived by students as something that only friendship could achieve.

This openness extended to the teachers' stance, the way the teachers present themselves as music makers. Students valued the openness of teachers to musical style, openness to take musical risks, willingness to try new things and even expose their own inability and weaknesses. These aspects will be examined further in the discussion of the psychological environment. Jessica, the drama and English teacher interviewed in the study, described the teacher's position in this as "valuing what the student brings" to the relationship (Jessica 1998, pers comm. with teacher, 22 January). It is important to stress here that openness is an essential element in the construction and interpretation of a nurturing environment.

What this means in concrete terms for the teacher is that they must seek opportunity for social interaction within the classroom through group creative work and ensemble performances. Beyond the classroom, social meaning is gained through the creation of large and small ensembles and the provision of opportunity for student-motivated activity to occur. In the case-study school, there were over twenty ensembles ranging from student-run rock bands and chamber groups through to larger choirs, wind ensembles and orchestras. The teacher can facilitate the beginnings of a new ensemble. They can direct the student to an existing one so that they might extend their access to musically challenging encounters and access social meaning in as broad a variety of ways as possible. Institutional and physical constraints such as time, space and people to supervise affect what is possible in this regard. These constitute the interpretive aspects of the teacher's role.

In the case study school, the variety of ensembles was the key to accessing socially meaningful experiences. A large number of senior ensembles were student run. Non-music staff directed many other ensembles with an interest in music making and all the others were directed by music staff whose course load included ensemble direction. These interpretations of the social environment involved institutional consideration of budget but more importantly, they involved openness to the interest-driven involvement of students and teachers and provision of the space and time for that intrinsic interest to grow. This is what I have described as the role of teacher as "animateur". The teacher creatively seeks opportunity for music to be made in a social and collaborative way and directs students and teachers in that environment to make productive use of the opportunity. The teacher's role in this is to act as a "cultural project manager"—interpreting the needs of the students and the community and finding ways to express those needs.

This aspect of the social also extends to the cultural and the teacher can find opportunity for ensembles and classes to experience sharing their musical expression with the community. In the case study school, this was done on two levels. The pragmatic or functional and the aesthetic, or art for art's sake, level, the teacher as builder looks for opportunities for students to perform within a safe open psychological environment. Sharing of music making occurred in the classroom, the concert hall and the community. Music was made for ceremonial purpose for church and school ceremony. It was made to explore aspects of innovation in the domain of music itself and it was performed to share with parents and peers within the community. Throughout the calendar year of the case study school, every ensemble had the opportunity to share its music making in a variety of settings which gave access to cultural meaning and affirmation of their value and worth within the community. These performances were built and interpreted by the teachers, the needs of the community and the students' own work. The intrinsic value of music provided the motivation for this access to meaning.

The psychological environment

In the section above, I spoke about openness as a requirement for effective relationship between teacher and student. The idea of a psychological environment that is open to what the student brings to the relationship is a complex one. The drama teacher Jessica's, notion of "valuing" was described as "genuinely valuing the child's interest in music" (Jessica 1998, pers comm. with teacher, 22 January). This is quite different from liking the musical style or the performance. The teacher need not be an authority on music of all forms, nor "like" all forms of music but needs to recognise that the student is attracted to and interested in music and as Aronoff (1969) suggests "build on the natural aesthetic response" that is inherent in human playfulness and developed by the cultural values of each community. This is a particularly sensitive area of building and interpreting of environment. The environment must be one where it is safe to express feelings verbally and in writing about music, safe to be expressive. The teacher must model this behaviour and provide a discipline structure that values and encourages open discussion and reflection.

The environment must be one where students are encouraged to take musical risks, where not achieving can be perceived as a valid part of the learning process that is enhanced by perceptive and reflective thinking. In the case study school, teachers were observed trying new things, attempting tasks they could not perform, to provide an environment where this kind of activity was not only permitted but also encouraged. The alternative to this environment is one where musical elitism excludes students from the discourse, where peer pressures ridicules or undervalues differences in musical taste and levels of achievement.

The teacher has control over these factors in their manner and the discipline structure of the classroom or studio. The teacher can shape this environment and interpret it as well as model behaviour, which nurtures a productive psychological environment where music making and reflection are valued and encouraged. Access to personal, social and cultural meaning is dependent upon a nurturing psychological environment constructed and interpreted by the teacher.

The institutional environment

The institutional factors that affect access to meaning are such things as school policy and curriculum. These structure what we are able to do as teachers, where we teach and at what times. School policy and curriculum can contain cultural, educational and aesthetic constraints, or they can nurture and develop understanding and participation in music making. The teacher's role in this is to interpret and build the institutional environment so that it facilitates access to meaning. History suggests that the institutional and physical environment have a large effect upon the art that is made within a community. The place and culture as a context has a profound effect upon what is possible; it shapes the art that is made—for instance, the kind of music that evolved in South American communities, where the physical context is one of rich physical resources from the fertile natural environment and where there are a large variety of resources available to make instruments. The cultural environment comprised Indigenous Indians, African slaves and European cultures combined with a powerful ceremonial structure from all of those cultures (Olsen. 1998). This cultural and physical interpretation of context expresses itself in an immensely complex and exciting musical form.

Comparatively, here in Australia, the physical environment is sparse and in many parts of Australia there are fewer resources for musical instrument manufacture. Indigenous groups here use music and call upon the resources in their country in quite different ways. Instruments that are well known internationally such as the didgeridu are really only found in regions where the trees and termites to bore the instruments out exist. Certainly instruments and techniques for playing instruments are traded between peoples but the didgeridoo has particular place regionally and relationally because of particular cultural values that surround the instrument. Because of seasonal movement of Indigenous groups following food gathering pathways, sound as cultural knowledge travels in more compact forms such as song. Songs are used as a means of "mapping" country and connecting location, lore and human understanding. Indigenous Australians integrates song with and spirituality in a very different way and is essential for the communication, storage and expression of culture and history (for example, see Bradley and Mackinlay 2007). While this is a rather rudimentary reading of both cultures connection between place and the interpretation of sound I have placed it here in this simple form to highlight how clearly place and culture influences and shapes the sounds of our cultures and communities. In both cases, we can see clearly that context has a great effect upon musical form.

Several teachers I spoke to talked about the notion that part of the attitude of the school was "in the bricks and mortar". They described a kind of "spirit of place". What this suggests in pragmatic terms is the profound effect that the place has upon what is done in that place and it became evident to me that the artist has a role in those contexts. The artist's role is often spiritual and interpretive. It is at some times as an educator and preserver of history. At other times, it is as a creative and expressive part of the culture. At other times, it is ceremonial and at still other times purely artistic. The artist in these communities is not unlike the music teacher in a school.

Schools are often described as artificial representations of reality, but are they? What institution is not artificial? What is artificial? The institution of "school" is a community of people a system of human interactions brought together for the purpose of initiation into culture and education of character. I would strongly suggest that the role of the music teacher in this be not unlike that of the artist in other societies. They are responsible for the cultures expressive needs and to its needs also. The institution places a demand upon the teacher to express and embody its values as well as reflect them to others. The teachers as builder and interpreter of context shape their actions to do this and are shaped by it.

How then does a music teacher build and interpret the institutional environment so that it gives access to meaning? First, their interpretation of curriculum must lend itself to giving access to meaning, providing experiences with making and reflecting music expressively, in such a way that it both responds to community and institutional need, and is relevant to the needs of the particular community. Second, they can be aware of the ceremonial needs of the community and utilise them as a means for aesthetic expression. This means that the teacher needs to seek to integrate music with the community and go beyond the classroom and school boundary. Music should be integrated with the ceremonial life of the school as well as for entertainment. The teacher responds to the community need for music as a unifying and expressive force and the community responds in affirming the music and the music makers, place in the community. This is where students truly gain access to social and cultural meaning. The personal and social meanings are gained through the encounter with the teacher's interpretation of curriculum, whilst the cultural meaning becomes most poignant in the co-curricular and extra-curricular interaction with the community. The teacher can facilitate this relationship or they can choose to isolate music as a subject that exists only on the timetable and deny real access to cultural meaning. Even the most hostile institutions (prisons and slavery) have produced access to all levels of meaning through the inspiration of musical leadership and our natural aesthetic response (Aronoff 1969).

The effects of the teacher upon access to meaning then, are both personal and constructed. In the intuitive sense, the teacher needs to have the ability to embody the intuitive and aesthetic aspects of musical expression. In an analytical sense, the teacher has to be able to be sensitive to the needs of the students. They need to be able to take into account the aspects of domain and curriculum that influence the nature of experience. Further, they need the ability to interpret and synthesize all of these into an environment that nurtures access to music meaning and fosters artistic growth. The importance of the teacher in this equation is paramount. The teacher creates the environment in which music meaning is both taught and caught. This is done most easily when the teacher is able to comprehend the meaning of music as a natural aesthetic response. They can then structure the environment so that it is able to occur or simply to enable the space for this response to take place unhindered.

The educational environment: Classroom and curriculum

One of the most powerful insights I have gained from my discussion with students and teachers relates to the way in which the environments of classroom music, and instrumental studio lessons are defined, framed and enacted.

The classroom environment

Classroom music was described by teachers and students in this case study as being:

- a gateway to deeper musical experience, where the teacher provides a variety of opportunities to experience music making with instruments both solo and in groups and then directs those who show interest to deeper experiences with studio teachers or within ensembles;
- the place where through the diversity of curriculum provides experience with music making from a variety of historical periods and global cultures;

- the place where students gain experiences with creative music making. Students compose songs and music through a variety of interactive groups and individual music making activities utilising a variety of composition methods and forms;
- the place where students learn to be perceptive about music they are making and to reflect upon their own music and the music of others, verbally in writing and as a physical and emotional response.

Students and teachers interviewed spoke of the classroom as a "poor cousin" to the deeper and more challenging experiences of ensembles and studio learning.

Nevertheless, the discussions also indicated ways in which the access to meaning in the classroom experience provided broader and more inclusive experiences. Classroom music is "general" and thus necessarily broad, so that all that participate has breadth of experience. It can be necessarily shallow so that the first experience with music making of any kind is achievable. These research findings suggest that the students gained the diversity of musical experience and developed the meta-cognitive skills of reflection through their classroom music experiences. These skills draw together music experiences from the disparate sources of studio, ensemble and classroom. In those experiences, there is little time for structured reflective practice except through the modelled behaviour of the teacher. In the classroom, however, this meta-cognitive skill of reflection and broad general experiences with music making combines to enable us to make sense of musical experience and contemplate its meaning and value to us. This is the true value of classroom music. Its strength is in its diversity of experience and the development of skills of reflection.

The access to meaning in this case is quite clear. It is through structured activity designed by the teacher and influenced by curriculum or it comes about through the teacher's choice of method. Group creative and ensemble work provides access to social meaning. Providing challenging but achievable individual activities in music making provides access to personal meaning. Reflection on music making gives further access to understanding and deepens the associated meaning. In the classroom, the cultural meaning can be simulated in a controllable and affirming fashion, if the teacher encourages the psychological environment of openness.

The instrumental studio environment

The instrumental studio is an environment where experience is intensely focussed. It concentrates upon the relationship between the student and a single musical instrument or voice. The opportunity for access to meaning is teacher dependent. Access to personal meaning is gained through the teacher and because of the teacher. In early music learning contexts, the student can be immersed in the teacher's own love of music. As students grows in their initiation into the discourse, the meaning becomes personal and the relationship with music making takes on the sense of ownership and of membership of a community of music makers.

The social meaning can also be gained through playing alongside or with the teacher. The teacher can also facilitate social music making experience. The access to cultural meaning is less likely in this context, but a teacher through examinations, informal performance and concert programs can facilitate it. This involves providing the opportunity for the music maker to share their music with others amongst the child's family, community and peers as a performance. The characteristics of the teacher as embodiment of intuitive understanding and builder and interpreter of contexts, is most important in the instrumental studio. Added to this is the need for the teacher to be sensitive to and value what the child brings to the relationship—to value the child's interest in music whatever that attraction might be.

Previously, I discussed the idea of a "micro-aesthetic" as a small part of an experience, which attracts students to the experience of an instrumental studio. In music, this might be the order of notes, the unique timbre of the instrument, the sound of one's own voice, the beauty of the woodwork in a violin. In interviewing of teachers and students for this research, I asked participants whether they could remember a first instance of attraction to music. What I believe is most likely is that the micro-aesthetic or micro-flow experience constitutes the first experience with something meaningful with music. Many of these initial attraction or micro aesthetic stories were either personal or social in nature.

They describe aesthetic responses about the qualities of music that are expressive because they have expressed something to us often without the complexity of form. If a single tone has the power to move our imagination, then a sequence of them would be even more expressive and attractive. It is the relationship with this fundamental attraction to music that is the responsibility of the instrumental teacher. For some though like Linda the violinist were attracted to the cultural imagery of music making as demonstrated by a model of performance. Linda saw a violinist whose "beautiful playing" moved an audience to applause (Linda 1997, pers comm. with student, 5 March). What she was experiencing as a four year old was an encounter with cultural meaning. James the keyboard teacher was attracted to the social activity of playing clarinet in a band personal Communication Interview Teacher James 28/10/96). It is these shining moments that the student brings initially to the instrumental lesson or finds at the lesson or through the teacher. The instrumental teacher needs to be sensitive to these attractions and value the interest in them whilst seeking to provide access to deeper experiences with all meaning.

The ensemble

Access to social meaning within the ensemble is assured by its nature. When an ensemble performs, it also has access to cultural meaning, an interaction with the community. These often subsume access to personal meaning and the depth of meaning in these contexts is relative to the kind of ensemble experience. Within this research, participants suggested that small, self-directed ensembles provide deeper kinds of human relationships. Larger ensembles serve a function of providing multiple levels of access to experience. In the large ensemble, students have access to social and cultural meaning in a highly structured environment. The challenge that provides flow for the participants is that of working together to produce a unified sound. Within the small ensemble and the undirected ensemble, the social interactions are closer and more dependent upon each person "getting it right". Participants suggest that these ensembles are the most challenging, educative and enjoyable. This is evidence of what Cage (1961) calls democratisation of the process of music making.

The access to meaning is partially determined by the nature of the ensemble experience but the understanding and educative aspects of these experiences are dependent upon the director or the facilitator of the self-directed ensemble. Jane, the wind ensemble conductor whose students imitated her reflective and perceptive problem-solving behaviour, gained a meaningful experience from this ensemble (Jane 1997, pers comm. with teacher, 13 February). The synthesizer players, described in the pilot study, spoke about how playing in this ensemble had changed them.

What I am saying here is that in performance, be it solos or ensemble of any description that music becomes what it is meant to be—an expressive aural medium. It is in performance that it has the potential to express something to others and about others. The ensemble and the solo performance are the object of music making. This is where the music ceases to be simply an experience that we are having and becomes an art object that we share with others. Access to meaning in the ensemble is simple. We need a variety of ensemble experiences with a variety of sizes, styles and degrees of direction and self-control. Students and teachers in the case study recognised the value of access to diverse experiences and the flexibility of the school to provide ensembles that reflected the community. Students need to experience the power and rigour of traditional large ensembles, the flexibility of chamber ensembles and the self-directed activity of jazz and rock ensembles. Just as ensembles in the Baroque times grew from whatever instrumentalists were available, schools should respond likewise by building ensembles from students rather than forcing students into ensembles.

The school environment

The school is a community, and as such provides opportunities for social interaction. The opportunity for access to music meaning within any community is relative to the perception of the arts within that community. This meaning is reciprocal and interactive. If a music department is elitist or separate from the community, then it becomes reflective only of a limited interpretation of the domain. In the case study school, where music was consciously integrated with the school ceremonial and spiritual life, the interaction with the school community became reciprocal and meaningful. This suggests that when music is part of the life of the school community, it has a unifying and involving effect on the participants. This is reflective of the role of music in any community and is not in itself unique. What this perspective differentiates is that music is used in these ways consciously and as an encounter, which provides benefit for the students who make the music and the community that shares in the music experience—this is the nature of cultural meaning. Recognition of the role of school as a community is reflective of the way in which music is made in the wider community and indeed in all cultures. Recognition and reflection upon music making wherever it occurs, be it in the classroom, school or concert hall, brings with it the possibility that the encounter has to be meaningful and ultimately educative. The school environment is an opportunity to understand and gain knowledge about how music is made in the world.

The school environment can provide access to personal and social meaning by providing a culture that values creative expression and innovation in students and staff and by affirming the place of its music makers as well as their artistic product. These characteristics of the institution or the community are both reflective of the community's character and expressive of it. These factors appear to be beyond individual control, nevertheless artists in primitive communities did not control the community—they merely responded to it and expressed, reflected and explored its nature through their art. This shapes the art and affects what is possible, constrains and encourages some aspects over others, but it is this reciprocal response that makes each culture unique and the art that is expressive of that culture unique. This opportunity is nonetheless available to artists in schools. Beyond this notion is the idea that all music making is potentially meaningful and educative in the hands of a skilful teacher.

The world beyond school

The community beyond school is worthy of our attention. It is where the student takes the meaning gained from their experiences with school and it is where they experience other meaningful encounters with music. I have said on many occasions that music needs to be made in a context that is both relevant and reverent to community. The discussion of meaning in the school community focuses upon its relevance and reverence to pragmatic and aesthetic purpose, as the world beyond is where we as educators are charged with the responsibility to initiate students.

What I am suggesting in this respect is not simply that in music education we initiate students into the culture, but rather, that we equip students to be expressive within it using the domain of music. We are charged with the responsibility of giving access to understanding and interpreting of music making of our culture and openness to new art and art from other cultures—it is a responsibility we hold to develop, gain and nurture reflective skills that enable us to be critical of art wherever we may find it.

In Chapter 9, I argued that music making has the potential to ground humanity in social interaction and act as a counterbalance to the more isolating aspects of contemporary culture. Music making gives access to personal, social and cultural meaning in communication with self, others and community. The sense of affirmation and belonging within a community can be enhanced by such interactions. This, I suggest, is a necessary counterbalance to the potentially isolating aspects of post-modern life. Sharp (1983, 1985) for example has argued that the conditions of post modernity affect the development of people so that they become constitutively abstracted in social practice. I argue that music making in the ways described here has the potential to counterbalance those abstract relations with meaningful encounters with self and others.

Participants in this study highlighted the gaining of meta-cognitive skills of self-contained criticism and reflection providing access to a broader variety of musical experiences. They spoke about openness to new ones, and an ability to be critical of music wherever they found it. The ability to differentiate and be critical of art in these contexts provides an informed perspective on what we perceive as art and the aesthetic qualities of commodities. With these skills as consumers, we are able to be more critical and informed. In school curricula, the idea that we might simulate the composition of an advertising jingle or compose a film score also assists in demystifying the abstraction of art in media. These are the kind of musical experiences that Walker (1996) suggests need to be a source for the way music is made in the world today.

Towards a shift in focus

What is being suggested here is the need for a shift in focus that is able to respond more readily to the multicultural, technologically developed and complex relationships of twenty-first century life. Despite the call for a shift in focus, in many ways it is a call for a reintegration of art and life as it was expressed in early European communities and as it appears in many non-Western cultures. In early civilisation music and art were integrated. Dewey (1989, 213) suggested that the arts "were part of the significant life of an organised community" and "music and songs were intimate parts of the rites and ceremonies in which the meaning of group life was consummated". The meaning and learning of music were integrated with social life and helped define and express it. In the nineteenth-century, European music became objectified—it became a subject of study and it was taught by instruction. In this period the focus was on knowledge about music—its history; theory and skills of practice—this was passed on to students by "instruction". In the middle of the twentieth century, Dewey's experiential philosophy (1970, 1989) and Bruner's discovery learning" (1966, 1972) shifted the paradigm of learning music to the experience of making art. As this idea grew in theoretical and practical application, there was an awareness of the need for reflective criticism and aesthetics. The focus of music education shifted to experience, practical making and critical listening.

What I am proposing here is a shift in focus equally inclusive of context, making and reflection. In a sense, this is a kind of reintegration of art and life. It constitutes a return to a life where art/music, life and learning about it become a "natural" process. This is not a kind of essentialism or even a contemporary romanticism—in educational terms, it might be considered "holism". What I am arguing for is a conscious and planned concept of music education that considers a context that is built and interpreted socially, psychologically and physically so that it facilitates music learning and access to music meaning. This environment considers and selects the aspects of context that enhance and give access to meaningful musical experiences. Experience and making music is done in those contexts, both real and simulated, and guided and structured reflection and evaluation occurs both during and after music has been made or experienced. During the process of production or making, perception about the process occurs that enhances and develops the product, and after the process is complete, there is reflection on the product.

I have suggested throughout this book that the teacher's role in this process is multi-dimensional—a builder of curriculum and contexts, a facilitator of experiences, an interpreter of culture, and a reflective practitioner. For a moment I would like to describe a simplistic and perhaps essentialist and romantic reading of the role of a cultural manager in a community. It is one that recognises the role of leaders of ritual, where music is integral to cultural knowledge, as being multi faceted. Keepers of cultural knowledge can be charged with the responsibility of storing culture and ritual, interpreting and performing it, inventing new ritual, which gives the culture growth, and passing these on to others. They may be historians, teachers, critics, cultural consultants and creative makers. They owe allegiance to their community and to the domain of magic and ritual that was are their art. They are both responsible for maintaining and advancing their craft. In Western cultures, the separation between performers, composers, producers, teachers and critics in European culture has compartmentalised or separated these roles. Yet in a school community, one that has village like qualities a music teacher is expected to be all these things and more simultaneously.

In the conception of this paradigm for music education, all these roles need to be reconceived to cope with the complexity of contemporary society and education, but the role is nonetheless unchanged. The difference is the consciousness of the position and the construction or interpretation of the context, the facilitation of encounters that allow students to experience the expressiveness of music in a real or simulated context. Most important is the guided and modelled perceptive, reflective and evaluation process that occurs during and after production. The focus is context, making and reflection- it is inclusive of all aspects of music making and locations where meaning can be gained. This paradigm allows access to personal, social and cultural meaning. In Chapter 5, Figure 5.1 was used to evaluate the context but in this setting we are able to also illustrates the numerous aspects and nature of demands upon the teacher's construction and teaching of curriculum.

If we reconsider the position of the teacher in this as one who attends to or balances and synthesises the demands represented in Figure 5.1 which we discussed in Chapter 5, we can begin to see the complexity of the notion of teacher as builder. The builder must also be the architect who considers all of the stakeholders in the process of education. Like the role of architect, the process is creative and practical, functional and aesthetic. The kind of structure built will be unique to the context and the needs of the stakeholders. In terms of music education, the only factors that can grow and change to respond to these needs are the teacher and the curriculum.

Building and interpreting context

I have read countless curriculum documents and philosophical works that say that music is intrinsic, and our response to it is natural. What does this mean for music educators? It means at the lowest level that we should not get in the way of this natural response. More clearly, though, the need is to build a context in which access to meaningful musical experience is assured and that reflective practice that reifies those experiences becomes part of the process of music education. This is a delicate balance to build and interpret context, to provide experiences with making music that are both broad and general and that lead to deeper and more challenging experiences and flow. Finally, it is important to build into this environment a culture of meta-cognitive reflective practice that becomes part of initiation into the music discourse.

Swanwick (1994) describes a dialectic tension between intuition and analysis in music education. I believe that this has been evident throughout this study. In curricula, we deal mainly with the analytical aspects of knowledge because it is most easily ordered into pedagogy. How do we teach the intuitive? Swanwick suggests that the intuitive is caught rather than taught. In schools, we catch knowledge from those who model it or from experiences that we have in a meaningful context. Students I observed in the case study who were members of a big band "caught" swing from immersion in a context that contained it and from the music teachers who modelled it for them. Swing is one of those concepts that we can feel and know aesthetically but it is difficult to describe or attribute cognitive understanding to. For the students I spoke, that context where swing could be caught was deliberately built and interpreted by a teacher whose lifelong passion was jazz. What this means is that teachers need to consider an approach to structuring and building a music teaching and learning environment so that students may encounter intuitive understanding in increasingly more complex ways.

Music education is indeed a dialectic tension between the analytic and the intuitive and, as Swanwick (1994) suggests, is initiation into a discourse. This study adds weight to this concept through the descriptions of context, observation of music making and biographies of people within the discourse. For these factors to combine usefully to provide music education to young people there needs to be a balance between the context of experience and reflection that provide access to meaning and understanding. This can be done through an approach that reintegrates art and life and seeks to give access to music as it is found in all human communities. However, it involves a little more than partitioning music into 50-minute lessons on the timetable.

In music education, we need to step beyond the access that students have to meaning and provide the opportunity for understanding that meaning. The teacher's role is to initiate students into a discourse where music reflects the ways in which it occurs in human life. In this task, we seek to provide the students with experiences that move from dependence through independence to interdependence but allowing the flexibility to swing freely between these. We strive to provide the opportunity for students to become self-contained, self-reflective and self-creative individuals. There is considerable evidence that Buber's (1969, 104) notion of "education of character" is what occurs when we enter a meaningful discourse with music making. Music is a part of every hearing human's life. Our experiences with it have the potential to educate our character, to move us towards more complex consciousness, and to educate our perception. The work of music education, then, is to initiate young people into the rich and valuable understanding of music as an expressively human activity, to give access to an understanding that music is capable of communicating with self and others, unifying and affirming human community and giving us opportunity for flow.

A changing environment: Tasks for the new millennium

It is quite clear that as the new millennium struggles to establish or redefine social life, change is the only constant. In music education there is a need to consolidate the knowledge that we have gained through philosophy and practice and ask what art means in this century. We need to continuously and dynamically examine what skills a music teacher needs today and to do so in our own unique cultural contexts. To establish clearly what a music teacher's work is in these new environments and with the diverse demographics that face us in classrooms and studios, we need to evolve strategies in curriculum and in teacher training that equip teachers with skills and the ability to structure analytical experience, and to facilitate and encourage experiences that enable students to reflect on intuitive experiences.

In this book, I have suggested that teachers can build and interpret environments where intuitive understandings might be caught but there is a need for further examples of how this kind of knowing might be transmitted located within a myriad of cultural contexts. As an Australian, I am patently aware of music's role in the colonisation of social contexts. Indeed the largest employer of musicians in my country is the military and the lack of a clear effect of curriculum to provide culturally inclusive music education and access to meaningful music making in schools and communities as a life long pursuit lacks philosophical unity. Yet as in most countries, the examples and anecdotes of how music has transformed the existence of individuals and communities abound. In school music, the analytical is emphasised because of the sense of control over environment and student that it represents. It is easy to assess and infinitely quantifiable. It is also the area of music, which is most often presented as the program and the area that turns students off in great numbers.

Alternatively, the intuitive aspects of music are difficult to quantify and exude an air of chaos that makes many teachers afraid of teaching creative music making. Yet we have no such qualms about asking a child to draw or paint, perhaps because it is quieter. Future research needs to outline strategies and examples that provide ways for teachers to create domain projects and evaluate their outcomes. They need to be able to do this in ways that allow them to feel comfortable about the level of understanding and skill that the child attains, and have confidence that this is meaningful and progressive. In many ways, we can look at health and physical education for a guide here. This discipline has moved successfully from a focus on elite athletes to health and sporting activity for life. These are issues for teacher training and for in-service training.

For the inclusive development of curriculum, we need to undertake further research that listens to children's voices about what is meaningful to them about music experience, and we need to consider that maybe the perceptions of teacher and student are not that different. In my discussion with students and teachers, both valued a teaching and learning relationship that was friendly, expressed openness, and where progress and teaching was made by example and immersion. In addition, the voices of children need to be heard within curricula alongside all the stakeholders within the school context. As Swanwick (1999) points out, we need to consider how we can fruitfully utilise the community as a resource in school music making. I have outlined here that the classroom is potentially the place where we can learn to make sense of the diverse music experiences that we encounter. We need to train teachers as managers of students' cultural lives, to give teachers experience in balancing the cultural life of a school and include a dynamic relationship with the community that build social capital and utilises the diverse ways in which music is represented in the community in culture and work.

The link between philosophical discussions of art and what actually happens in schools and the community is rarely made. Philosophy needs to be continuously tested in practice and practice must be evaluated for its meaning. The reality is that philosophy rarely moves beyond the written curriculum statements. Teachers learn to use the language to justify their aims but revert to draconian survival methods to teach children. Fortunately, music's own intrinsic qualities allow students access to music meaning without the need for school input. The kind of approach to music learning I am suggesting here considers these things and seeks to make music useful, expressive, relevant and meaningful. The over-emphasis upon the less intrinsic aspects of music making suggests a lack of good teacher training in ways of taking advantage of what attracts us all to music. Teachers who ignore curriculum change and teach in mimetic and boring ways are proof of this phenomenon. Others focus heavily upon skill-based methods to the detriment of expressiveness.

The focus of further research in music education needs to consolidate what it is we know about music education, examine the implications for curriculum and teaching, and respond to the changing meaning of art in contemporary social life. I feel we need to examine more narratives about how children and adults develop musically, to ask composers, musicians, new media artists and creative thinkers generally, about what influenced their creative lives and seek to distil these ideas for replication in schools.

At present, much music learning is based upon pedagogical beliefs that are largely grounded in European tradition, and have evolved from distinctly nineteenth century artistic values. Interestingly though, only other people still make a distinction between high and low culture, segregate music from other creative arts and the technologies and see cultural otherness as alien rather than a refreshing encounter with new expressive possibilities. Children in this century move unselfconsciously between these and other adult constructs of binary oppositions. This is most evident in the new multimedia playground of sound, movement and story. Sound, movement and story are part of the tradition and ceremonies of all cultures. In music education research, we need to examine the interaction between these modes of engagement and explore the expressive possibilities rather than perceive them as a threat to existing concepts of music.

The school as village and technology

The ways in which technology facilitates and encourages community is integral to the sustainability of the technology itself—just as the ability of a community to adapt to technological change affects a community's resilience and cultural health. As described earlier technology, as we perceive it in music education contexts, takes on different roles depending upon its function. Our relationship with it also shifts depending on the ways in which we are able to use these tools for the purpose of creative production of music or learning about music. Philosophically it is important to recognise that much of the music technology we use in classrooms is based upon print based metaphors for learning, focusing upon skill acquisition. In interaction design terms and educational ones it often represents an abdication of responsibility for the musical knowledge rather than an integrated approach, which uses the technology to enhance expressive activity. The classic observation of this in classrooms happens around aural training software. Using software in this case amplifies the teachers' insecurity about their own skill level, though in many cases the software provides extension activity and access for the student to practice aural training without the teacher. What is evident from observations about music teachers' relationship with technology is the lack of a critical perspective on its use.

In previous chapters, I have presented some simple approaches for observing and evaluating music technology software/ hardware and the potential for the software to provide access to learning music. I have suggested that we need to examine what the technology reveals and conceals and what the concealing of functions or knowledge lends to the focus of music learning or to its detriment. I have drawn heavily on the work of Andrew Brown whose work deals with these ideas in more detail philosophically, practically and from the dual perspectives of music education and interaction design. Just as music is intrinsically motivated so too are many pieces of technology we use today. Andrew Brown and I have spent many hours observing children's responses to technology and examining the relationship, the interface and the nature of the engagement (Brown 2000, 2003, 2006, Brown and Dillon 2007, Dillon 2001b, 2003, 2004b, 2004c, 2005b, 2006c, 2006d).

The sad truth is that most music software is not culture creating. Nor is it collaborative and social. Most of it is solitary and isolating. It is only through parallel play of children in computer laboratories that it becomes remotely social. The teacher is responsibility for designing engaging environments and technology can be simply a resource in that environment or what Papert calls a "micro-world" (Papert 1980, 1994). The notion of creating a world where a particular discipline was the focus is akin to Papert's "mathland"—the philosophy of which he built into a computer programming language for children called logo, which used "turtle" symbols to move around the computerscreen in geometric shapes. He gave these computer design principles a concrete representation by also having children use Lego building blocks. The computer provided a visual design tool to represent geometric shapes and mathematical models while the Lego made these shapes into concrete realisation. These ideas are still innovative education today more than 20 years later. In Papert's Mathland primary/elementary school aged students were able to learn and creatively manipulate engineering level mathematics using the computer tools available at the time. Logo computer language also had a musical aspect, which enabled a sonic construction to be made using similar principles of design and programming. The creation of micro-worlds and the idea of the school as village both have origins in children's" and adults imaginative play as a way of learning by immersion. They have their philosophical origins in Rousseau's Emile and have been explored thought Bruner's discovery learning (Bruner 1960, 1966, 1972, 1973, 1986) and Deweyan experiential learning (1916, 1963, 1970, 1989). Gardner's (1993) theory of multiple intelligence and its manifestation as curricula in Arts Propel's

Domain projects (Davidson 1992, Gardner 1993b, Gates 2004) all explore this notion of playfulness in virtual worlds. What eludes me is why such an engaging methodology as the playful use of themes and micro-worlds as represented over a hundred years in these approaches, are not wide spread, and why the intrinsic nature of playfulness with technology is also not applied either to the design or application of music technology.

Building community with technology

The ability for technology to create or be the coalescing point for community is a major focus of the interaction design and business world today. YouTube and Myspace are massive communities of interest and based around making and sharing music and creative visual materials. Earlier I discussed Dennis' who was a young electronic musician. When the technology of the Internet was quite young, he participated in chat rooms about music and traded MIDI files via email. The process of collaboratively working on composition was called "Mods" it involved sending a composition in MIDI file format between members of a community of 2 or more composers who modified, added and changed the music until it reaches final production. Then the participants would record it on tape and move on to the next composition. This approach had a profound effect on the musicianship of the students and the development of their production skills. This kind of activity occurs today with audio samples, loops, sounds, plug-ins and computer code yet this intrinsically motivated community whose collective interest is music and sound is mostly ignored in schools.

For technology to be a community building device rather than an isolating one we need to examine the role of technology and our interaction with it as described earlier. We also need to pay attention to the communities that exist today that have music at their centre. iPod song lists are used by youth to present their identity; the trading of music files, making music and performing it using technology enables the creation of communities of interest. As teachers and experience designers, we must see how we can utilise these ideas within our communities. In the same way as we examine the intrinsic qualities of music we need to examine the intrinsic qualities of technology. Each time we use a computer as a boring "drill and response" learning device we not only demean music we demean the technology as a potential for learning inductively.

The simple question that needs to be asked here is: how is music made and distributed in the world today? Next, we ask how we can design curriculum so that it simulates this. In the case study school, there was a wonderful example of a multi-media church service where a "stations of the cross" performance was composed, arranged and performed by the students under the direction of a music teacher. This technologically mediated performance that involved video images of the crucifixion of Christ underscored by electro acoustic performances, readings and song replicated the role of European church musicians—in the same way as Bach used the technology of the organ and the church surrounded the congregation with a stained glass light show, this performance immersed the audience in a spiritual experience that created a sense of community and unity of purpose. Music technology in this case served as a tool for developing skills of sound design, a medium, as scores and charts were prepared and an instrument when used in live performance.

The principle here is to examine the potential for both music and the technology to be intrinsically engaging and meaningful. We need to distinguish what both have to offer to our context and then design an environment where it can replicate or simulate a real world application. Also we need to look beyond our traditional notions of static twenty-first century technology to be able to utilise existing music communities such as Myspace and YouTube. As it is in many Indigenous Australian communities, music can be a valuable "currency" for knowledge transfer and containment or as with Western society a commodity in both circumstances music provides an opportunity for understanding about how a community uses and trades musical ideas and its value and role in that community.

As described earlier the role of music in aestheticising commodities and the commodification of aesthetic products such as music is an area that students need to be familiar with if they are to be at least informed consumers. So too is the understanding of music as a container and communicator of cultural knowledge. Rather than delineating the quality of music between the purely aesthetic and the functional, both perspectives need to be experiences if a student is to gain openness. The role of technology in this is critical. Music and technology both provide materials that engender playfulness. For that playfulness to create or sustain communities we need to harness their intrinsic qualities.

The school as village and culture

This chapter has considered the idea that a school might be reinterpreted as a village-like community. Many schools today could better be described as global villages; indeed my own daughter's school boasts students from 60 nationalities from every continent except Antarctica. Global villages however can be mono-cultural or multi-cultural, and even when the demographic is largely non-Western in makeup, the cultural frameworks act as a colonising process. Music has powerful value as a frame for cultural values. This is sometimes an affirmation of belonging and other times an endorsement of otherness alienation. Politically this is a difficult issue for schools and teachers but I think we have to acknowledge that it *is* political and that culture always presents inherent tensions. As Nakata (2002) suggests, unless we engage with theses tensions someone is being colonised or compliant and someone else is imposing values on a community that may not share those values.

For this reason, I suggest that the most culturally appropriate way to engage with these tensions is by firstly undertaking a context analysis as described in Chapter 6. Following this, we need to draw upwards from what the community values and then refer to curriculum documents and pedagogy. This is clearly not simply about "consulting" the community but beginning a relationship with parents and Elders in communities. It is at this point, where the real global village concept begins. The teacher who is in touch with the community can call upon the resources within the community and manage the cultural lives of the children in their care. For example, in one of the schools in the case study in suburban Brisbane, a teacher has regular contact with Indigenous Australian elders who facilitate other community members to tell stories and teach songs and dances. In this context, South Sea Islander dancers regularly teach their songs and dances, and local pop musicians run workshops with students to write songs and produce them. In this location music making becomes a common ground and a place where students from diverse background experience cross-cultural musicianship in an ethical way.

Alternatively, a mono-cultural school community seeks to integrate into a single set of values. For a community like Australia that still bears the imprint of its colonial history, this represents a distortion of values systems inherited further mutated by waves of immigration and refugees. While early in white Australian history mainly Christian and European migration dominated the ethnic mix and the values remained relatively cohesive except perhaps for the tension between cultural conservatory practices and the need to forge a national identity. Today however, integrationist approach to immigrant populations is less homogenous. The spiritual beliefs and values of non-Western, non-Christian immigrants question the validity of integrationist approaches. The Australian connection with Europe also comes into question here.

These kinds of cultural shifts in values comment on the value of European approaches and systems, which is further reflected in our music making and our music classrooms. Acknowledgement of diversity is relatively simple if religious and cultural values are similar but when spirituality and culture are radically different, this presents problems. Westerners do not easily understand indigenous constructions of music as knowledge. Islamic notions of song as prayer and too powerful an emotional effect to be trivialised also presents problems for music educators in multi cultural communities. Yet in Australia, we are located in a largely Islamic region and the origin of our country has a history of at least 40,000 years of Indigenous Australian culture, connections to and ownership of country.

Indeed, I have been challenged many times when I have asked whether a Hungarian folk song presented in a European aural and visual representation system is appropriate to Indigenous Australians or even my fifth generation Irish descendant child. It is not that I am questioning that the folk song contains important cultural knowledge or pedagogical knowledge that is worthy of attention but what concerns me is that that we do not ask that question. We need to question what values and knowledge does the music we choose contain, and how does it help us to understand others and ourself? Culture is political and teachers need to make this acknowledgement and then actively engage with those politics.

In a school, culture can be simulated, it can be appropriated, or it can be subjugated. The teacher as manager of the cultural lives of students and designer of experience can utilise the unique characteristics of a range of cultures to increase the expressive range of students. The teacher can also facilitate music as cultural common ground, and through experiential music making that involve embodied learning of other cultures, can facilitate learning about culture and humanity. A failure to acknowledge cultural diversity and to engage with the political tension of music and culture misses an opportunity for greater expressiveness in music and ethical syncretism, which leads to new music, which is greater that the sum of its parts and new understanding that bridges the gaps between cultures. We need to aim for an open and ethical relationship with, between and across cultures—for music education in an increasingly global focused world, introversion and colonial values have no place.

What we can do

- *What kind of village do you work in as a music educator?*

- *Evaluate your context and audit it regularly do not assume that because an approach worked last year it is still appropriate today. Use situational analysis models to audit your context and your own values so that curriculum responds directly to your unique context.*

- *Discover the values that you have as a teacher or music coach that are most important to you and compare these against the situational analysis.*

- *Your personal philosophy is dynamic—it will evolve in relation to your experience and context. You need to examine the tensions and congruencies to establish which are productive and enabling and which need attention. Note that tension is not necessarily a bad thing. Swanwick for example talks about a productive tension between analytical and intuitive musical knowledge. You'll know if the tension is unproductive when one becomes more dominant than the others.*

- *The role of the music teacher in each context is different but overlaps. You do not have to be all things to all people or have extensive knowledge of every facet of musical knowledge. You do however have to manage the cultural lives of students and the experiences that they have in music both in and out of school. The classroom teacher is the gateway to deeper experiences with the studio teacher or the ensemble director.*

- *It is reflection that unifies the disparate experiences of the music maker and connects them. All teachers need to model reflective and analytical behaviour. Reflection and response in music is not always a verbal or written response it might be notated or an improvised phrase or an expressive example of a performance. In music learning and teaching we need to express ourselves through modelling and presenting knowledge in symbolic form.*

CHAPTER TWELVE

MEANINGFUL MUSIC MAKING FOR LIFE

Introduction

It has been necessary to make this book an intimate text so that I could model the idea of a music teacher's journey of engagement with philosophy in practice. It has been a kind of brain-dump for me beginning with a seven year participant observation case study and then adding a subsequent seven years of academic and philosophical research. The journey has been personal but it has also been a rigorous one bounded on one hand by a doctoral study, and on the other, engagement with the international community of music educators through scholarly journal publications and diverse research across disciplines of education, the arts, computer study and multi-media in the creative industries. Being a music teacher, as with being a musician, is a voyage of self-discovery and I have described here the relationship between making music and forming identity through meaningful engagement with music making. The perspective I have offered is one that seeks to focus on the student or music makers experience of meaning and engagement with music making. It is one that seeks to enable access to meaningful music making as a lifetime pursuit. I have argued that this educates character (Buber 1969), and that this is influential in self-formation and has an effect on how we might engage with contemporary life. The design of the book has incorporated my own journey of observation and discovery about how students gain access to meaningful engagement in music making.

A summary of the journey

I have provided some simple ideas about what we can do as teachers to engineer this engagement and meaning. I have presented some analytical tools that I have found useful in engaging with the more complex ideas of a "relational" approach to music learning and teaching that considers context, culture and human relationships before suggesting pedagogy or strategies for music learning. I have suggested that "methods" as such, though useful for pedagogical sequence, are often culturally It can also framed and sometimes not appropriate to context. This is a rather controversial claim and will perhaps attract criticism. It is difficult for musicians and music teachers whose identity has been formed through a deep relationship with a particular methodology to reconcile this kind of criticism because it does attack our very identity. The identity formed by our relationship with music is an emotional one and it is not my intention to attack identity in this way only to suggest that when we teach music we need to take into consideration many factors before deciding how to teach.

The colonial imposition of music as a means of social control is not able to provide the kinds of educational outcomes that we need in an increasingly global context in this century. Certainly cultural identity is necessary and a large part of music education should be about understanding how the community we belong to communicates itself in sound and how it values its construction and product. We do need to be grounded in our senses of what music means in our community but we also need the capacity of openness to engage with music across cultures and times and understand the importance of music as an intrinsically motivated human pursuit that does indeed form our character and make us human. I have begun to suggest here that this process also need to move towards more political engagement with decolonisation of music education.

Many teachers of music are indeed eclectic in their approach and attend to the student as maker of music with energy and enthusiasm. The difficulty with these eclectic approaches is that they have no "off the shelf" framework or text books like "traditional methods" and it is less easy than teaching from a text book or through a pre arranged sequence of identifiable skills, techniques and processes. I am not suggesting any abandonment of structure, sequence and pedagogy in music education—far from it. What I am suggesting is that music teachers continuously question and develop their personal philosophy of music education as they would a relationship in an ensemble, considering audience and context and how the sounds we make effect our selves and others and communicate with the culture in which we belong.

As I suggested earlier being from the southern hemisphere and from colonial origins presents a series of contexts and values which problematise music education. The biggest of these problems is that methods that appear to function in the northern hemisphere or in the last century or in one context might not work in a fresh context or at this moment in time. This notion is in a sense a realisation of the post-modern concept of distortion and fetishism occurring when we move the local narrative to the grand (Lyotard 1984). This stance is not proposed as a criticism of traditional music methods but to ask those who design curriculum and experience and teach music to continuously question the relevance and appropriateness of what they do and how they do it. When pedagogy ceases to be meaningful and relevant and reverent to the community it serves then we need to review what it is we are teaching and learning and why.

What I have tried to describe and model here is that teachers need to engage with their own personal philosophy of music education as a dynamic process. This is a difficult but satisfying approach to understanding the musical experiences that we love so much and those we embody and communicate to others and which is so much part of our identity. What I present here are examples and tools for analysis that seem to work for music teachers in the field and pre service teachers in engaging with this journey in diverse communities. As a wonderful music teacher once said to me, "'it is what happens when you ask the community" (Templeton 2006, pers comm., 12 July).

This is a continuous process of questioning and at the core of it I have also suggested the need to question what musicianship is in the twenty first century and how it can be reconceived to be more culturally ethical and able to accommodate the very real expressive qualities of contemporary music and technologically mediated production and performances of sound. The approach I have sought to advocate in this book is one that does not suggest a conclusion or any kind of general claims.

I began by asking where music in your life is. Before we know what motivates children and indeed any other characters we hope to educate we need to know about the intrinsic motivations, values and tensions in our own musical lives. We need to identify what gives us flow and what has sustained our interest and allowed it to grow so that we engage with music making in our lives as natural part of it. From here I questioned, where is music in the life of a child? What are the locations of meaning? Who influenced it? What contexts and people nurture connections with music making which lead to transformation?

I then asked where music is in the life of a school. I suggested an alternative here—one which sees a school not as an artificial environment but as a community where music can serve a purpose beyond education alone to serve community and foster belonging, social inclusion and identity. The purpose of this has been to demonstrate a personal philosophical journey that proposed to examine philosophical principles and put the meat on the bones of theory through field research that allowed the participants voices to be heard. These questions simply move from the personal though social meaning to an understanding of how our perspectives become part of the culture we belong to. I believe that if each of us asks these three questions then we may begin to understand that philosophy of music education is a continuous and dynamic process. It allows us to engage with the tensions at the interfaces between cultures, to understand the kinds of contemporary musicianship that technology and popular culture now affords and most importantly to shift the focus of music education from a cultural framing to one which focuses upon the student as maker realised thought the teacher as builder and transmitted and translated into culture by the ideas of the school as village. This framework can confidently and seamlessly move between cultures, genres, and periods of history.

I have tried to be practical and suggest solutions but please be wary of "solutions" because they are highly contextual and influenced by a range of factors and value systems. The most logical solution is to examine context and values as described so that the differences are clear. I hope to model this behaviour here rather than advocate a definitive way of working. Appendix B provides a tool for analysis for this purpose. This chapter then is not a conclusion because this process is continuous and dynamic. I hope that readers will continue to ask these questions and generate new ones from practice that critique the philosophy of music education that we have inherited from a Western art music and Northern hemisphere practice, history and context. This chapter simply asks you where we are now with our thinking about how music might be meaningful for life. While I do not think it appropriate to propose any general principles, I would like to present a summary of some of the insights observed here that are useful in practice and research. What I would also like to do is tag some large ideas that need further discussion and research in a variety of cultural settings.

A summary of insights

In presenting these insights, I have drawn from each chapter in the book and integrated the notions of technology and culture within the discussion and the implications of these on transformation. Transformation is difficult to evaluate. We are often unable to self report it but while this is problematic it is not impossible to measure. As Buber suggests, "any education worthy of the name is the education of character" (1969, 104). There is no doubt that music has transformative effects but what kind of music making has this effect and where is the change in self-located and to what end? The notion of measurement and evaluation of music's impact on education and health is not within the bounds of this book but it is perhaps the next most important step in this enquiry and needs to be pursued rigorously and accountably. For now, I am taking a position that music is and has transformative effects on people of all ages and cultures (Hallam 2001, Simpson, Bodlovich, Harvey and Owens 2003).

Personal meaning

"Personal meaning" describes the personal relationship we have with music making. It is what engages us wordlessly with self in the act of making or perceiving music. It is intrinsically motivated and leads to flow through the challenge of music making. For this experience to lead to transformation it should lead to and involve a dialogue with self. The research also suggests it should be a process that becomes self-actuated. Personal meaning should be evident in the relationship we have with the process and product of music making. It requires an understanding of how we engage with the creative process. It requires the understanding that some knowledge is intuitive and can only be modelled or caught from someone who knows. Alternatively, analytical knowledge requires an attachment to the source musical so that it does not become isolated from its function to support and enable expression.

For the teacher this suggests a need to understand how intuitive and embodied activities can be "caught" through creating an environment where this knowledge can be encountered in context. It also requires an understanding of how to allow analytical knowledge to emerge from a connection with practice. Most importantly, the idea of becoming self-actuating is dependent up in developing a dialogue with self and this is achieved through reflective practice. This kind of practice stems from a combination of modelled self-critical behaviour by the teacher and an understanding of the unique nature of musical reflective practice. This kind of practice involves a discourse about music but one, which involves a conversation about music with music present. It is not an abstract behaviour and in many cases can be non-verbal reflection or may for example involve an improvisational response. Music is only abstract because it is temporal if we utilise technology to capture artefacts such as recordings or graphic representations the conversation about music becomes a rich media experience and a present one. Indeed one of the affordances of technology in music education is that we now have access to multiple positions to discuss analyse and observe musical knowledge.

Our multi-cultural classrooms and communities provide an opportunity to engage with understanding about culture. Music has the capacity to engage people personally in experience with the values represented in the sounds of culture. An open approach to this modelled by teachers, coaches and parents provides a gateway for students to experience "otherness", which contributes to their personal, musical and cultural growth. The implications here for teachers/coaches and parents are about how this behaviour is modelled. Rather than a politically correct way this needs to be an ethical and embodied approach that allows students the opportunity to experience musical otherness with music as the intersection point as a common ground.

Social meaning

Social meaning describes an experience, which leads to broader social engagement and it does so on several levels. Music making in ensembles provides a wordless form of communication between people who share the same measured temporality through rhythm the same intensity of timbre and pitch organization. Collaborative music making communicates in ways, which words cannot and this is useful as a basis of understanding between people; secondly, the music making and its associated discourse provide a focus for discussion about music which is structured by the musical experience rather than any specific social rules. For many this structured way of relating can be a way of achieving social relationships successfully and feelings of belonging that are not dependent upon words and age, gender and cultural politics. Finally the different kinds of socially meaningful experiences replicate human social life—we are partnered in duets or small ensembles, work in teams or families and are a part of larger social entities where we have to behave in unified ways.

Certainly, music as a means of social control is a distortion of this and may be seen in the military use of music as a means of large-scale people coordination and management. Nevertheless, social meaning is important to students learning for precisely these reasons they replicate expectations in social life and provide clear structures for interaction and behaviour. Understanding the power of music making as a means of creating environments, which facilitate social inclusion and community, is valuable for community music making and for schools where community needs to be unified. The role of music in social inclusion and engendering resilience in individuals and communities is critical and as observed in this research offers non-verbal means of collaboration within and across cultures. This aspect needs to be more rigorously documented and perhaps measured in new ways but it is clear that music has a significant role to play in community engagement.

Alternatively, an understanding of the role of social meaning for teachers designing pedagogy and implementing curriculum, is essential. To simply turn parallel learning in groups into collaborative learning provides a multi layered approach and a strategy for handling multiple abilities and capacities in groups and classrooms. Yet many small group instrumental studio teachers teach in parallel approaches despite the availability of ensemble and recordings that feature full instrumental backing with the live instrument muted for ensemble practice and arrangements that frame collaborative performance. It is a simple shift in perspective to always include a collaborative and socially meaningful activity within classes or rehearsals. It is also not difficult to use the opportunity of a social music making activity as site for a conversation about music as reflection in action. This is where modelled behaviour about how to be interpretive, analytical and focused upon increasing expressiveness becomes an opportunity to learn about music with music present in the conversation. Social meaning offers opportunities for both pedagogical and social development of self and it is undeniably a transformative experience.

Cultural meaning

Meaning through cultural engagement is also essential to music making, its sustainability and capacity to enact transformative experience. It is important not only to the individuals' sense of self but their sense of self and others and the sense of self and community. It is where the music maker makes music that they present to their community, that is, "of" the community. The music contains and is creative with the sonic value systems, which characterise the community. Added to this is how the community itself constructs its own identity through the music makers it appreciates as signifying or adding to the collective character. While this is most prominent with national pride in songwriters and composers who articulate what it is to be Australian or Greek or Chinese, it operates on the local level. We see it in the wind ensembles that play in shopping malls; we see it in the eyes of parents at school concerts. We see it in a rock bands compact disc and a DJ's dance floor. Cultural meaning contributes simultaneously to self-formation and community identity. The relationship is reciprocal and the music maker gains a sense of well being and belonging through this process.

It is trivial to consider that at the end of every class or rehearsal or studio lesson there be some kind of presentation of our music making that allows cultural meaning to occur. The Suzuki method practitioners talk of mother tongue approaches. Music making is a "family" activity in that philosophy and practice and teachers facilitate cultural meaning through mini concerts to families and major concerts to others in the Suzuki community. The secret here is that the cultural event is engineered for success. It is a safe environment to undertake cultural activity. For example, the music teacher's organising mini concerts in the classroom. So too is this possible in the instrumental studio and ensemble. For composition and music production then other metaphors for presentation should be encouraged—an exhibition of works, artist talks—both allow a conversation about production to occur with music present in the conversation. It is an opportunity to "reflect on action". Using technology to record, revisit compositions and performances allow the discourse about music to occur and for meaning to be formative.

Designing meaningful and engaging environments

Cultural meaning is useful on its own but needs to be connected to activities, which encourage social and personal connections to be transformative. It is these considerations that

> Education must therefore begin with a psychological insight into the child's capacities, interests and habits. That we have been examining here and this leads to being continually interpreted – [to] know what they mean [and] translated into terms of their social equivalents (Dewey in Eisner 1994, v).

It is this understanding that forms the basis of designing meaningful and engaging environments. The notion of designing environments where musical knowledge can be encountered is different to that of mimetic teaching and learning practice. It has its origins in Dewey's Experiential learning (Dewey 1970, 1989) and Bruner's notion of Discovery learning (Bruner 1960, 1966, 1972, 1973, 1986). These ideas were central to my own formation as a teacher and seemed to answer the question of how we encounter intuitive and embodied knowledge in music as well as deal with ever-increasing amounts of information. These ideas have been further refined in the last twenty years by such innovative educators as (Papert 1980, 1994, 1996) constructionist notion of "micro-worlds" provided virtual worlds for children to engage with meaningful experience. So too has this work been enhanced by Gardner's theory of "multiple intelligences" (Gardner 1993b) and the practice based realisation of these ideas in Harvard Project Zero: Arts Propel (Davidson 1992). Each of these approaches enriched the fundamental Rousseau notion of engaging children with intrinsic play as learning.

These approaches also utilise constructed and existing environments and simulations as a principle for learning. It still intrigues me that these more natural learning approaches are still not widespread and discipline and mimetic approaches still abound. The concern for many teachers is to structure analytical experience and knowledge in ordered sequence is not problematic but to facilitate intuitive and embodied experience is not personally confronting, exposing and challenging for teachers. To seek to have these in productive tension as Swanwick (1994) describes for musical knowledge or to actively engage with the politics of culture at the interfaces between cultures is perhaps more difficult to enact and certainly impossible to contain within a text book or a pedagogy.

I have advocated here an approach that begins with the intrinsic nature of music experience and presented some analytical tools I have found useful in getting information about the nature of a school or community and the culture and values of those who inhabit these contexts. The use of these tools for situational analysis (See Appendix A) is an important step in shifting from colonial imposition to a bottom up approach, which considers culture and people ethically and empathetically. To then observe the interaction between music maker and the creative process and examine the presence of meaningful engagement using the matrices provides a way of evaluating the effectiveness of a program or approach (See Appendix B). It seeks to identify gaps in the access to meaningful engagement and then suggests what kind of response might fit the situation for curriculum/experience design. It is then that we are able to examine philosophy in practice and check our fundamental beliefs and values against wider understandings of music education theory and philosophy. Philosophy needs to be dynamic and interact with culture and practice. What is separated out of this process in this discussion are the areas of technology, culture and popular music. I have argued that each of these problematises a Western art music framing of musical culture and education.

What I am suggesting, as a rule of thumb, is a politically active approach which engages with the tensions at the interfaces between cultures, and which draws upon music as a common ground for syncretic interaction between cultures and across them in ethical ways. With technology we simply need to ask what it is that the technology reveals, what it conceals and whether what it conceals can act as a pedagogical focusing mechanism to direct activity. It is important to consider these ideas when examining the creative process so we need to know what the role of the technology is in production of music. These ideas suggest quite strongly the need to re focus our concept of musicianship and aural perception so that they are culturally inclusive, sho an understanding of technological mediated expressions and performance.

The primary focus here then is on the development of a new form of musicianship and aural perception based on a time and space model of aural analysis but able to accommodate culture ethically and technology as an amplifier of musicality (Brown 2006) and transcends twentieth century concepts of "tool". We need to also examine the idea that there are new performances spaces such as the internet, compact disc, DVD and these too require a different way of working and performing. The purpose of music education in this environment needs to facilitate an understanding of how music is expressive of culture and provide opportunities for embodied and intuitive learning in a productive relationship with analytical and technical knowledge. In the post-modern sense teachers and music coaches need to be able to equip students with critical tools and reflective frameworks that allow them to move towards self contained engagement with music making as a lifetime pursuit. It needs to provide students with a means of critical of the abstraction of music's presence in commodities and the aestheticisation of commodities.

Music is all around us and we need to be aware of its purpose and effect on us and there is not better way to do this than through direct experience of making music and critiquing reflecting and responding to these experiences in words, writing, visual representation and sound. Hence, it is making music that is at the core of this philosophy and practice of music, which leads to transformation

The student as maker

The concept of the "student as maker" of meaning and self suggests that through making music and reflecting and responding to these experiences that the outcome will be self-formative—it will lead to transformation. What I am arguing here then is multi layered. On the first level, the student needs to have access to making music in a relevant and reverent way and in a context, which replicates or simulates how music is made in the world. The student also needs to have access to experience possible worlds as well as actual through exploratory and innovative experience (Bruner 1973, 1986, Papert 1980, 1994, 1996). In this way students can encounter and be critical of how music is made in their own community, experience something of the reality of "other" cultures and times through making music in common ground experiences and finally discover the limitless possibilities of music making through developing or experimenting with new forms and sounds.

All of this activity needs to be accompanied by a conversation about music, its effect, cultural significance and a drawing out of musical knowledge in relation to the context. This kind of reflective activity certainly subscribes to (Saatchi and Saatchi 2000, Schon 1984, 1987) notion of reflection on action and in action but we need to further acknowledge that the musical discourse is more than words and textual descriptions these conversations should be had with the music present in the conversation either live or through artefacts that represent it. Music notation, computer wave forms and sound and video recordings allow us to now have these conversations in a present rather than abstract way.

In our work on ePortfolio systems (Dillon 2002, Dillon and Brown 2006, Dillon and Nalder 2004, Dillon, Nalder, Brown and Smith 2003) in relation to evaluating and assessing music and arts activity perhaps one of the most significant aspects of using these kinds of digital systems in assessment and evaluation was that participants in the research valued the presence of music in the conversation about music. The technology allowed them to revisit music, apply different lenses to it to analyse and examine it. Beyond this it also allowed a response to music to also be music rather than a sentence describing music. So it is argued here that not only do we need to make music and reflect but we need to make music that is meaningful and engaging and reflect on it in new ways so that our reflections engage with music as a discourse (Swanwick 1988, 1994). The other issue this raises is that evaluation, assessment and reflection that leads to an engagement with musical knowledge is not a separate entity for documenting progress in school reports but an integral part of the learning—it is the learning. Students in the case study here valued teachers who they perceived they learnt from not those who were just friendly. They wanted to feel that they were making progress and becoming more effective, expressive and critical musicians. They compared their own understanding with their "less musically engaged" friends as "seeing and hearing in 3D".

Reflection is a natural process. When my own child was a baby I experienced watching her review and practice new words and sentences she had encountered during the day. She practiced their sound and their effect before she went to sleep each night. I wondered what it was that happened to children to stop this seemingly natural reflective practice. Was it the absence of playfulness or the seriousness of school in? We need to encourage reflective practice through building an environment where this too is modelled by the teacher and frameworks for analysis and language and processes for discussion are available that have music present in the discussion about music and methods to allow for multi media responses. The role of technology in this is obvious but we need to reframe music reflective practice to understand that recording and representative music technology reveals that temporality and the abstract and ephemeral aspects of music which text response assumes it's a factor that no longer applies. Music making and its artefacts are now as present as visual art. Therefore, the student as maker of music and self can construct themselves through encountering an environment built by a teacher who understands the essence of practice and reflection in twenty first century music education as being present entities.

The music teacher as builder

Building involves design and planning based on a thorough architectural knowledge of materials and their properties, an understanding of the location of the structure and knowledge about the function and users needs. The music teacher as builder has examined this kind of holistic, contextual and community approach to curriculum and teaching practice. The teacher as builder understands the student as maker of meaning through making and reflecting as described above. The teacher as builder then seeks to enable a student to become a self-actuated and expressive music maker. The student becomes open to music experiences from a broad range of cultural and chronological contexts.

The idea of becoming self-actuating and autotelic music makers allows a student to manage their own lifelong music learning and access music making in a range of way over their lives. This self-actuation is not a linear process we do not simply move from dependence through independence and then to interdependence although this is the impression we get when we outgrow one teacher and move to another. In many concepts of musical knowledge, we revisit them many times at progressively deeper levels as Bruner suggests, but we also shift in confidence about our achievement of the inherent challenges in the musical experience and the concept. As an example from my own experience as a singer I have sung across and sailed over the groove as a jazz musician and popular performer for many years. I have been known for my sense of phrase and rhythmic ability and it has been a feature of my personal style.

Recently I began singing bass in an Acapella group that sings complex polyrhythmic and polyphonic repertoire. I am now responsible for the groove. For holding it together, for grounding the whole ensemble, I am currently seeking movement lessons so that I can locate my feeling of rhythm in my body rather than my head. I have moved from an articulate interdependent understanding of rhythm in one context to one where I am dependent on manually stomping for several minutes before beginning any tune and totally dependent on the physical and embodied notion of the pulse. I am relearning what rhythm means to me. This kind of process is endless for musicians not just a part of early musicianship. We need to learn this behaviour also. To recognise when we are dependent in some contexts and how we might approach learning this new skill or recognising that we perhaps need to visit a new teacher to engage with this knowledge.

What arises, as a central issue for music education is what the role, responsibilities and characteristics of good practice are in music teaching? What contributes to teacher identity? The picture of the music teacher which I have created in this study has particular characteristics. These are not simply personality types but stances that an effective teacher adopts so that the environment they construct reflects those kinds of values and nurture creative making and reflection. The teachers model and engender values of openness to music from across cultures and times. Interestingly, when compared with more recent interview data with Music teachers who are considered by their community to exhibit good practice in music education, almost without fail these teachers were either from a non-Western cultural background or had experience with cross-cultural musicianship. At very least these teachers crossed genres in their experience of Western art music, jazz and popular music (Dillon 2005a, 2006a). This suggests that openness may not be a personality trait but is teachable and further that our music teacher training should include cross cultural and cross-genre embodied experience with music making. It is this kind of openness that students and teachers alike presented in interviews. I would suggest here that experience of being "the other" and challenging the musical skill level of an individual provides a model of openness and an opportunity to learn how to engage with the unknown.

The teacher as builder then engenders an approach to teaching music that allows students to encounter knowledge in the environment on one hand and a process of direct modelling of intuitive and embodied knowledge to and with students. So on one hand the teacher models an approach to performance, composition and analytical listening to the students and on the other the teacher constructs and environment where musical knowledge can be encountered.

The school as village

Recognising that a school or community space has its own cultures, activities and ceremonies is a fundamental understanding. If we imagine the school as a village with pragmatic reasons for music making then this is the beginning of understanding the resources of place and culture in music education (Dillon 2000). This concept seeks to reintegrate art and life or at least recognise the significance of functional music making. The school is a village with its own culture and values and recognition of this makes its very culture a site for learning. The idea that a school is an artificial environment and that what this enables is for experiences to be designed that is controlled for their focus and safety. Further, more the environment enables a flexible space where new ideas can be realised and old ideas experienced as imaginative play or simulation that replicate "real world" practice.

The school as village allows knowledge to be encountered in a managed school or community one where the learning is focused and the outcome has been designed to provide a safe, ethical and musical knowledge focused environment. These are indeed managed micro-worlds. The benefit though of this approach is that it feeds directly into an understanding of how music is made in communities and how its functional and aesthetic qualities become blurred such that both are educational experiences. As our world becomes more complex and more abstract it is this kind of approach, which allows us to experience music making first hand and to adopt an approach to analytical thinking which allows students to be critical of music wherever they find it and be able to reconcile the effects and meaning of the context.

Just as Arts Propel advocates "domain projects" (Davidson 1992), I am advocating that our own contexts and environments have the capacity to contribute to our knowledge of music. Simultaneously this approach also affects how we might respond to social change and other cultures as well as integrated multi media and even as Papert (1980) suggests software based environments. Networked musical environments also amplify this thought and raise further questions twenty first century musicianship, cultural politics and understanding of the role of technology. What then becomes the role of the teacher in this kind of context?

Knowing where we need to go next

These ideas constitute the beginning of further discussion that seeks to flesh out a refocusing of music education and involve others in the discussion. Western music education has evolved from a musical world that reifies soloists, conductors and solitary composers while the philosophy tends to congregate around gurus and whilst I am thankful for their critical thinking, I am also conscious of the idea that "I think therefore I am" which focuses around individuals perhaps needs to learn from the Indigenous Australian notion of "I am because we are" (Chalmers 2005) and consider a world of productive tensions rather than binary oppositions as the norm. In the same way that much music technology was about solitary activity with a computer and now congregates around creating communities of interest through networks of collaborative interaction, music education needs to also move from the solo focus of the previous centuries to the collaborative frameworks of the twenty first century which encourage and nurture, support and enable us to engage with the tensions at the interfaces between cultures and discover productive tensions between intuitive and analytical knowledge in the construction of pedagogy. We need to reframe musicianship so that it is inclusive of cultural constructions of meaning and application rather than simply aesthetic and mono-cultural. We need to acknowledge that where we are, whom we are, our values, experiences and relationships all contribute to unique perspectives on how music is made, perceived and valued.

Music is important to humanly organised societies (Blacking 1995). The ways in which we make music, perform it, integrate it into our ceremonies and rituals affects us personally, socially and culturally. It contributes to how we define ourselves as persons it provides non-verbal means of communicating important knowledge and emotional qualities between others and ourselves in small groups. It signifies our place in a community and captures the values that identify the community simultaneously. It can be a common ground where we can wordlessly communicate between cultures. It has the most surprising ability to blend in syncretic ways with other human societies and form new expressive experiences.

Music has the power to heal, communicate and affirm our self. It also has the power to transform self and our understanding of our self in relation to other people and cultures. All this is intrinsic. For music experience to be meaningful and for it to lead to transformation in these kinds of positive ways and to educate character at the core of this is simply recognition of this idea. Music is intrinsically motivated—if I have a child in a room with a drum, the child will hit the drum. If we do nothing else then we should not get in the way of the child's desire for playfulness with sonic materials. If we do however decide to initiate the student into a musical discourse, then perhaps we can consider first the student as maker. We can then build an environment for them to be playful in so that they can encounter musical knowledge. Second, we can consciously recognise our context as a village where we can provide a safe and encouraging environment for students to understand where music is in their lives. Perhaps then, we can realise music as meaning and transformation and give access to meaningful music making for life.

APPENDIX A

MEANINGFUL ENGAGEMENT MATRIX

← X axis

	Appreciate	Direct	Explore	Participate	Select
Personal					
Social					
Cultural					

↑ Y axis

Key to using the matrix

X axis

An appreciator: Listening carefully to music and analysing music representations.

A director: Managing music making activities.

An explorer: Searching through musical possibilities and assessing their value.

A participant: Involved in intuitive music making.

A selector: Making decisions about the value of music or musical elements.

Y axis

Personal: The activity is intrinsically enjoyable.

Social: The activity connects the student with others and these relationships are valued.

Cultural: The activity is regarded as valuable by the community and, by participating (or succeeding) in it; the student achieves a sense that they too are important.

APPENDIX B

PHILOSOPHICAL CHECKLIST

Beliefs supported by theoretical references

Music is an intrinsically motivated activity (Abbs 1990, Aronoff 1969, Dewey 1989, Dillon 1995b, 2001c, Dillon and Stewart 2006, Dillon, Stewart, Brown, Arthurs, Dodge and Peacock 2004).

What this means is that humans are playful beings and being playful with sound and organising it is widespread and universal amongst human cultures. So if children will naturally make sounds and be playful with sound and expressive with sound why do so many of us here have such bad memories of school music teachers and classes. Why is music NOT intrinsically motivated in schools except by the elite 'gifted'? It must be to do with the teachers values, the curriculum and the approach or method so at the very least we should not get in the way of the intrinsic nature of music activity and aim to build on the child's natural aesthetic responses- create environments where they can both be playful with artistic materials and learn.

What music/activity is intrinsic in this context?

Activity and reflection should ideally complement and support each other. Action by itself is blind, and reflection impotent. (Csikszentmihalyi 1996, Schon 1984, 1987)

We need a balance of these activities of experience and reflection and we need to provide structures and habits of making and reflecting. Activity and experiences in making music in real or simulated way need to be made into cognitive understanding through structured reflection. Reflection needs to be in another medium ie verbal, written, video audio tape- this allows another lens or perspective on the experience.

Alternatively, over attention to reflective and abstract learning is impotent. Make it come alive by giving it purpose, context, and relevance and make it concrete- a making activity. The secret is a balance between analytic and intuitive learning between that which is 'caught' and that which is "taught" (Swanwick 1994).

How can the environment we construct contain making and reflecting activities?

Music lessons should include both making and reflective activities and be taught within a context that is real or simulated so that it is relevant to life. (Bruner 1960, 1966, 1972, 1986, Dewey 1916, 1970, 1989, Dillon 2004a, 2004d, 2005a, Dillon and Stewart 2006, Durrant and Welch 1995, Hallam 2001, Papert 1996, Swanwick 1981, 1994).

In practical terms, this means to make music i.e. create or perform music in the classroom based upon real life activity and discuss and draw out the process and evaluation of each product through reflection both formal and informal.

What is a real world or simulated context that contains this experience?

Music lessons should have activities that involve Composing or a creative aspect, Performing or a presentation aspect and listening/audition/ analytic response (Swanwick 1981, 1988, 1994, 1999, Swanwick and Franca 1999, Swanwick and Tillman 1986).

Every lesson should involve the possibility of children making aesthetic judgments or creative thought. Even if it is simply deciding on the timbre and dynamic of singing the "pop" in "Pop goes the weasel" the students should be involved in making those decisions. They should always present or perform work at the end or during a lesson and they should always discuss each work in a reflective way using the vocabulary that of musical elements. Devise ways in which a lesson containing all these elements can be devised?

The musical aspects of curriculum refer to consistently revisiting the fundamental concepts of the elements of music in increasingly deeper and more complex ways that build on understanding of music (Bruner 1960, 1966, 1972, 1973, 1986, Swanwick 1981, 1988, 1994, 1999, Swanwick and Franca 1999, Swanwick and Tillman 1986).

The elements of music are used to:
• Develop compositions in expressiveness and form.
• Develop performances in expressiveness and impact
• Develop critical listening frameworks and criteria for aural analysis of sound/music (Dillon 2001c, Pratt 1990).

What is the musical knowledge contained in this activity?

Music is a part of life and community - treat it as such in schools (Burnaford, Aprill and Weiss 2004, Dillon 2006f, Dillon and Chapman 2005, Dillon, Stewart, Brown, Arthurs, Dodge and Peacock 2004, Dillon 1999a, 2000, 2001c, Fiske 2000, Gardner 1993a, 1993b, Hallam 2001, Robinson 2001, Rusinek, Burnard, Evelein, Economidou-Stavrou and Sæther 2005).

Music is not just part of the curriculum but can be used as an effective learning tool in other subjects. More importantly, it can be used as a unifying cultural force within the school community and as a way of projecting the image of that community to the world beyond school/community

Is there some way this can become a whole school or community experience?

If students gain broad general music experiences in the classroom and they also learn to be reflective and self critical about music then this skill enables them to make sense and gain access to the meaning of music wherever they find it. (Dillon 2001a, 2001c, Fiske 2000, Saatchi and Saatchi 2000, Schon 1984).

What are the lifetime education implications?

Music is meaningful in personal, social and cultural ways—students need access to all of these through the classroom and school environment if they are to make sense of the world they live in- a world where music plays an important role (Csikszentmihalyi 1994, Dewey 1989, Dillon 2001a, 2001c, Elliott 1995, Fiske 2000, Paynter and Aston 1970, Reimer 1989, Saatchi and Saatchi 2000, Swanwick 1994, Vella 2000).

Does the project/process give access to all three areas of meaning?

Examine the teaching methods, resource, curriculum design and policies that allow access to this kind of interaction. Focus perhaps first on a "real world scenario" that demonstrates the problem in practise then construct an approach and or policy that embeds all of these ideas drawn from the previous questions and make sure that it includes a making, skill development and reflective/presentation stage that allows access to all three areas of meaning. Next, re-use the notions of personal, social and cultural meaning as a checklist for the potential for your strategy/plan to deal with the problem.

Writing up your personal philosophy in context

Step 1
Use all the data from the above to write a rationale that begins by describing and stating the problem, describing your context succinctly.

Step 2
Then examine the aspects of the context drawn from the context analysis diagram that will identify the constraints and positive aspects of the whole context including the student's and communities need.

Step 3
Next include the theoretical understanding drawn from the checklist and perhaps look at readings drawn from this checklist (refer to the bibliography for wider reading)

Step 4
Finally construct a solution in terms of an approach, which will include strategies, lesson and project plan ideas, policies and a teacher's stance, which describes the values inherent in the approach, that is, attitude such as "music is musi" or a focus on creative and imaginative product rather than technical perfection or an attitude of full and enthusiastic participation over technical perfection but with strategies to build skills.

Step 5
Summarise by describing how the approach addresses the personal, social and cultural meaning issues. For example:
- Personal meaning from composing, creating, or achieving a challenging task.
- Social meaning: the activity may be developed in a collaborative interactive group.
- Cultural meaning: the activity has a presentation in a positive feedback environment ie concert, exhibition, or recording. The idea here is that the music conveys something to a community to which the community can respond by sharing and can value both the work and the maker.

REFERENCES

Abbs, P. 1990. *Living powers: The arts in education.* London: Falmer Press.

Agardy, S. 1985. *Young Australians and music.* Melbourne, VIC: Research Branch, Australian Broadcasting Tribunal.

Aronoff, F. 1969. *Music and young children.* New York, NY: Rinehart and Winston.

Askew, G. 1998. *Music education in the primary school.* South Melbourne, VIC: Addison, Wesley and Longman.

Baker, F. 2004. Results from the questionnaire and school data for *The Band Thing project.* Unpublished report on questionnaire research The Band Thing, School of Music, University of Queensland.

Bamford, A. 2006. *The wow factor: Global research compendium on the impact of the arts in education.* New York, NY: Waxmann Munster.

Barwick, L. 2005. Performance, aesthetics, experience: Thoughts on *yawalyu mungamunga* songs. In *Aesthetics and experience in music performance*, ed. E. Mackinlay, D. Collins and S. Owens, 1-18. Cambridge: Cambridge Scholars Press.

Bernstein, B. 2000. *Pedagogy, symbolic control and identity.* Lanham, MD: Rowman and Littlefield Publishers Inc.

Blacking, J. 1995. *Music, culture and experience.* Chicago, IL: University of Chicago Press.

Borg, W. R., and M. Gall, eds. 1983. *Educational research: An introduction*, 4th ed. New York, NY: Longman.

Bradley, J., and E. Mackinlay. 2000. *Songs from a plastic water rat: An introduction to the musical traditions of the Yanyuwa Community of the Southwest Gulf of Carpentaria.* Ngulaig 17. Brisbane, QLD: Aboriginal and Torres Strait Islander Studies Unit, University of Queensland.

—. 2007. Singing the land, singing the family: Song, place and spirituality amongst the Yanyuwa. In *The soundscapes of Australia: Music, place and spirituality*, ed. F. Richards,75-92. London: Open University Press.

Bresler, L. 2004. *Knowing bodies, moving minds.* Urbana-Champaign, IL: Kluwer Academic Publishers.

Brown, A. 2000. Modes of compositional engagement. Paper presented at the Australasian Computer Music Conference *Interfaces*, June 19 - 21, Brisbane, Queensland, Australia.

—. 2003. Music composition and the computer: An examination of the work practices of five experienced composers. PhD thesis, University of Queensland, Brisbane, Queensland, Australia.

—. 2006. *Computers and music education: Amplifying musicality*. New York, NY: Routledge.

Brown, A., and S. Dillon. (In press). Networked improvisational musical environments: Learning through online collaborative music making. In *Teaching music in the digital age*, ed. J. Finney and P. Burnard. London: Continuum International Publishing Group.

—. 2001. *Sound reflections: Your music learning diary*. Brisbane, QLD: Exploding Art Music Productions.

Brown, A., S. C. Dillon, and K. Purcell. 2005. *Reading and writing rock*. 2nd ed. Sydney, NSW: Science Press.

Brown, A., A. Sorensen, and S. Dillon. 2002. *jam2jam*. Version 1. [Interactive generative music making software]. Brisbane, QLD: Exploding Art Music Productions.

Bruner, J., S. 1960. *The process of education*. New York, NY: Vintage Books.

—. 1966. *Towards a theory of instruction*. Cambridge, MA: Belknap Press of Harvard University.

—. 1973. *Beyond the information given: Studies in the psychology of knowing*. New York, NY: Norton.

—. 1974. *The relevance of education*. Harmondsworth: Penguin Education.

—. 1979. *Essays for the left hand*. Cambridge, MA: The Belknap Press of Harvard University.

—. 1986. *Actual minds, possible worlds*. Cambridge, MA: Harvard University Press.

Buber, M. 1969. *Between man and man*. trans. R. G. Smith. London: Fontana.

—. 1975. *I and thou*, 2nd ed, trans. R. G. Smith. Edinburgh: T & T Clark.

Burnaford, G., A. Aprill, A., and C. Weiss. 2004. *Renaissance in the classroom: Arts integration and meaningful learning*. Mahwah, NJ: Lawrence Erlbaum and Associates, Publishers.

Chalmers, G. 2005. Tigershark Dreaming. Lecture presented in *Music and Spirituality Series*, 30 August, Queensland University of Technology, Brisbane, Queensland.

Cox, E. 1997. *A truly civil society: 1995 Boyer Lecture Series*. Sydney, NSW: Australian Broadcasting Corporation.

Csikszentmihalyi, M. 1994. *Flow: The psychology of happiness*. New York, NY: Random Century Group.

—. 1996. *Creativity: Flow and the psychology of discovery and invention*. New York, NY: Harper Collins.

Curriculum Corporation of Victoria. 1994a. *A statement on the Arts for Australian schools*. Melbourne, VIC: Curriculum Corporation of Victoria.

Curriculum Corporation. 1994b. *The arts: A curriculum profile for Australian schools*. Melbourne, VIC: Curriculum Corporation of Victoria.

Custodero, L. A. 2002. Seeking challenge, finding skill: Flow experience and music education. *Arts Education Policy Review* 103(3): 3-10.

D'Cruz, J. V., and W. Hannah. 1979. *Perceptions of excellence*. Melbourne, VIC: The Polding Press.

Davidson, L. 1992. *Arts Propel: A handbook for music* (with video of evaluation methods and approaches). Cambridge, MA: Harvard Project Zero.

de Bono, E. 1991. *I am right, you are wrong: From this to the new renaissance, from rock logic to water logic*. Harmondsworth: Penguin.

Denzin, N. K., and Y. S Lincoln. eds. 2000. *Handbook of qualitative research*. 2nd ed. London: Sage Publications Inc.

Dewey, J. 1916. *Democracy and education*. New York, NY: Macmillan.

——. 1954. *Art as experience*, 2nd ed. New York, NY: Capricorn Books.

——. 1963. *The child and the curriculum and the school and society*, 7th ed. Urbana, IL: University of Chicago Press.

——. 1970. *Experience and education*, 12th ed. London: Collier-Macmillan.

Dillon, S. C. 1997. The student as maker: A narrative for a pragmatist aesthetic. Paper presented at the Australian Society for Music Education (ASME X1), 4-8 July, Brisbane, Queensland, Australia.

——. 1995b. The student as maker: An examination of making in music education and the implications for contemporary curriculum development. Master of Education Minor thesis, Latrobe University, Melbourne, Victoria, Australia.

——. 1999a. The student as maker: An analysis of the meaning attached to early childhood musical encounters. *The Weaver: A Forum for New Ideas in Education*, http://www.latrobe.edu.au/www/graded/SDed3.html, 3. (accessed 28 February, 2007).

——. 1999b. The teacher as builder of music learning contexts. Australian Association for Research in Education and New Zealand Association for Research in Education Joint Conference Proceedings [CD-ROM].

——. 2000. The school as village: Reintegrating art and life in a school. *Primary Arts* 1: 9-12.

——. 2001a. Arts education 21C: The meaning of arts in the twenty first century and the implications of this meaning for teaching learning and research. *Primary Arts* 2: 1-10.

——. 2001b. Making computer music meaningful in schools. *Mikropolyphonie-online journal* 6, http://www.mikropol.net/ (accessed 28 February 2007).

———. 2001c. The student as maker: An examination of the meaning of music to students in a school and the ways in which we give access to meaningful music education. PhD thesis, La Trobe, Melbourne, Victoria, Australia.

———. 2002. Digital multi media portfolios (D-MAP) in music learning. Paper presented at the *Closing the Loop: 2002 Evaluations and Assessment Conference*, 14-15 November, Brisbane, Queensland, Australia.

———. 2003. jam2jam-Meaningful music making with computers. Paper presented at the *Artistic Practice as Research* 25th Annual Conference of the Australian Association for Research in Music Education, 27-30 September, Brisbane, Queensland, Australia.

———. 2004a. Documenting cases of "good practice" in Music Education. *Queensland Journal of Music Education* 1(1): 23-52.

———. 2004b. Meaningful music making with music technology. *Queensland Journal of Music Education* 10: 23-52.

———. 2004c. Modelling, meaning through software design. Paper presented at the 26th Annual Conference of the Australian Association for Research in Music Education, Southern Cross University, 25-28 September, Tweed Heads, New South Wales, Australia.

———. 2004d. Music, Meaning and Transformation. Paper presented at the 26th International Society for Music Education Conference, 14-16 July. Tenerife, Spain.

———. 2004e. Save to DISC: Documenting innovation in music learning. Paper presented at the 26th Annual Conference of the Australian Association for Research in Music Education, Southern Cross University, 25-28 September, Tweed Heads, New South Wales, Australia.

———. 2005a. El profesor de música como gestor cultural (The teacher as cultural manager: Identifying the qualities of music teachers that promote social inclusion in secondary schools). *Revista Electrónica Complutense de Investigación en Educación Musical* 2: 1-10.

———. 2005b. Meaningful engagement with music technology. In *Aesthetics and experience in music performance*, ed. E. Mackinlay, D. Collins and S. Owens, 327-341. Cambridge: Cambridge Scholars Press.

———. 2006a. Assessing the positive influence of music activities in community development programs. *Music Education Research* 8(2): 267-280.

———. 2006b. Before the eyes glaze over. *Music Forum* 13: 32-33.

———. 2006c. jam2jam: Networked Improvisational Musical Environments. In *School music and teacher education: A global perspective in the new century*, ed. M. Moore and B. W. Leung, 19-30. Hong Kong: Department of

CAPE, the Hong Kong Institute of Education & International Society for Music Education (ISME).

——. 2006d. jam2jam: Networked jamming. *Media Culture* 9(6), http://journal.media-culture.org.au/0612/04-dillon.php (accessed 28 February, 2007).

——. 2006e. Maybe we can find some common ground: Indigenous Perspectives, a music teachers' story. Paper presented at the *(Re)Contesting Indigenous knowledge and Indigenous studies* Conference, 28-30 June, Gold Coast, Queensland, Australia.

Dillon, S., and A. Brown. 2006. The art of ePortfolios: Insights from the creative arts experience. In *Handbook of research on ePortfolios: Concepts, technology and case studies*, ed. A. J. and C. Kaufman, 418-431. Indianapolis, IN: Idea-Group Inc.

Dillon, S., and J. Chapman. 2005. 'Without a song you are nothing': Songwriter's perspectives on indigenising tertiary music and sound curriculum. In *Cultural diversity in music education: Directions and challenges for the 21st century*, ed. P. Shehan Campbell, J. Drummond, P. Dunbar-Hall, K. Howard, H. Schippers and T. Wiggins, 189-198. Brisbane, QLD: Queensland Conservatorium Research Centre with Australian Academic Press.

Dillon, S., G. Nalder, A. Brown, and J. Smith. 2003. Digital multi media portfolios (D-MAP) in music learning. Paper presented at the *Artistic Practice as Research* 25th Annual Conference of the Australian Association for Research in Music Education, 27-30 September, Brisbane, Queensland, Australia.

Dillon, S., and D. Stewart. 2006. Songs of resilience. Paper presented at the Proceedings of the 27th World Conference of the International Society for Music Education, 16-21 July, Kuala Lumpur, Malaysia.

Dillon, S., D. Stewart, A. Brown, A. Arthurs, G. Dodge, and C. Peacock. 2004. Building culturally sustainable communities through expressive music making. Unpublished document, Queensland University of Technology Brisbane, Queensland, Australia.

Durrant, C., and G. Welch. 1995. *Making sense of music*. London: Cassell.

Edwards, B. 1999. Inside the whale: Deep insider research. Paper presented at the Australian Association for Research in Education and the New Zealand Association for Research in Education joint conference, 29 November–2 December, Melbourne, Victoria, Australia.

Eisner, E. 1985. *Learning and teaching the ways of knowing*. Chicago, IL: National Society for the Study of Education.

——. 1994. *Cognition and curriculum*, 2nd ed. New York, NY: Teachers College Press.

—. 1991. *The enlightened eye: Qualitative inquiry and the enhancement of educational practice*. New York, NY: Macmillan.
Elliott, D. J. 1995. *Music matters: A new philosophy of music education*. New York, NY: Oxford University Press.
Ellis, C. 1985. *Aboriginal music: Education for living*. St. Lucia, QLD: University of Queensland Press.
Encarta® World English Dictionary. 1999. ed. Microsoft. Corporation, Bloomsbury Publishing Plc.
Fiske, E. B. 2000. *Champions of change: The impact of the arts on learning*. Washington DC, WA: Arts Education partnership, The President's Committee on the Arts and the Humanities.
Gans, H. J. 1975. *Popular culture, high culture: An analysis and evaluation of taste*. 2nd ed. New York, NY: Basic Books.
Gardner, H. 1993a. *Creating minds: An anatomy of creativity seen through the lives of Freud, Einstein, Picasso, Stravinsky, Eliot, Graham and Ghandi*. New York, NY: Basic Books.
—. 1993b. *Frames of mind: The theory of multiple intelligences*. London: Fontana Press.
Gates, A. 2004. *A multiple intelligence approach to teaching music*. Unpublished manuscript no. 1425920, Wayne State University, Michigan United States.
Green, L. 1988. *Music on deaf ears: Musical meaning, ideology, education*. Manchester: Manchester University Press.
—. 2001. *How popular musicians learn: A way ahead for music education*. Burlington, VT: Ashgate.
Hallam, S. 2001. *The power of music: The strength of music's influence on our lives*. London: Performing Rights Society.
Heidegger, M. 1977. *The question concerning technology, and other essays*, trans, W. Lovitt. New York, NY: Harper and Row.
Hinkson, D. J. 1992. Misreading the deeper currents: The limits of economic rationality. *Arena* 98: 112-132.
Jorgensen, D. L. 1989. *Participant observation: A methodology for human studies*, 2nd ed. Newbury Park, CA: Sage Publications.
Leirse, A. 1999. The effectiveness of music programs in Victorian government secondary schools 1995-6. PhD thesis, Monash University, Clayton, Victoria, Australia.
Lincoln, Y. S., and E. G. Guba. 1985. *Naturalistic enquiry*. Beverley Hills, CA: Sage Publications Inc.
Lyotard, J. 1984. *The postmodern condition*. Minneapolis, MN: University of Minnesota Press.

Mackinlay, E. 2004. "Without a song you are nothing". Lecture presented at Queensland University of Technology, 9 August, Brisbane, Queensland, Australia.

—. 2005. Moving and dancing towards decolonisation in education: An example from an Indigenous Australian performance classroom. *Australian Journal of Indigenous Education* 34: 113-122.

Marett, A. 2005. *Songs, Dreamings and ghosts: The wangga of North Australia*. Lebanon, NH: Wesleyan University Press.

McLuhan, M. 1967. *The medium is the massage*. London: Routledge and Kegan Paul.

Ministry of Education (Schools Division). 1988a. *The arts framework: P-10*. Carlton, VIC: Curriculum Corporation of Victoria.

Ministry of Education (Schools Division). 1988b. *The school curriculum and organisation framework: P-12*. Carlton, VIC: Curriculum Corporation of Victoria.

Mussen, P. H., Conger, J. J., and J. Kagan. 1974. *Child development and personality*, 4th ed. New York, NY: Harper and Rowe.

Nakata, M. 2002. Indigenous knowledge and the cultural interface: Underlying issues at the intersection of knowledge and information systems. Paper presented at the 68th International Federation of Library Association Council and General Conference, 8-24 August, Glasgow, Scotland.

Papert, S. 1980. *Mindstorms, children, computers and powerful ideas*. New York, NY: Basic Books Inc.

—. 1994. *The children's machine: Rethinking school in the age of the computer*. New York, NY: Harvester Wheatsheaf.

—. 1996. *Constructionism*. Mahwah, NJ: Lawrence Erlbaum and Associates.

Paynter, J., and P. Aston. 1970. *Sounds and silence: Classroom projects in creative music*. Cambridge, MA: Cambridge University Press.

Perkins, D. N. 1986. *Knowledge as design*. Hillsdale, NJ: Lawrence Earlbaum Associates.

Perkins, D. N. 1988. Teaching for transfer. *Educational Leadership* 46(1): 22-32.

Pratt, G. 1990. *Aural awareness: Principles and practice*. London: Open University Press.

Reimer, B. 1989. *A philosophy of music education*, 2nd ed. Englewood Cliffs, NJ: Simon and Schuster.

Reimer, B., and R. A. Smith. 1992. *The arts, education and aesthetic knowing*. Chicago, IL: National Society for the Study of Education, distributed by the University of Chicago Press.

Reimer, B., and J. E. Wright. Eds. 1992. *On the nature of musical experience*. Niwot, CO: University Press of Colorado.

References

Vulliamy, G. 1981. Music education and Music language. *Music Education* 26: 25-28.

Vulliamy, G., and E. Lee. 1976. *Pop music in schoo* Cambridge University Press.

—. 1982. *Pop, rock and ethnic music in schools.* Car University Press.

—. 1982. *Popular music: A teachers guide.* Cambridge: R Paul.

Vulliamy, G., and T. Shepherd .1984. A response to Swanw *of Sociology of Education* 5(1): 57-76.

—. 1985. A further response to Swanwick. *British Jouri Education* 6(2): 225-229.

Walker, C. 2000. *Buried country: The story of Aborigii* Sydney, NSW: Pluto Press.

Walker, R. 1990. *Musical beliefs: Psychoacoustic, mythica perspectives.* New York, NY: Teachers College Press.

—. 1996. Music education freed from colonialism a new pi *Journal of Music Education* 27: 2-15.

Will, U. 2000. Oral memory in Australian Aboriginal song pe Parry-Kirk debate: A cognitive ethnomusicological *Proceedings of the International Study Group on Music* X), ed. E. and R. Hickmann, 1-29. Columbus, OH: Ohic Columbus.

Zillmere State School. 2002. *Aim high: From little things* [Unpublished video recording]. Brisbane, QLD: Zillmere Lifeline Brisbane City Council and Education Queensland.